INTERNATIONAL ENCYCLOPAEDIA OF ISLAM

Vol.-2

Faith in Islam

INTERNATIONAL ENCYCLOPAEDIA OF ISLAM

Vol.-2

Faith in Islam

Editor

A.H. Qasmi

ISHA BOOKS

DELHI-110 033

International Encyclopaedia of Islam
(*Religion*)

ISBN: 81-8205-320-X (Set)

ISBN: 81-8205-322-6

Published in 2006 in India by
Isha Books, D-43, Prithviraj Road,
Adarsh Nagar, Delhi-110 033

Printed at : Rajdhani Printers, Delhi.

Contents

Preface

Man is a social creature. It is the society where he learns how to live in this vast cosmos. Apart from society, people are divided into different castes, cultures and creeds. All these factors go in developing a man's personality. Of all the factors, mentioned above, religion is most important.

There exist about more than two thousand religions in the world today. A religion is regarded as a sacred institution, which governs a man's life here and hereafter and teaches him how to lead a happy and prosperous life.

What's unique to Islam is its endowment to humanity from the divine creator or the Almighty. It is not a set of principles and dogmas scribed by a scholar or thinker. It was sent on the earth circa fifteen hundred years ago, but its principles and preachings hold good even today. Besides showing humanity a straight way to the eternal success, it also has a say in various other walks of human life, such as economy, politics, human rights, social relations, judiciary, marriage and so on and so forth.

Another distinguished feature of Islam is that apart from being the latest religion, it is also the last one. That is to say, whatever is there in Islam, it is valid upto to the doomsday. Now, there will not come any other religion till the Day of Judgement. Therefore, it is the most powerful and as well as the most human-nature-friendly.

Given the present global scenario, there was being felt a dire need to bring out such a mini-encyclopaedia of Islam which may cater to the maximum needs of man in the least possible sheet of paper.

The present series is an humble attempt in the same direction. It comprises ten volumes which cover all the major disciplines of human life like, Prayer, marriage, justice, human rights, social justice and so on.

We are sure that the endeavour would prove to be a capsule of treasure of knowledge about Islam, prepared perfectly. Nevertheless, considering the adage 'to err is human', we would be obliged if the readers suggest some improvements for further editions.

Editor

1

The Backdrop

The Hebrew Bible records that Christianity centres on the personal teachings of Jesus Christ. To Christians, the Jesus of Nazareth, was and continues to be promised Messiah of God in the prophesies of the Old Testament.

Rome was founded nearly 725 years prior to Isa (Jesus), a s., and some time later Zoroaster came up in Persia (628 B.C.), which was followed by yet another eventful century, 6th century B.C., when Confucius and Tao rose in China and Buddha in India giving rise to the philosophy which was promoted by Socrates, Plato and Aristotle in Greece in the coming Centuries. Then came Jesus, a.s., deeply versed in the Rabbinical lore, who devoted almost completely his short ministry in reforming his society particularly the poverty stricken peasantry and fishermen of Galilee and strove to lift humanity towards ethical and spiritual purification. Jesus, like David and Moses, was sent for a specified people 'people of Israel' which is evident by Mathew's (15: 12-28) and Mark's (7: 24-30) Gospels when Jesus replies to a call of Canaanite women, 'I have been sent to those lost sheep, the people of Israel' Jesus Christ, a.s., was born in 4 B.C.' (a disputed date among the chronologists) and crucified in 29 B.C.

The word 'Christ' originally 'Christos' in Greek, is the translation of the Hebrew word for Messiah meaning anointed' 'a paganised Christian doctrine of incarnation wherein God becomes man'. The Jewish expectations of a Messiah didn't identify the Messiah with God. Indeed, nature of Jewish Monotheism wholly excludes such pagan connotations. The word 'Christ' is a title, not a name, as the priests and kings were also 'anointed' when declared sacred to their office which is evident from the book of Isaiah (45:1), the Old Testament, when the title was conferred on a heathen king of Cyrus, 'thus said the Lord to his 'anointed', to Cyrus ....' From the study of the Old Testament it transpires that anointing kings was a symbol of their power as representative of God in a theocracy (1 Samue l- 10: 1, 16:13; 2 Samue-2:4; 2 kings - 9-6; Psalms 89:20). Thus it generally became associated with Daud (David), a.s., in the Old Testament and also became surname of Isa (Jesus), a.s., in the New Testament representing the Christian belief that he is the anointed one of the God.

Holy Scripture : Bible is the Holy book of Christians. The word bible has its origin in Greek word 'biblia' meaning books. The Holy Bible consists of two parts, first, the Old Testament, sacred writings of Jewish people, originally written in Hebrew language except certain portions in Aramaic. The second part composed in Greek language called The New Testament, records story of Jesus and advent of Christianity. The Old Testament consists of 46 books' (including 5 books of the Law/Torah, 18 prophetical books, 16 historical books, and 7 poetical or wisdom books- Psalms is included under this category).

New Testament : The New Testament consists of 27 books (including 4 Gospels - according to St. Mathews (Matt.), according to St. Mark (Mark), according to St. Luke (Luke), and according to St. Jhon (Jhon); 1 book on Acts of Apostles, 21 books on Epistles (Letters) of St. Paul, and 1 book on Revelation. Compared to the Old Testament, the books of the New Testament, are precise.

Regarding several versions of the Bible, it is said that ancient versions are in Greek, old Latin, Syriac, Coptic, Armenian and other languages. Later, parts of the Bible were reproduced in the Anglo-Saxon and Middle English. Jhon Wycliffe came with the first English versions during 1380-93 A.D. using the Latin text. It was followed by the translations into modern languages particularly that of German by Martin Luther and English by William Tyndale. The following are from among the later versions: Miles Cover-Dale's Bible (1535), Mathew's Bible (1537), the Great Bible (1539), Geneva Bible (1560), King James, or Authorised version (1611), English Revised version (188185), American standard version (1946-57), New English Bible (1961-70), Jerusalem Bible (1966), New American Bible (1970), Today's English version (1966-76), and the Revised standard version (1971).

The Gospels were authored by Mathew, Mark, Luke and John around 60-100 A.D. (though opinion on dates differ) the saints, said to be the disciples of Jesus. The writings of the Gospels have been attributed to these saints who are believed to be the witnesses to the crucifixion of Jesus, a.s., some scholar name them as 'alleged authors'. Surprisingly, Christians themselves term their Gospels 'according to Matthews' etc. One of the scholars of eminence, who is known globally for his analytical and thought provoking research on Christianity, Mr. Ahmad Deedat, writes in his 'Crucifixion or Cruci-fiction' that 'the translators of the "New International version" have unceremoniously expunged the. "according to's" as these words signify non-books.

Another mystery hovers the reality of these writers as half of them were not among the twelve elated disciples of Jesus, as., and on top of it St. Mark tells us, ` AH his disciples foresook him and fled' - (Mark 14:50). Consequently, the so-called eye-witnesses do not seem to be the real eye-witnesses ` unless St. Mark', opines Mr. Deedat, ` is not telling us the whole truth, the `Gospel truth'.

Over the years, maybe because of non-seriousness or otherwise, the expression ' bible' has assumed different astonishing names' which make it a laughable issue. For instance 'Breeches Bible'- the Geneva Bible, it is called so because in the book of Genesis 3:7 occurs expression ' made themselves breeches'(in Authorised and Revised versions the word is 'aprons'). ' Treache Bible', an English Bible of the year 1568, in which Jeremia vii: 22 reads,' is there no tryacle (in Authorised and Revised version it is balm). Likewise 'wicked Bible or Devil's Bible' a Bible printed in 1631, in which the word not is omitted from the commandment 'thou shall not commit adultery'- Exodus XX : 14. 'Vingegar Bile', an English Bible printed at Oxford in 1717, with the heading to Luke, xx, as the `parable of the vinegar' (instead of vineyard.)

Introduction of New Beliefs

After the crucifixion of Jesus, a.s. St. Paul, the Chief Christian missionary, laid the foundations of Christian theology, by the middle of Ist. century A.D. His role is transforming the Christianity from a mere sect of Jews to a world religion has been prominent. The original Christians being Jews, followed the dietary ritualistic laws of the Torah and asked non-Jewish converts to observe the same in the manner they did. This condition was lifted by St. Paul and other missionaries for the Gentiles and thus Christianity became attractive.

Nearly a decade back, an American mathematician and researcher, Michael H. Hart, wrote a book: 'the 100, the top hundred or the Greatest Hundred in History'. The writer gives the names of hundred most significant personalities in history supported by his reasons. The writer puts Prophet Muhammad, on him be peace, First, for genuine reasons. And equally for good reasons puts Jesus, a.s., at number Third. The writer divides the credit for founding Christainity between St. Paul and Jesus, a.s., and gives the major portion to St. Paul and as such puts him at Second. Every knowledgeable Christian accepts

St. Paul to be the real founder of Christianity. During the 4th century A.D. Christianity spread throughout Rome where it was declared as the state religion. Thereafter, the institution of Church saw its rise the world over, and thus became a major religion.

***Church* :** After the fall of the ancient Jewish state in 586 B.C., the institution of Church, as a religio-political organisation, was formed. The process of separation of Christianity from Judaism was started by St. Paul and was completed following the destruction of Jerusalem Church by the Romans during the Jewish Revolt (66-70 A.D.). Till the recognition of Christianity as the state religion by the Roman Emperor Constantine I (331 A.D.), it was strongly resisted by the Ruler as faith killing numerous Christians. The Church institutionalised the Christian religion as a political and social force, and later broke-up into two major groups, the Western Church under the pope in Rome and the Eastern Church under the Patriachates of Antioch, Alexandria and Constantinopole. After some period, it broke-up more when Roman Church got divided by Protestantism, whereas in Eastern Church several communities setup their own Patriachates like Ethiopians, Armenians, Russians and Italians.

The Church became ruler of the thinking and living of society on adding temporal powers to its spiritual leadership in the year 476 A.D., while barbarism, bloodshed, ignorance, tribal rivalries, and wars of nations engulfed the West badly.

The division of Church into Latin (Western Europe) and Greek branches (Byzantine or Orthodox) took place during the middle ages. It may be mentioned here that orthodox Roman Catholics lay more significance to the Church tradition in defining context of faith and Roman Catholicism, whereas Protestants stressed on scripture as the only source of external revelation. Pope or Bishop of Rome is regarded by the Roman Catholics as absolute authority on matters of faith. The division of the Western Church into the Protestant Churches and the Roman Catholic Church came in sixteenth century A.D.

Regarding governance of most of the Churches, it may be mentioned that they have a distinction between the clergy and ordinary believers. The Orthodox Churches and the Roman Catholic Church possess three-tier ministry, i.e., of bishops, priests and deacons (and many minor orders). Pope heads the Roman Catholic Church who functions through the papacy- a centralized bureaucracy in consultation with his fellow bishops. The Protestant Churches now mostly allow women clergy which is disallowed by the Roman Catholic Orthodox Churches. The Roman Papacy claims to have uninterrupted chain of Popes, beginning St. Peter to John Paul II till now.

In spite of the fact that Romans recognised the Christian faith but controversies continued about its being purely monotheistic concept given the doctrines of Monarchism (God the Creator was Supreme but shared its power with Jesus, the Logos or the Word), Modernism (three persons Trinity were aspects or modes of same God), Arianism (the Son was inferior to the Father), Nostorianism (denied that Mary was the mother of God), Monophysitism (stressing divinity of Jesus over his humanity). The Church rejected all these doctrines and the dismissal of Monophysitism broke off the Church of Mesopotamia, Syria, Egypt and Armenia, developing friction in the Byzantine Empire.

Christians follow Monotheism but the early Church developed the characteristic doctrine of Trinity, which shadows the pure concept of Monotheism.

During the middle ages, Feudalism emerged in the Christendom and officers of Church, bishops and even cardinals became powerful princes governing huge estate and possessing private armies.

'The laws of Moses and the example of Jewish history were

hastily, perhaps erroneously, applied by the clergy to the mild and universal reign of Christianity .... But among the Christians the worship of saints and relics and similar practices multiplied; it must ingenuously be confessed that the ministers of the Catholic Church imitated the profane model which they were impatient to destroy'- Gibbons.

The Protestant reformers like Martin Luther and John Calvin, during the Reformation period (16th century A.D.), revolted against the papacy by securing support of secular rulers. Then followed the wars of religion, such as 'thirty year's war', when Protestants fought against the Catholics for control of the State-Churches and the people's faith. The Reformation movement swayed Church of England also primarily on the denial of papacy to break the marriage of Henry VIII and Catherine of Aragon. Consequently, Henry VIII and the English Parliament cut off all the links between the English Church and Rome. And through the Act of Supremacy (1534) Henry VIII was declared as 'Supreme head' of the Church of England.

'The many Churches of Christianity are so much at variance one with the other, and their 'Divines' have made such an inextricable tangle of Christian teaching, and the dogmas are so hopelessly bewildering, that clear reasoning mind and open ingenuous heart of man both crave for a religion which is tangible and convincing, as well as simple' - Lord Headley.

Jesus in the Bible : There has been unthinkable human interference by way of editing, re-writing and dogmatisation in the writings of Bible (The Old Testament as well as New Testament) over the centuries to such a level that close study of the scriptures reveal that Jews, a.s., was unwilling and reluctant to die! wailing! Sweating! Crying and Complaining! It is seen that Gospel writers have been in thunderous speed in putting words into the mouth of Jesus, a.s. word for word, as fulfilment of prophecies. It shall be my endeavour to mention precisely some of the biblical contradictions.

Doctrine of Trinity : *'For there are three that bear record in heaven, the Father, the word and the Holy Ghost, and these three are one'*- Ist. Epistle of John 5:7 (the New Testament) whereby, God is thought as a Creator (Father), Redeemer (Son), and Sustainer (Spirit or Holy Ghost)'. This Christian doctrine erodes the concept of Monotheism and tends towards incarnation of God into a human being. Christian teaching tells us that man disassociated himself from God by his original sin and built a wall between himself and God which was unconquerable from the man's side. This wall, they believe, is the main source of all strife, like struggle between reason and passion, conflict between men and the life. Unless this wall is conquered the discord prevails.

Thus salvation of mankind came in the incarnation of Jesus, a.s., who being God is equally a man, and being man he is equally God. This doctrine is clearly objected in the Holy Quran (4: 171): 'O People of the Book, exceed not the limits in your religion nor spew anything about Allah, but the truth. The Messiah, Jesus, son of Mary, is only a messenger of Allah and His word which he communicated to Mary. So believe in Allah and His messenger And say not, three Desist, it is better for you, Allah is only one God. Far be it from His glory to have a son....'

Surprisingly, the words concerning the doctrine of 'trinity' have been expunged unceremoniously as falsification in the Today's English version and Revised standard version-the most updated translation of the Bible. Fortunately, I was able to lay my hands on one of the early versions, King James or Authorised version (1611 A.D.) published by the British and Foreign Bible Society, London. On comparing page nos. 1244 and 1245 of this version with the relevant chapter/verses of the Today's English version (1966-76) Bible, published by American Bible Society (in India by the Bible Society of India, Bangalore titled Good News New Testament) 'the disastrous human interference' assertion of Sulaiman Shahid Mufassir proves beyond doubt. It is startling to see how the verses from 6 to 21 of Ch. 5 are throughout certifying the skillful art of editing the portions of the Bible.

Crucifixion : Crucifixion, historically speaking, was a method of execution used by the Romans to punish slaves and foreigners. The naked victim, hung from a crossbar with legs apart on an upright peg, was allowed to hang as a public spectacle until dead. In such a way death was a slow and agonised process with no damage to vital human organs. And before execution the victim was abused and cursed and driven to carry the crossbar to the site of crucifixion. As per the Gospels (Jhon 19:7 and Mark 15:15) the crucifixion of Jesus, a.s., followed the same order. Crucifixion continued till 337 A.D. when it was banned by Constantine-1. Earlier Phonecians had attempted various ways to eliminate political prisoners, murderers etc., by stoning and drowning and later tried crucification to bring about slow painful death because the earlier methods brought quick death.

Since Jesus, a.s., was crucified, the 'Cross' has obviously assumed theological significance for Christianity and became mainstream of their faith. Prof. Jurgen Moltmann in his book *The Crucified God* says that, ' The death of Jesus on the cross is the centre of all Christian theology .... All Christian statements about God, about creation, about sin and death have their focal point in the crucified Christ.' In short, without crucifixion, there is no Christianity!

It would be unjust to touch this debatable topic without appreciating the research works of Mr. Ahmad Deadat, who has logically, using biblical references, elaborated it neatly in his tract 'crucifixion or crud-Fiction'. Basically, the conflict of crucifixion stems primarily from the Holy Bible itself. Compared to the teaching of the Master (Jesus) that salvation only comes through keeping of the commandments (Mathew's Gospel 19:

16-17), St. Paul flatly denies it by claiming that salvation comes through the death and resurrection of Jesus, a.s., 'And if the Christ be not risen (from the dead), then is our preaching vain, and your faith is also vain' (1 Corinthians 15: 14, the New testament). Whereas, the Muslim stand on the so-called crucifixion is clear as per the Quranic belief (ch. 4:157). The problem of crucifixion would never grip the Christians had they affirmed the Holy Quran as the word of God. Mr. Ahmad Deedar in his above tract quotes the words of Thomas Carlyle, 'they (the Christians) have been trained to hate the man Muhammad (PBUH) and his religion'.

No Crucification : Christians object to the revelation (Jesus was neither killed nor crucified) of the Holy Quran to Prophet Muhammad, on him be peace, by claiming how can a man (The Prophet, on him be peace) thousand miles away from the scene of happening, and 600 years after the event declare as to what had transpired? The Muslims reply, those were the words of Allah who is All-knowing and All-seeing, and the words were not 'authored'.

If one ought to take the 'crucifixion' a reality, then he would begin with eyewitnesses. But St. Mark in the Gospel writes, 'they all forsook him and fled'- Mark 14:50. Dean Farrar in his book *Life of Christ* says,' Jesus was on the cross for only three hours - when taken down'.

Jesus, a.s., was blamed with two charges, (i) claiming son of God - blasphemy, and (ii) claiming kingship - insurgency. Both the charges were false. The first one not being blasphemy because as per Jewish theology God ought to have numerous sons. The Jewish Scribes and High priest seemed adamant to crucify Jesus, a.s., 'what need have we for any further witnesses? And they all condemned him to be guilty of death' Mark 14: 63-64. Both Jews and Christians wanted the Jesus, a.s., to dig:; one for 'Good Riddance' and the other for 'Good Redemption'. The Roman king's consent was required to crucify Jesus, a.s., and they took him to Pontius Pilate, the Governor, as the Jews said, 'It is unlawful for us (Jews) to put man to death ' Jhon in Gospel 18:31. Pilate passed the buck w Herod who sends him back to Pilate.

The Bible goes about the second charge, 'we found this fellow perverting the nation, and forbidding to give tribute to Ceasar, saying that he himself is Christ, a king' Luke in Gospel 23:2. But Mathew in Gospel (22:21)9 contradicts, ' render unto Ceasar the things that are Caesar's, and unto God, the things that are God's'. And Jesus, a.s., replies, 'My kingdom is not of this world...' Jhon in Gospel 18:3336. So man of God couldn't disavow his spiritual status. The spiritual kingdom of Jesus, a.s., didn't outrage the Romans, and Pilate tells Jews, ' I find him no fault at all' Jhon in Gospel 18:38 and pleaded innocence of the blood of this righteous man (Jesus)- Mathews in Gospel 27:24.

It would be appropriate to reproduce chapter 18 of Mr. Deedat's tract 'Crucifixion or cruci-fiction' for the interest of readers.

"none so blind .....take stock the truth shines through"

Let me give you a quick summary of the points we have discussed so far, concluding that Jesus Christ was neither killed nor was he crucified, as alleged by the Christians and the Jews, but that he was alive!

1. Jesus was reluctant to die!

   He had worked out a strategy of defence to repel the jews. Because he wanted to remain alive!

   Luke 22:35,36,38, Matt 26-51

2. He beseeched god for help.

   With strong crying and tears for God Almighty to keep him alive! Luke 22: 44, James 5:6

3. God 'heard' his prayers

Which means that God accepted his prayers to keep him alive! Matt 26: 39, 13:13, Hebrews 5:74.

4. An angel of god came to strengthen

   Him:

   In the hope and belief that God will save him alive! Luke 24:43

5. Pilate finds Jesus not guilty!

   Good reason to keep Jesus alive! Jhon 18:38, 19:12

6. Pilate's wife shown a dream in which she was told that- "No harm should come to this just man." In other words that he should be saved alive! Matt. 27: 19

7. Supposed to be on the cross for only three hours.. According to the system in vogue, no man could die by crucifixion in so short a time which means that even he was fastened to the cross - he was alive!

8. The other two - his "coruscates" on their respective crosses were alive

   So Jesus too, for the same period of time; must be alive!

9. Encyclopedia biblica under article 'cross'- column 960: Says that when the spear was thrust - Jesus was alive!

10. "Forthwith" came there out blood and water:

    "Forthwith" means straightway, immediately which was a sure sign that Jesus was alive! Jhon 19:34

11. Legs not broken - as a fulfillment of prophecy

    "Legs" can be of any use only if Jesus was alive!

12. Thunderstorm, earthquake, and darkening of the sun all within 3 hours!

    To disperse the sadistic mob to enable his 'secret disciples' to help, keep him alive!

13. Jews doubted his death:

They suspected that he had escaped death on the cross that he was alive! Matt. 27: 62-64

14. Pilate "marvels" to hear that Jesus was dead

    He knew from experience that no man can die so soon by crucifixion. He suspected that Jesus was alive! Mark 15:44

15. Big roomy chamber:

    Close at hand, and big and airy for willing hands to come to the rescue. Providence was out to keep Jesus pest.

16. Stone and "winding sheets" had to be removed:

    Only necessary if Jesus was alive!

17. Report on winding sheets..

    German Scientists who carried out experiments on the "Shroud of Turin" said that the heart of Jesus had not stopped functioning - that he was alive!

18. Ever in disguise!

    Disguise not necessary if Jesus was "resurrected".

    Only necessary if he was alive!

19. Forbade mary magdalene to touch him.

    "Touch me not" for this reason that it would hurt; because he was alive!

20. "Not yet ascended unto my father"

    In the language of the Jews, in the idiom of the Jews, he was saying, " I am not dead yet", in other words, " I am alive!

21. Mary magdalene not afraid on recognising Jesus.

    Because she had seen signs of life before. She was looking for a Jesus who was alive!

22. Disciples petrified on seeing Jesus in the upper-room

All their knowledge about the "crucifixion" was from hearsay, therefore, they could not believe that Jesus was alive!

23. Ate food again and again in his post 'crucifixion' appearances.

    Food only necessary if he was alive!

24. Never showed himself to his enemies.

    Because he had escaped death by the "skin of his teeth." He was alive!

25. Took only short trips

    Because he was not resurrected, not spiritualised, but

26. Testimony of men around the tomb:

    "Why seek ye the living among the dead?" (Luke 24:45): That he is not dead, but alive!

27. Testimony of angels:

    " angels who had said that he was alive!" (Luke 24:23) Did not say, "resurrected" but the actual word uttered by the angels was alive!

28. Mary magdalene testifies

    ".... they heard that he was alive, and had been seen by her, they believed not." - (Mark 16:11): Mary did not vouch for a spook, or ghost or spirit of Jesus but a live Jesus. What they could not believe was that the Master was alive!

29. Dr. Primrose testifies:

    That the "water and the blood", when Jesus was lanced on the side, was on account of an upset in the nervous vessels because of the scourging by staves which was a sure sign that Jesus was alive! Jhon 19:34

30. Jesus had himself foretold that his Miracle. will be the Miracle of Jonah!

According to the *Book of Jonah*, Jonah was *alive*, when we expected him to be dead. Similarly when we expect Jesus to he dead, he should be alive! Matt. 12: 38-40

These thirty points and many more arguments are fully expounded in the proceeding pages of this book. "Please read and re-read the arguments and practise them on your friends. The pleasure is yours. I pray for your success!"

The Christian world has been infamous for exploiting Jesus, a.s., to make money by making films and about 'Cross' they find themselves at the' 'crossroads'. Even some Christian groups, over the years, have given peculiar concepts of crucifixion like Jehovah's witnesses - a growing Christian cult who claim crucifixion of Jesus, a.s., on a pole instead of cross. Yet some have exhibited crucifixion merely by remaining hung on the wooden cross bars nailing their hands and thighs and some performers have repeated the ritual several times.

Resurrection: To my thinking, the three tracts of Mr. Ahmad Deedat aie more relevant to this topic, viz

(i) What was the sign of Jonah

(ii) who moved the stone, and

(iii) Resurrection or Resuscitation.

Besides other sources, I have tried to centre my discussion mainly around these booklets.

Literally, resurrection means an act of rising again from the dead. This concept is found in many religions. The idea is variously conceived. In one sense it centres around transformation of human life from the dead into a transcendental mode of existence (a spiritual sense). Another concept is resuscitation or a return to this worldly existence, as narrated in the raising of Lazarus '2 and others attributed to Jesus, a.s. But it is believed by the scholars that the above concepts are separate.

According to Mathew's Gospel (1238) some of the Scribes and Pharisees, learned men among Jews, asked Jesus, ' Master, we would see a sign from thee.' In tact they were looking for some magical illusion or miracle ,to which Jesus, a.s., replied: '.... An evil and adulterous generation seeketh after a sign (miracle or a trick), and there shall be no sign given to it, but the sign of Prophet Jonah: For as Jonah was three days and three nights in the Whale's belly; so shall the son of man be three days and three nights in the heart of the earth' (Mathew 12:39-40). Jonah was crying and praying inside the belly of that fish who finally vomited him out upon the dry land or sea shore. There is unanimity in the beliefs of Jews, Christians and Muslims that Jonah (Younis) was alive for 3 days and 3 nights. Thus, one can say that Jesus, a.s., would have been alive in the tomb as he himself prophesied (Mathew 12: 40) after he was removed from the Cross. Here our Christian brethren deny aliveness of Jonah in the death of Jesus, a.s., and in turn refuse prophecy of Jesus, a.s.

According to Christian belief 'Good Friday' is celebrated as the day of Christ's death on the Cross to wash off sins of mankind. Now let us elaborate verse 40 of Ch. 12, Mathew's Gospel, further. It reveals from the study of Gospel that Jews were in much hurry in taking Jesus, a.s., off the Cross as they were in taking him on the cross in view of the apprehension of Sabbath, which commences around 6.00 p.m. on Friday, as they were alarmed in their scriptures (Deuteronomy 21: 23) that the victim of the crucifixion was an accursed of God and shall not be allowed to remain hanged on the Sabbath day. Writes Mr. Deedat ' that, to satisfy the religious scruples of the Scribes and Pharisees the 'secret disciples' of Jesus took down the body from the Cross.

They gave the body Jewish burial 'path, plastered it with "one hundred pounds weight of aloes and myrrh" (John 19:39), then placed the shrouded body into the Sepulchre before night fall. Now, it is to be seen whether Jesus, a.s., was there in the tomb exactly for 3 days and 3 nights, which can be analysed from the following table:

Easter Week	In the Sepulchre Days	Nights
Friday		
Placed in the tomb just before sunset	Nil	1 Night
Saturday		
Supposed to be in the tomb	1 Day	1 Night
Sunday		
Missing before sunrise	Nil	Nit
Total	1 Day	2 Nights

It transpires that Jesus, a.s., was in the tomb just for one day and two nights but not for three days and three nights. The Gospels clearly indicate that 'before sunrise the first day of the week (Sunday morning) Mary Magdalene went to the tomb of Jesus, a.s., and found the stone rolled and the tomb empty (Gospels; Mathew 28:1, Mark 16: 12, Luke 24: 1 and John 20: 1). Writes Mr. Deedat, Mr. Robert Fahay of the *Plain Truth* magazine, delivered a lecture recently at the Holiday Inn Durban where I was present. Mr. Fahay attempted to prove to the Christian audience that Jesus Christ was crucified on a Wednesday and not on Friday as is supposed by Orthodox Christianity for the past two thousand years. According to him if one counts backwards from Sunday morning deducting 3 days and 3 nights, one ought to get Wednesday as the answers. So it is clear that Mr. Fahay wants the Christian world to celebrate' rather than 'Good Friday'- which they have been doing nearly for the last 2000 years. And what contradictions arise out of Mr. Fahay's findings, readers might well understand. No one can safely say that the prophecy of Jesus, a.s., (Mathew 12: 40) is flatly denied by his followers.

Theologians are worried as to who moved the stone or 'rolled the stone?' (Mark 16:3.) A famous Bible scholar, Mr. Frank Morrison in his *Who Moved the Stone* tried to solve the puzzle but has failed. Whereas, the Gospels solve the problem when thoroughly studied.

When Mary Magdalene went to the tomb of the Jesus, a.s., on the first day of the meek, Sunday morning, before sunset, she went to 'annoint' him (anoint here refers to rub or massage). But do Jews, Christians and Muslims massage the dead bodies after three days? Absolutely not. Isn't it clear that she was looking for a live Jesus, a.s., Gospels tell us that she was the only woman beside Joseph of Arimathea and Nicodemus, while giving 'final' rites to the body of Jesus. Except Jhon, the rest of three Gospel writers are silent about Nicodemus. Dr. Hug J. Schoufield, one of the leading Bible scholars, writes, 'it is difficult to avoid concluding that the omission in the synoptic tradition of the mysterious disciple was intentional.' So the scholar admits that three Gospel writers have remained wilfully silent about Nicodemus.

> As Mary was talking to Jesus, a.s., she was supposing him to be the gardener as he was disguised so because of being apprehensive of Jews, when finally Jesus, a.s., called her 'Mary'. 'Jesus with unto her Mary. She turned herself, and with unto him, Rabboni; which is to say Master' (Jhon in Gospel 20: 16).
>
> On Mary's try to come forward and grab her spiritual Master, Jesus, a.s., responds, 'touch me not, for I am not yet ascended into my father' (Jhon 20:17).

In simple language the expression of this verse goes, 'I am

not dead yet; so logically speaking he is not resurrected from the dead. Since Jesus, a.s., had not died and thus was not resurrected which is why he was afraid of Jews. Mr. Deadat says, ' Had he died and resurrected, he wouldn't have been afraid. Why? Because the resurrected bodies can't die twice. Why says so? The Bible says so'.

'......it is ordained unto all men once to die, and after that the judgment' (Hebrew 9: 27, the Old Testament). The further prophesies of Jesus, a.s., lend credence to the fact that resurrected ones cannot die twice. The Scribes and Pharisees from among the Jews came once with a puzzle to Jesus, a.s., regarding a woman having seven husbands in turn 'in the resurrection therefore whose wife shall she be of the seven? For they all had her' (Matthew 22: 28). In reply to this fabricated notion Jesus, a.s., replied, 'Neither shall they die any more, for they are equal unto the angels, and the children of God, for such are the children of the resurrection.' (Luke 20: 36). Is it not clear then that the resurrected persons are immortalised, no second time death, no thirst, no hunger as angelised (spiritualised) bodies become like spirit and the means of death fail before the resurrected persons. That is why Jesus, a.s., tells Mary Magdalene:

'For I am not yet ascended into my Father' meaning ` I am not dead yet: Now, see what St. Luke writes in the Gospel:

> '.... Jesus himself stood in their midst, and said unto them, peace be upon you'
>
> '.... But they were terrified (affrighted), and supposing they were seeing a spirit. And he said unto them..—'
>
> 'Behold my hands and my feet, that it is myself, handle me and see; for a spirit has no flesh and bones, as you see me have
>
> 'And showed them his hands and feet'

'And while they yet believed not for joy and wondered, he said unto them, Have ye here any meat?'

'And they gave him a piece of broiled fish and of a honeycomb'

'And he took it, and did eat before them'

Luke 24: 3643.

One is confronted with a simple question. Why the disciples were terrified? The answer is that they thought they saw a ghost. Did he look like a ghost? Christian reply is No. Then why to get terrified. The answer is given by St. Mark (Mark 14:50), 'they all forsook him and fled' means the disciples of Jesus were not exactly the eyewitnesses or the ear witnesses to the actual happenings of the previous 3 days as they forsook Jesus, a.s., at the most critical time of his life and that is why they had heard their master was hanged on the cross. They had heard he was dead and buried for 3 days; they heard that had given up the ghost. Writes Mr. Deadat, 'If one is confronted by a person with such a reputation then the conclusion is inescapable; they must be seeing a Ghost. Little wonder these ten brave men were petrified'.

That is why Jesus, a.s., tells them 'Behold my hands and my feet....' which in simple language means ' can't you see I am the same person'. Then Jesus, a.s., tells them in most clear terms that he is not what they are thinking of resurrected. For a spiritual body is resurrected, brought back from the dead. And finally Jesus, a.s., asks them for something to eat; because he was not a spiritualised body immune from hunger, thirst and the like. Jesus, a.s., tells plainly that he is not resurrected and spritualised, but the Christian world believes him otherwise.

The Christians today are groping for truth. Writes Mr. Deadat, 'He (Christian) is asking questions which he did not dare to ask a few centuries ago. Questions like :

(a) Is Jesus God?

(b) What was the sign of Jonah?

(c) Is the Bible God's word?

(d) Who moved the stone?

(e) Was Jesus Christ an importer?

(A Christian Magazine, ' plain truth' - April 1977)'

The Holy Quran commands the Muslims to demand from the Jews and Christians their authority in support of their forceful claims that 'salvation' is exclusively their right. 'And they say: None shall enter the Garden except he who is a Jew, or the Christians. These are their vain desires. So, produce your proof if you are truthful' (2: 111). That is why the Holy Bible is used to refute the Christian claims, as he is programmed to believe in dogmas without reasoning.

Jesus, a.s., in the Holy Quran : The personality of Jesus, a.s., is rightly, like other Prophets, glorified in the Holy Quran. The Muslim perception of Jesus, a.s., is simple and clear as enshrined in Holy Quran to answer unambiguously the questions as,

(i) Jesus was neither killed nor crucified;

(ii) sin is not inherited;

(iii) The 'Trinity' is a fabrication;

(iv) Jesus is not God; and

(v) God does not beget sons/daughters.

Let me quote some of the Quranic verses in support of the above assertions:

Is Crucifixion a Truth ?

> And for their saying: We have lifted the messiah, Jesus, son of Mary, the messenger of Allah, and they killed him not, nor did they cause his death on the cross, but he was made to appear to them as such.

> And certainly those who differ therein are in doubt about it. They have no knowledge about it, but only follow a conjecture, and they killed him not for certain.
>
> Holy Quran 4: 157

Inheritance of Sins - a Dogma : 'They speak not before He speaks, and according to His command they act'

Holy Quran 21: 27

> 'I will raise them up a Prophet from among their brethren, like unto thee, and will put my words in his mouth; and he shall speak unto them all that I shall command him.' Deut. 18: 18

The Holy Quran nowhere mentions a Prophet to have committed a sin; so the doctrine of sinlessness of the Prophets is unassailable. Allah has praised every Prophet in Holy Quran, pointing to the fact that every Prophet speaks the 'spoken' words of God and act to his commandment. So their words and deeds flow from the fountain of Divine Will, then how come the alleged inheritance of sin is attributable to them. Despite distortions, even the Holy Bible points to sinlessness of Prophets like Nuh, a.s., Ibrahim, a.s., Moses, a.s., etc. when it says:

> of Ibrahim , a.s., '... and said unto him, I am the Almighty God, walk before me, and be thou perfect',
>
> Genesis 17:1
>
> of Nuh, a.s, '.....Nuh was a just man and perfect in his generations and Nuh walked with God.'
>
> Genesis 6:9
>
> of Moses, a.s., 'Thou shalt be perfect with the Lord thy God.' Deut. 18: 13
>
> 'The mouth of the righteous speaketh wisdom, and his tongue talketh of judgement. The law of his God it is his heart; none of his steps shall slide.'
>
> Psalms 37: 30-31.

It can thus be observed that according to Christianity the sinfulness of the earlier Prophets has stemmed from the 'sonship' of Jesus, a.s., which is flatly rejected by the Holy Quran and the undistorted portions of the Holy Bible.

Trinity - a Fabrication : The doctrine of Trinity is outrightly rejected by Allah (Holy Quran 4: 171). Dramatically , some of the Christian scholars have tried to justify Trinity in the light of Holy Quran by including God, Jesus, a.s., and Mary ; but for this false notion too, they are groping to give Mary divine status; so sad about their scholarly pursuits. But Holy Quran rejects the doctrine of Mary worship by Christians (which is common to Roman Catholic Church Catechism) in the following verse:

> 'And when Allah will say: O Jesus, son of Mary, didst thou say to men, take me and my mother for two gods besides Allah? He will say: Glory be to Thee! it was not for me to say what I had no right to (say). If I had said it, thou wouldst indeed have known it'.
>
> (5:116)
>
> The word 'rich' used in verse 4:171 of Holy Quran, and its application cannot take Jesus, a.s., beyond the limits of mortality as Holy Quran is clear about the status of Jesus, a.s., to that of Adam, a.s., 'I breathed My spirit into him,' (15:29)
>
> 'Then He made him complete and breathed into him of His spirit, and gave you ears and eyes and hearts....'
>
> (32:9)
>
> ***Godship of Jesus a.s., an Exaggeration*** : Certainly they disbelieve who say: Surely Allah is the third of the three And there is no God but One God, and if they desist not from what they say, a painful chastisement shall befall such of them who disbelieve'
>
> Holy Quran 5:73

> The Messiah, son of Mary is but an apostle; apostles before him have indeed passed away, and his mother was a truthful woman; they both used to eat'-
>
> Holy Quran 5:75

Hunger and thirst does not affect mortality.

The Christian doctrine of 'Atonement' raises Jesus a.s., from a mortal to a divine status of God which being erroneous and tainted with idolatrous notions, takes Christian world away from God. And see what Allah says:

> 'Say- O People of the Book, exaggerate not in the matter of your religion unjustly, ...'
>
> Holy Quran 5:77

Jesus, a.s., is explicitly and always referred in the Holy Quran as ' the son of Mary'

> 'The likeness of Jesus with Allah is truly as the likeness of Adam' Holy Quran 3:58

> ***Sonship of Jesus, a.s., - an Invention*** : 'And wee sent no messenger before thee but We revealed to him that there is no God but Me, so serve Me. And they say. 'The Beneficent has taken to Himself a son. Glory be to Him! Nay they are honoured servants ...'
>
> Holy Quran 21:25-26

This verse clearly answers the false belief that other Prophets like Jesus, a.s., are referred as sons of God in the Holy Quran, but this title signifies nothing more than that they are 'honoured servants' of Allah. Thus, the 'doctrine of sonship' of Jesus, a.s., as propounded by the Christians attributes unwarranted sinfulness of all mankind including prophets, which is direct assault on the sinlessness or perfection of all the apostles of Allah.

He does not beget sons/daughters.

A careful study of the Holy Bible reveals that one verse

contradicts with another, therefore, the human interference and dogmatization cannot be ruled out.

'.......and a party from among them indeed used to hear the word of Allah, then altered it after they had understood it, and they know (this).

> Woe! then to those who write the Book with their hands then say: This is from Allah .....
>
> Holy Quran 2:75,79

Whereas, a thoughtful reading of the Holy Quran transpires that one verse testifies the other, free from error and human interference being the ultimate book. 7th Section of Chapter 5 of Holy Quran provides a comprehensive explanation of this argument.

Will Durant writes that Julian 'the apostate' loved philosophy too much to be dissuaded by the conduct of philosophers who gave reasons for abandoning Christianity. ' The Gospels' he writes, in a preview of Higher Criticism, contradict one another, and agree chiefly in their incredibility; Gospel of Jhon differs substantially from the other three in narrative and theology; and the creation, story of Genesis assumes plurality of gods. Will Durant quotes Julian as saying, 'unless everyone of these (Genesis) is a myth involving, as I indeed, believe, some secret interpretation, they are filled with blasphemies against God'.

> '.... This day have I perfected for you your religion and completed my favour on you and chosen for you Islam as a religion ....' Holy Quran 5:3

2

Faith before Islam

The awareness of man slowly developed down the ages to the presence and admission of a Supreme Force managing all existence. And finally the recognition of this Ultimate Truth, through the consecutive revelations, got fulfilment in the religion of Islam from among the major faiths of the world exhibiting universality through oneness of humanity and eternal and worldly peace.

It has been my endeavour to understand the religion of Islam, while looking back to the transition of faith from totemism to monotheism necessitating a look at the pre-Islamic religions, religious philosophies, religious beliefs of archaic cultures and primitive faiths of mankind.

What is Religious ? : The word 'religion' is a complex phenomenon defying definition or summary. Scholars emphasise to look to its fundamental characteristics that lie behind the historical manifestations of a particular religion. Archaeologists and anthropologists have done a lot in deep understanding of religious phenomenon, in addition to the role of historians. Generally, religious belief or expression is manifested in terms of sacred or the holy, carrying with it the sense and realisation of the Supreme and Ultimate reality, as against profane expression (evil spirits or ungodly manifestations). 'The holy is experienced in religion as an initiating power, coming to human life and touching it from beyond itself. Usually revelations are considered the fountain-head of a religion signifying distinctive and unique experiences of the holy coming into human life. Religion-unites the instinctive criteria of working and living; that is egoism and the criterion which ought to be the basis for working and living, in order to guarantee (for mankind) happiness, prosperity and justice.

Faith is not a mere belief but an attitude of persons in which they commit themselves to the sacred and voluntarily accept its claim upon them. In a perfect religious sense, commitment of faith tends to shape all that person's life and character. With the successive development of religious beliefs, systems of belief rose concerning both practice and doctrine. This practice and doctrine, in earlier times, most probably found expression in the bodies of myth or in ritual law. The importance attached to the right belief, generally termed as orthodoxy, has varied from time to time and religion to religion. Religious experience of mankind raises the question about its validity, which can be judged about its being in favour or against the existence of a Supreme Force.

Religion : Early Jesus : The name given to religious beliefs and practices of the culturally backward societies is primitive religion. The religious beliefs of Archaic cultures—Paleolithic, Mesolithic and Neolithic Ages—are called as primitive religions. Rituals, creator, gods and myths generally dominated the primitive beliefs. Fear, wonder, dreams, the soul and animism provided the basis of such beliefs. Some of the historians have classified the objects of religious worship into six classes: celestial, terrestrial, sexual, animal, human and divine. But it can't be said exactly as to which object was worshipped first. Historians believe the moon probably to be the first object as the early folklore speaks of the 'man in the moon'. There existed a distinction between the sacred and the profane: sacred signified the world of reality genesis of all meaningful forms, and behaviours in a society. The concept of profane just opposite of sacred. Most of the ancient societies relate to the Supernatural through some religious form, though crudely, like totemism, ancestor worship, animism, etc.

Given the multiplicity of these beliefs, there has been enormous number of so called gods. Writes Will Durant, 'an official census of gods, undertaken in the 9th Century before Christ, counted them as some 65,000—oldest of all were the astronomic gods'. Historians believe that every family had household gods and with the passage of time, the number of gods came down by interpreting the minor ones as attributes or forms of the major deities.

From fear of death followed dreaming and wondering, the primitive men are seen to have affirmed some soul behind ultimately paving the way for adoration of astronomical gods, then to respect for animals and ancestor worship. In ancestor worship, perhaps the notion of God as Father took the form of a 'totem'. Sigmund Freud in his *Totem and Taboo* believes that the totem was a transfigured symbol of the father, revered and hated for his omnipotence and rebelliously murdered and eaten by his sons. Thus, it was in their reverence or hatred they treated totems 'sacred' and 'unclean'. No sharp distinction is seen between men and gods as, for example, to the early Greeks their ancestors were their gods and their gods were their ancestors. Yet another situation arose, when out of mixture of ancestors, few men and women who had been uncommonly distinguished were spotted for clearer deification, thus great kings became gods, at times prior to their death.

Will Durant refers Allan Grant, who in his book *Evolution of the Idea of God* (ICY. 1897) believes that among several primitive men the word for god actually meant, 'a dead man' and even today the English word 'spirit' and the German word 'geist' mean both ghost and soul. 'The Greeks invoked their dead precisely as the Christians were to invoke their saints'. The belief in the continued life of the dead was so firm amongst the primitive people that sometimes messages were sent to dead in the most literal way. A chief of a tribe for conveying such a letter, recited it verbally to a slave and later cut off his head for special delivery of message and if he forgot something to recite he would then behead another slave as a post-script.

It is surprising to see that among primitive men atheists are also found who denied existence of Supreme natural power and few are still found like some Zulus, the dwarfs of Cameroon or some pygmy tribes of Africa who don't observe any ritual or follow any cult; they are called primitive atheists.

The primitive religions count by thousands. In fact, they are now very small communities with handful of votaries in aboriginal tribes of Australia, the Americans, India, Burma, South-East Asia, Indonesia and Africa.

Religions in the Beginning

> "You are the best of the Peoples, evolved for mankind,
> enjoining what is right, forbidding what is wrong and
> believing in .Allah; if the People of Book had faith,
> it were best for them: among them are some who have
> faith, but most of them are perverted transgressors".
>
> Holy Quran 3:110

Muslim belief is that Allah granted Taurat (Torah) to Musa (Moses), A.S., Zebur (Psalms) to Daud (David), A.S., Injil (Gospel) to Isa ,(Jesus), A.S. And the manner in which such holy scriptures are before us today shall be explicitly cleared from the following paras.

Judaism : The word 'Jew' is derived from the Kingdom of Judah, which included two of the twelve Israelite tribes, loyal to the family of king David, (Daud, A.S.) and 'Israel' referred mainly to the northern kingdom of ten Israelite tribes richer kingdom. This division took place after the death of king Sulaiman (Solomon, A.S.)

Since 1948, the word Israelite is linked to the citizens of Israel. Whereas, Hebrew is a biblical name for Israelites. Hebrews believed that their religion was founded on covenants that God had with their Prophets starting from Ibrahim (Abraham, A.S.), and special covenant with Musa (Moses), A.S. Yahweh had agreed to make them his specially chosen people and protected them, but only if they obeyed his Law. After separation of Jews into two kingdoms, the Northern kingdom (Israelites comprising ten rich tribes) and the Southern kingdom (Judah comprising two tribes), the latter believed that a special covenant had also been made with king David and his royal descendants (the Psalmists). So they believed in the revelation of Zebur (Psalms) to Daud (King David), a.s., by Lord God.

The Hebrew language, which belongs to Canaanite branch of the North West semitic family of languages, is more than 3000 years old which is also evident from the 'Dead Sea Scrolls' found by the archaeologists in the Caves near the ancient Essence monastery – Qumran dating from 2nd Century B.C. to 1st century A.D. These scrolls are preserved in Jerusalem, the Israel Museum.

Jews are first from among the people who are called 'the people of Book' or, 'the Ahle-kitab' to whom Allah revealed the Taurat (Torah) through his Messenger Musa (Moses), a.s., so Hebrews or Israelites had the privilege of prophesying monotheism, after the prolonged ' history of polytheism, prior to all nations. Historians write that religion of Hebrews was in existence long before its first law-giver Musa (Moses), A.S., came on the scene. The first among Hebrews is Patriarch Ibrahim, who left Ur in Chaldea (Sumeria) with the Hebrew tribe around 2100 B.C., to take them out of wrong doing and superstition nearly 900 years after Phoenician (Philistinian) settlement on the Syrian coast with centres at Tyre and Sidon, when Pharaoh became God-King in Egypt (2980 B.C.). After a long period of wandering in the Arabian desert, the Hebrews finally settled in Egypt, where mighty Pharaohs enslaved them.

Holy Scriptures : It was left to Musa (Moses), A.S., at the age of 80 years to liberate Hebrews from Egyptian bondage who led them out of Egypt, in 1450 B.C. across the Red Sea, to a promised land of milk and honey (Palestine). On the way at Mt. Sinai Musa (Moses), A.S., received 'the Ten Commandments' from 'Yahweh' or 'Jehovah', the Supreme God. By the time the Hebrews had settled in the promised land, the first five books of Moses, the Mosaic Law 2, had been written. Thereafter, king David (1013-973 BC.) established Hebrews hegemony in Palestine.

The Law, the Prophets and the Psalms remained as separate holy books until the time of Isa (Jesus), A.S., when they were put together as the Hebrew Bible or the Old Testament.

'In 1854 A.D., two Englishmen uncovered the sites of Ur, Eridu and Uruk .... and many others have exhumed the primeval city of Ur, where Sumerians appear to have reached civilization by 4500 B.C.' 'The Jews believed that the people of Ibrahim had come from Ur in Sumeria, and had settled in Palestine (ca 2200 B.C) a 1000 years or more before Moses and the conquest of the Cananites was merely a capture by the Hebrews of the land promised by their God'

The Hebrew Bible consists of 39 books comprising: 5 books on the Law (Torah), 21 books on the Prophets and 13 books on the Writings - Psalms is included under this category. The Mosaic Law consists of the following books

Genesis - tells about creation of universe; the first human beings.

Exodus - how Moses led the people from Egypt and received the revelations at Mount Sinai.

Leviticus - mostly contains legal code.

Numbers - contains story of migration towards the promised land.

Deuteronomy - partly repeats narrative, re-coding other laws, and concludes death of Moses.

Western scholars are of the opinion that Torah or Pentateuch is based on four principal sources:

i. The old Testament (J) was probably written in Judah, the Southern Kingdom, (950 B.C.).

ii. Israelite version of Northern kingdom, Ibrahim (E) around 900-750 B.C.

iii. Deuteronomy (D) compiled around 7th century B.C.

iv. Priestly source (P) being final addition to Torah around 550 B.C.

Torah (Taurat) : A Hebrew word meaning 'instructions', in the broader sense is the entire body of Jewish teachings included in the old Testament, Talmud and in later rabbinical commentaries.

In the early biblical times, the term 'Torah' signified the oral instructions of the priests on legal, moral or ritual questions. Slowly, the term was applied to written collection of the priestly decisions contained in the first five books of the Bible, called the Mosaic Law, or Pentateuch 1. In the latter sense, the Torah is preserved on scrolls kept in the ark of every Synagogue reading. Reading of the Torah is central to the Synagogue service among Jews.

Book of Psalms (Zabur) : Literally, Psalm means a sacred song or a hymn. It is the major collection of Hebrew religious poetry, in the Old Testaments. Psalms consist of 150 pieces and 5 sections, originally spoken or sung in various worship settings. According to Hebrews the Psalms have been composed individually from 10th through 4th century B.C. and completed in their present form by at least 200 B.C. King David is named the Psalmist who used to sing these sacred songs. But the titles of some psalms name Moses, Solomon, Ethan, Asaph and the sons of Korah as authors. The influences of Babylonia, As Syria, and Egypt are also seen in the Psalms.

Talmud: The word Talmud means teaching. It is also termed as a record of rabbinical opinion, history, folklore, medicine, trade and commerce, and a code of religious laws and ethics. Jewish teachings were initially transmitted orally, apart from the Written. Law or the Pentateuch and were eventually compiled in the Mishnah (Oral teaching) by Rabbi Judah the Prince, the spiritual head of the Palestinian Jewish community by 200 A.D. The Mishnah served as the basis for Babylonian Talmud - a work of great scope, covering every aspect of daily life and was completed in 500 A.D. Writes Will Durant 'In the Temple, the Synagogues, and the schools of Palestine and Babylonia the scribes and rabbis composed those enormous bodies of law and commentary known as the Palestinian and Babylonian Talmuds. Moses, they held, had left to his people not only written law in the Pentateuch, but also an oral law. It had been the main point of issue between the Pharisees and Seduces of Palestine whether this law was also of divine origin and binding Force'. The Mishnah is similar in both the Talmud's – Babylonian and Palestinian – but the commentary (Gemara) is four times more in the former. Will Durant continues, 'the new teachers did to the Mishnah of Jehuda what they had done to the Old Testament : they debated, analysed, explained, amended, and illustrated the text' The rabbis were called 'tannain teachers of the oral law'. 'The Talmud's God is frankly anthropomorphic: He loves and hates, gets angry, laughs, weeps, feels remorse, wears phylacteries', sits on the throne surrounded by a ministering hierarchy of Cherubim and Seraphim, and studies the Torah three times a day.' This clearly speaks of the distortion in the divinely revealed books of Torah and Psalms.' Of all the ideas the most distasteful to

Judaism is that of a plurality of Gods'. To the Jews right conduct is more important than the right belief. Talmud had hardly been completed when Justanian outlawed the book (553) as, 'a issue of puerilities, fables, inquisities, insults, imprecations, hearsies and blasphemies.' The rigorous, tudy of Talmud gave Jews sharpness of intellect and retentiveness of memory 'consistency and persistency' over the years but still tended to narrow the range and freedom of their mind.

Historians write that Exilarch Solomon died in the year 762 and Anan ben David stood in succession but the heads of Sura and Pumbeditha, rejecting the hierarchy principle installed Anan's younger brother named Chanaya which embittered Anan who fled to Palestine and found his own Synagogue, and called upon Jews everywhere to reject the Talmudic Laws and obey only Torah (Pentateuch). Writes will Durant, 'he protested against the changes that Talmudic rabbis had made in the Mosaic Law by their adaptive interpretations, and insisted on the strict fulfilment of the pentateuch decree, hence his followers received the name Qaraites- adherents of the Text. Anan praised Isa (Jesus), a.s., as a holyman who desired not to set aside the Written Law of Musa (Moses), a.s., but only the Oral Law of scribes and Pharisees; Jesus in Anan's view had aimed not to found a new religion but to cleanse and strengthen Judaism.'

Israelites : The analytical study of some authentic books on religion transpires that Israelites, or Hebrews gave toughest time to their Prophets - Moses (Musa), a.s., King David (Daud), a.s., and later Isa (Jesus), a.s. in denouncing polytheism. They even attributed King Solomon's glory to certain devilish crafts and thus lied against him. Western scholars have also maintained that Solomon was not a polytheist, though he had Israelite and non-Israelite wives but he didn't make separate places for their worship.

While studying the existing scriptures (Moses in

Deuteronomy 18: 15, 18, 19 and Jesus in John l: 23, 25 14: 16,17 16: 13, Acts 3: 21-23) it seems that Jews were still waiting for a promised Prophet even after Christ's alleged Crucification. And yet at another place, it reveals (Mathew 21: 43)' that such Prophet will rise from a nation different than Israelites. This Fact is evident from the Holy Quran also, 'O Allah, Owner of the Kingdom, Thou giveth the Kingdom to whom Thou pleasest, and takest away from whom Thou pleasest....' Contrary to their Scriptures, the Jews believed to obey only what was revealed to Israelite Prophet but then why they attempted to kill even Israelite Prophet (Jesus), shows their hard heartiness in affirming the truth, whether it was revealed to a non-Israelite or Israelite Prophet (see Holy Quran 2: 91).

In response to Muslim and, to some extent, Christian tolerance towards Jews in practising their religion, they (Jews) intrigued and conspired on the same land they dwelt against the host nations. Writes S. Amir Ali in the introduction to his *Spirit of Islam*, 'the series of disasters which one after the another had befallen the doomed nations of Moses, had culminated in the wars of Titus and Hadrian... their own sufferings at the hands of ruthless persecutors had faded to teach that the value of humanity and peace. The atrocious cruelties which they committed in the cities of Egypt, of Cyprus and Cyrene, where they dwelt in treacherous harmony with the unsuspecting natives, takes away all sense of pity for their future fate. The house of Israel was a total wreck; its members were fugitives on the face of the earth, seeking shelter far and wide but carrying everywhere their indomitable pride, their rebellious hardness of heart, denounced and apprehended by an endless succession of Prophets'. Writes Will Durant, 'the first out break of intolerance was among the Jews themselves. In 1149 Jehuda ibn Ezra, steward of the palace of Alfonso VII of Leon and Castle turned powers of his master's govt. against the Qaraite Jews of Toledo, the details are unknown, but from that time the once numerous Spanish Qaraites are heard no more'. For one reason or the other Jews were expelled from France thrice, in 1181 A.D.,1254 A.D., and 1306 A.D., and from England in 1290 A.D.

Jewish Doubtful Faith : The teachers of the Law and the Pharisees are the authored interpreters of Messes' Law. So you must obey and follow everything they tell you to do; do not, however, intimate their actions, because they do not, practise what they preach Mathews Gospel - 23: 1-3

> 'And the Jews say, the Christians follow nothing (good) and the Christians say, the Jews follow nothing (good) while they recite the same book ....'
>
> Holy Quran, 2: 113

In the illusion of their doubtful faith, Jews often vexed Muses (Moses), a.s., with different questions and demands, which is evident from this holy verse;

> 'Rather you wish to put questions to your Messenger, as Moses was questioned before. And whoever adopts disbelief instead of faith he indeed had lost the right direction of the way' Holy Quran - 2: 108
>
> '......the chief priests and the teachers of the law and the elders jeered at him (Jesus). He saved others but he cannot save himself' Isn't he the king of Israel; If he comes down from the crass we will believe him!
>
> Mathew Gospel - 27: 41-42

Historians say that on entering the historic scene, for the first time, Jews are seen as nomadic Bedouins who were scared of the jinns of the air. They also worshiped cattle, rocks, sheep, and sometimes spirits of the hills and even caves. In the Old Testament (Exodus - 32: 25-28) the indulging of Jews in a naked dance before the Golden Calf is written clearly and how Levites, priestly class, following the orders of Musa (Moses) a.s., slew three thousand of such dancers.

Will Durant says, 'Moses could never quite win his flock

from the adoration of the Golden Calf, for the Egyptian worship of the bull was still fresh in their memories'. Western scholars admit that Jews were comprising of 12 tribes (2 Judas and 10 Israelites) and Holy Quran lends credence to this historical fact, 'and we divided them into twelve tribes as nations, These Israelites, in whom defiance, adultery, idolatry, and similar other things were rampant vices, would also offer their sons and daughters for sacrifice to the Cannan idols.

Even after the successive messages of God through Musa (Moses), a.s., Daud (David), a.s. and Isa (Jesus), a.s., the plight of Jews continued to be disorderly with worsening tendencies as idolatry and plural worships became common features. And some adrifted claimed false prophethoods. Records book 1 of the Kings, in the Old Testament, that 450 Jews claimed prophethood having been inspired by the idol 'Baal' (18: 18, 21-22) 'Baalism'. Will Durant rightly says, `the Synagogue never fully replaced the Temple in the heart of the Jew. The hope that he might one day offer sacrifice to Yahveh before the Holy of the Holier on Zion's Hill, inflamed his imagination, and left him open to repeated deception by false messiahs and Gibbon is seen upright in his melancholy duty as a historian when writing, the Jewish religion was admirably fitted for defence, but it was never designed for conquest. The obligation of preaching to the Gentiles the faith of Moses had never been inculcated as a percept of the Law, nor were Jews inclined to impose it on themselves as a voluntary duty.

The inherent doubt in their perception made Jews more ritualistic than holistic in pursuit of their faith. Judaism sought unity through uniform ritual - it was first of all a law of worship to be performed in Synagogues which succeeded the Temple. 'The ritual was a mark of identity, a bond of unity, and continuity, a badge of defiance to a never forgiving world'

Torah or Pentateuch **:** A distorted book in its present form.

The Pentateuch was a book rarely remembered completely

by the Israelites as it was initially read-out only once in seven years and there remained every apprehension of its distortion through Scribes and Pharisees. 'Certain rabbinical edicts frankly voided the laws of the Pentateuch, or interpreted them into harmlessness.

Study of the Old Testament reveals that during the reign of king Jehoiakin, the king of Jerusalem, the Babylonian king, Nebuchadnezzar attacked and besieged Jerusalem and took away all the treasures from the 'House of God'. 'And Nebuchadnezzar king of Babylonia came against the city, and his servants did besiege it.. And he carried out thence all the treasures of the house of Lord, and the treasures of the king's house, and cut in pieces all the vessels of gold which Solomon long before Israil had made in the Temple of the Lord, as the Lord had said'.
Book of II kings 24: 10, 13 the Old Testament.

'...... Came Nebuzar- adan, Captain of the guard, a servant of the king of Babylon, unto Jerusalem: And he burnt the house of Lord, and the king's house, and every great man's house burnt it with fire'
Book of II kings 25: 8,9.

'And Captain of the guard took Seraiah the chief priest, and the Zephaniah the second priest, and the three keepers of the door.. including an officer, 5 men present before the king, principal scribe of the host, and three score men.. found in the city .. And the king of Babylon smote them, and slew them at Ribah in the land of Hammath- So Judah was carried away out of their land'. Book of II kings 25: 18, 19, 21.

In this period of turbulence and turmoil, Jews remained Babylonian slaves, and were getting slowly mixed with the Babylonian prudence and morals. Under these turbulent circumstances, how can the originality of the Jewish scriptures

(Pentateuch) be assured as with the limitations of printing, the copies of Pentateuch were obviously not accessible to common believers and whatever was available with notables of the city and in the 'House of God' that was either robbed off or set aflame in the ruthless fires. John Mills, a catholic, writes, 'all agree that the real manuscript of Pentateuch was destroyed by the soldiers of Bakhtanasr (Nebuchadnezzar). Will Durant also supports what is written in the Book of II Kings, on the outrageous attacks by Nebuchadnezzar on Jerusalem. Even Greeks massacred Jews for possessing copies of the Torah. 'Every Jew who was found possessing the Book of Law, was to be jailed or killed, and the Book, whenever found was to be burned' says Will Durant.

> When Cyrus, King of Persia came to Babylonia he freed all Jew slaves who left for their motherland, Jerusalem. Scattered in their efforts but firm in the support by the Persian kings, Cyrus, Darius, and Artaxerxes, the Israelites built 'House of God'. Then Ezra the Priest came from Babylonia to Jerusalem to teach the Law of Moses as the captivity had taken their belief and restoration of temple renewed it. 'This Ezra went up from Babylon; and he was a ready scribe in the Law of Moses, which the Lord God of Israel had given... For Ezra had prepared his heart to seek the Law of the Lord, and to do it, and to teach in Israel statutes and judgements... And thou, Ezra, after the wisdom of thy God, that is in their hand, set magistrates and judges, which may judge all the people that are beyond the river, all such as know the laws of thy God; and teach ye them that know them not'
>
> (Book of Ezra 7: 16, 10,2,5) The Old Testament.

Around 444 B.C., a learned priest of Jews, Ezra, compiled the Pentateuch. It is believed by some scholars that Ezra reclaimed holy books by intuition; whereas his Prophethood remains in doubt and thus this intuition cannot be agreed upon. So the genuineness of the Pentateuch by Ezra is unreliable. Will Durant writes that for seven days Ezra and his Levites read the book of the Moses Law from the scrolls and then solemnly affirmed this Law as their constitution and conscience. 'From those troubled times till ours that Law has been the central fact in the life of Jew'. Another Jewish priest, Hilkiah, is believed to have told Josiah the King, about discovery of a surprising scroll in the secret archives of the temple. Around 621 B.C., the king summoned notables and elders of Judah to the temple, and among the gathering of thousands of people read to them the 'Book of the Covenant' followed by oath ceremony to abide by this Book. It is believed by the scholars that this Book would have been Deuteronomy or Exodus. It is also seen that the 'Book of the Law of Moses' might not have been exactly the same as that 'Book of the Covenant', because Ezra read out the former Book in seven days while Josiah read-out the latter twice a day. 'We can only guess that the larger scroll constituted a substantial part of those first five books of Old Testament which Jews call Torah, or the Law, and which others call Pentateuch'. Historians have also failed to see exactly as to when these books were written, which constituted that 'Mosaic' Code. This Code is pivotal to the Ten Commandments received by Mesa (Moses), a.s., from God (Exodus 20:1-22) towards the end of third century, the scholars of the Great Assembly had finished the editing of the older literature thus closing the Old Testament Canon. 'It was their judgement that the age of the Prophets was ended... The result was that many works of this epoch, full of wisdom and beauty, lost the chance of divine collaboration.

Apart from literary editing, the successive attacks on Jerusalem by the Babylonians and Romans after Ezra, marked the worst episodes of its chequered history when loots, fires and persecutions dominated the scene, the survival of the original Pentateuch remains a question unanswered.

Contradictory Translations : The outstanding translations of the Torah or Pentateuch are available in Greek, Hebrew and Summerion languages, despite several others. The Greek Church and the Church of East take Greek version as authentic; when Jews take Hebrew version authentic. 'On account of their enmity with the Christians, the Jews distorted a portion of the Hebrew text so that it does not agree with the Greek translation thereby, rendering the Greek translation as unauthentic' said Augustine as reported by Henery Wescott. Adam Clark in his commentary on Pentateuch, Vol. I, p-817, writes, 'the Jews effected distortions in the text of Pentateuch because of their enmity with Sumerians... and since like most of the ancient books, there has been large scale distortion in it, consequently any interpretation of it is nothing but an exercise in futility.' Philistin Charlott in his 'short story of Great Religions' confirms that in 17th century a Jewish philosopher of Holland, Spooiza, recounted the contradictions in the Holy Book. He ridiculed the scholars who believed that these contradictions were only extraneous, and objected its originality in Hebrew as the earliest manuscript in that language does not go beyond 10th century A.D.

One needs enough of time and space to go through and brief various scholarly comments on the distortion of Pentateuch. Precisely, the distortions in the holy Book arose from constant fires, raids, persecutions, conspiracies amongst Pharisees, Rabbis and governors, amiable relation of Jews with the idolaters and the like. However, its absolute wrongness cannot be hurriedly claimed or it cannot be rejected off hand in toto. While going through the Holy Quran, one comes across several verses about the distorted Books of faith (Torah and Psalms) and a few verses are reproduced here for ready reference:

> '....... and a party from among them index used to hear the word of Allah, then altered it after they had understood it, and they know (this)' (2:75)

The corruption and distortion of the Jewish scriptures is beyond doubt in the light of what has been put forth by the historians and researchers also.

> 'O People of the Book, you follow no good till you observe the Torah and the Gospel and that which is revealed to you from your Lord- And surely that which has been revealed to thee from thy Lord will make many of them increase in inordinacy and disbelief......' (5:68)

This speaks of their (Jews) holding the revelations not in purity.

> 'And some of them arc illiterate; they know not the Book but only (from) hearsay, and they do but conjecture.' (2:78)

Conjecture means following the guess-work, as the holy Books were not accessible to Jew masses; only men of learning, Scribes , Pharisees, knew and possess them, which is revealed by the historians also.

> 'Woe! then to those who write the Book with their hands then say, this is from Allah, so that they may take for it a small price......' (2: 79.)

> 'And when Allah took a Covenant from those who were given the Book: you shall explain it to men and shall not hide it. But they cast it behind their backs and took a small price for it...' (3: 186)

> 'O People of the Book, indeed our Messenger has come to you, making clear to you much of that which you concealed of the book.......' (5:15)

> '......they alter the words from their places and neglect a portion of that whereof they were reminded, (5: 13)

'And (I am) verifier of that which is before me of the Torah and I allow you part of that which was forbidden to you....'

Here Isa (Jesus), a.s. is seen addressing the Jews.

> 'And if they had observed the Torah and the Gospel, and that which is revealed to them from their Lord, they would certainly have eaten from above them and from beneath their feet.......' (5: 66)

> If anymore there remains doubt about the falsification of the Old Testament or the Hebrew Bible, then one should read the book of Deuteronomy carefully which narrates, 'so Moses the Servant of the Lord died there in the land of Moab, according to the word of the Lord. And buried him in a valley in the Lord of Moab, over against Bah-poor: but no man knoweth of his sepulchre unto this day.... And the children of Israel wept for Moses in the plains of Moab thirty days : So the days of weeping and mourning for Moses were ended' (34: 5,6,8)

These verses from chapter 34 point to a fact that the Old Testament seems a job of a historiographer but not Musa (Moses), a.s. Had it been the job of Moses, how come he would narrate the above story. A western scholar, Dummelow, in his 'Bible Commentary' writes, on close examination, however, it must be admitted that the Pentateuch reveals many features inconsistent with the traditional view that in its present form it is the work of Moses. For instance, it may be safely granted that Moses did not write the account of his own death in Dt. 34 (Deuteronomy). The statement in Dt. 1:1 that Moses spoke these words beyond Jordan is evidently made from the standpoint of one living in Canaan, which Moses never did ... Other passages which can with difficulty be ascribed to him are Ex. 6: 26-27, 11:3, 16:35-36, Lv. 18: 24-28, Nu. 12:3 and Dt. 2:12'.

The Jews till date continue to be in confusion about the authenticity of the Old Testament which could sustain reason. It is astonishing to see how Israelite parliament's (Knesset) member recently took an outrageous liberty in using blasphemous language against Daud (King David), a.s., apparently in referring to the ungodly or distorted portions of the Old Testament. The press clipping of *The Hindustan Times* dated 14th February, 1993, is reproduced here in original:

The Transgressors : There is no second thought about the transgression of Israelites who unceremoniously infringed and violated the holy Messages and exceeded the limits that paved the way for unending chaos and confusion in the matters of their faith which was once linked by them to Divination, a ritual, probably still used by some of them, to ascertain the will of gods by shaking a dice (Urim and Thumunim) out of a box (Epod). One gets amazed to see as to what is written in the Scriptures about the transgression of Israelites.

> Ezra, the learned priest of Jews, says, 'then were assembled unto me every one that trembled at the words of the God of Israel, because of the transgression of those that had been carried away; and I sat astonished until the evening sacrifice'
>
> Book of Ezra 9: 4; The Old Testament.

> 'O my God, I am ashamed and blush to lift up my face to then, my God: for our iniquities are increased over our head, and our trespass is grown up unto the heaves' Book of Ezra 9:6

Iniquity refers to wickedness and unrighteousness.

> 'So far the iniquity of Jews, we forbade them the good things which had been made lawful for them and for their hindering mater (people) from Allah's way'
>
> Holy Quran 4: 160

> 'He said (Moses): My Lord, I have control of none but my ownself and my brother; so distinguish between us and the transgressing people'
>
> Holy Quran 5:25

'O people of the Book, exaggerate not in the matter of your religion unjustly.......' Holy Quran 5:77

' .... And if People of the Book had believed, it would have been better for them. Some of them are believers but most of them are transgressors'

Holy Quran 3:109

'And ask them about the town which stood by the sea. When they violated the Sabbath, when their fish came to them on their Sabbath day on the surface, and when it was not their Sabbath they came not to them. Thus did we try them because they transgressed'

Holy Quran 7:163

The above verse refers to the temptation of Israelites to violate the Law, as Sabbath was the day of their prayer (seventh day of the week, i.e., Saturday). Scholars generally believe that it is the town of Ela, as referred in this verse, which stood by the Red Sea.

'For I know thy rebellion, and thy stiff neck; behold, while I am yet alive with you this day, ye have been rebellious against thy Lord; and how much more after my death? For I know that after my death ye will utterly corrupt yourselves, and turn aside from the way I have commanded you ....'

Moses in Deuteronomy 31:27 and 29

Says Ezekiel the priest,

'But when the righteous turneth away from his righteousness and committeth iniquity, and doeth according to all the abominations that wicked man doeth ....' Bk. of Ezekiel 18: 24 the Old Testament.

'For there is no faithfulness in their mouth, their inward part is very wicked; their throat is an open sepulchre; they utter with their tongue'

David in the Book of Psalms 5:9

'Depart from me, all ye workers of iniquity'

David in the Book of Psalms 6:8

'O Jerusalem, Jerusalem, thou that killest the Prophets, and stonest them which are sent unto thee ......

Jesus in Mathew's Gospel 23:37, Luke's Gospel 13:34

'How terrible for you, teachers of the Law and Pharisees, you hypocrites, you lock the door to the kingdom of heaven in the People's faces, and you yourself don't go in, nor do you allow in those who are trying to enter... you are like white washed tombs, which look fine on the outside but full of bones and decaying corpses on the inside— on the outside you appear good to everybody, but inside you are full of hypocrisy and sins'

Jesus in Gospel Matthew 23:13.27,2H Luke 11:39,40,52

'And because; the iniquity shall abound, the love of many shall wax cold'

Jesus in Gospal.Mathew 24: 12

Israelites - Cursed by the Prophets : It is generally seen that all the Prophets cursed the Israelite unfaithfuls for their persistent disbelief and warned the transgressors the divine punishment so that they refrain from unrighteouness. While going through the history of nations, one observes with amazement the treatment Israelites received over the centuries. The Babylonian kings and later Romans savaged Jerusalem and persecuted Jews inhumanely and those survived were taken as slaves. Even the events of present century concerning Jewish persecutions are fresh in our memory.

'Those who disbelieved from among the children of Israel were cursed by the tongue of David, and Jesus, Son of Mary, because they, disobeyed and exceeded the limits' Holy Quran 5: 78

'Behold, your house its left unto you desolate'

Jesus in Gospel, Mathew 23: 38

Here Isa (Jesus), a.s., curses Pharisees and Scribes (Jews) for their wickedness. Desolate means solitary, neglected, miserable, depopulate, devastate, and the like.

> 'They shall fall by the edge of sword, and shall be led away captive into all nations...'
>
> Jesus in Gospel, Luke 21:24

> 'And he (a far off nation) shall besiege thee in all thy gates until 'thy high and fenced walls come down ....'
>
> Moses in Deuteronomy 28: 52

> 'Those who conceal the clear proofs and the guidance that We revealed after We have made it clear in the Book for men, these it is whom Allah curses, and those who curse, curse them (too), except those who repent and amend and make manifest (truth) ....'
>
> Holy Quran 2: 159-60

> 'His (unrighteous) mischief shall return upon his own head, and his violent dealing shall come down upon his own pate' David in the Book of Psalms 7: 16

In Archaic language 'pate' means seat of intellect.

> 'And thou shalt not go aside from any of the words which I command thee this day – if thou wilt not hearken unto thee the voice of the Lord thy God, to observe to do all his commandments.....,that all these, curses shall come upon thee; and overtake thee....'
>
> Moses in Deuteronomy 28: 14-15

Israelites - in the Holy Quran: On studying all the Scriptures including reliable commentaries one gets satisfied the way Holy Quran narrates most profoundly and unambiguously the story of Hebrews about their belief, Prophets and Revelations, their iniquity, their arrogance and aversion, and their depredation and desolation.

3

Propagation of Islam

Law's Supremacy

The institution of law exists in human society from time immemorial. Every race, every religion and every group of men has made some contributions in this sphere.

Law, as defined in an English dictionary is a rule of actions established by an authority, such as the government in a country. A citizen has to abide by the law and show respect to it, otherwise there are prescribed penalties for actions contrary to the established laws.

According to the Holy Quran, the greatest of Ruler and the Supreme Law-Giver is Allah. All His creatures have to obey His commands and to follow His laws. No man can change Allah's law. Those who refuse to obey or judge according to His law as contained in the Quran are wrongdoers, unbelievers and rebels.

Islam is the greatest law-giving institution in the world and its laws are supreme in all matters. These laws are restricted within the limits prescribed by the Shariah. The commandments of Allah and His Prophet are unchangeable and cannot be amended. They are to be accepted and obeyed and no legislative body can make any alterations or modifications in them or make any law that is against their teachings.

In the eyes of Islam, every person is equal and everyone has equal rights to seek redress through a court of law. Everyone has equal rights to protection of life, property and honour. Islam proclaims equal treatment in law, irrespective of one's status or position in life. Even the ruler is not exempted. He has to appear before a court of law, if called. The teaching as well as the practice of Prophet Muhammad (PBUH) followed by that of his successors show that judges never hesitated to decide against the rulers in cases of default.

Khalifa Hadrat Umar, in a case filed against him, appeared personally before the judge with the appellant, who was a Jew, and so did Hadrat Ali, the fourth Khalifa of Islam, in yet another case.

An incident is noted in *Sahih Bukhari* that in Medina, a woman of the Banu Makhzum tribe committed a theft. She was likely to be subjected to the punishment of the cutting off her hand. The chiefs of this powerful tribe prevailed upon Usama bin Zaid, who was held in high esteem by the Holy Prophet (PBUH), to intercede for her. On Usama's intervention the Holy Prophet (PBUH) said angrily, "Would you intervene in the punishment prescribed by Allah?"

Then he turned to those who were present and said:

> "What has been the cause of the downfall of the previous nations is that when a thief of noble origin was caught, he was allowed to go without punishment, whereas a thief of humble origin was subjected to punishment. I swear, by Allah, that if Fatima, daughter of Muhammad, committed a theft, I would have her hand cut off."

This tradition is a significant example of the supremacy of law in Islam.

Another incident is that of Amr bin Aas, who was the Governor of Egypt. A man accused him of whipping him without any just cause. Khalifa Hadrat Umar, after making enquiries, ordered that the man should lash the Governor with an equal number of stripes. Some of the men present there persuaded the aggrieved man to forgive Amr bin Aas and accept monetary compensation for the injury caused to him by the Governor.

The third incident relates to Jabalah, a convert from Christianity to Islam and the chief of his tribe. During tawaf of the Kaaba, the edge of his shawl accidentally came under the foot of an Arab villager. Jabalah, in anger, slapped the man on his face and broke his tooth. Khalifa Hadrat Umar permitted the villager to take revenge from Jabalah by slapping him on the face and breaking his tooth. When Jabalah came to know about this, he fled from the Islamic territory. With all his tribe, he went back to his old religion.

In Islam, therefore, nobody is above law; the ruler and the ruled are subject to the same law and there can be no discrimination on the basis of power or position. If the ruler himself committed a prohibited act, he would not be able to reproach others for the same act. Therefore, Islam has struck at the root and source of this kind of evil by emphasizing the supremacy of law, it declared that nobody is above law, not even the Prophet and his family.

Fellow Beings and their Rights

The Quran guides man with regard to his dealings with other individuals of the society. It lays emphasis on justice, trust, respect for life and property, patience, humility, thankfulness and forgiveness. The fundamental relations between a man and other individuals are those of parents and children, husband and wife. It also includes relations between relatives, neighbours, the poor and the needy, orphans and non-Muslims. The Quran says:

"Treat with kindness your parents and kindred and orphans and those in need; Speak fair to the people."
(2: 83)

Parents and Children : Among worldly relations, the relations between parents and children have the highest status. Islam has given great importance to this relationship placing respect and kindness to parents next only to belief in Allah and the command to be grateful to Allah is immediately followed by the command to be grateful to one's parents. The Quran says:

"Show gratitude to Me and to thy parents."(31.-14)

It further says:

"We have enjoined on man kindness to his parents."
(46:15)

Allah says:

"Be kind to parents. Whether one or both of them attain old age in thy life, say not to them a word of contempt, nor repel them, but address them in terms of honour.

And out of kindness, lower to them the wing of humility, and say:

"My Lord! Bestow on them Thy Mercy even as they cherished me in childhood." (17:23-24)

The Holy Prophet (PBUH) received very little of his mother's love and upbringing; yet whenever he visited her grave, he wept and prayed to Allah to have mercy on her soul.

Once a person came to the Holy Prophet (PBUH) and asked:

"O messenger of Allah, what are the rights of parents on their children ? "

He replied:

"For you, they can be heaven or hell."

It is clear from this that, kind and gentle treatment of parents leads to heaven and their ill-treatment to hell.

Among parents, the status of mother is higher, because she undergoes more sufferings for the sake of her children. The Quran says:

> "In travail upon travail did his mother bear him, and in years twain was his weaning:" (31:14)

The Holy Prophet (PBUH) said:

> "Heaven is beneath the feet of mothers."

The rights of children on their parents are that they should bring them up in the best possible manner, to cherish and nurture them, to protect them from all kinds of evil and to provide them with the best education and training.

The Holy Prophet (PBUH) said:

> "No father has given his child anything better than good manners."
>
> "He who is not affectionate to God's creatures and to his own children, Allah will not be affectionate to him."

Husband and Wife

> "And they (women) have rights similar to those (of men) over them." (2: 228)

This verse clearly shows that both husband and wife have equal rights over each other. In his Farewell Pilgrimage, the Holy Prophet (PBUH) declared:

> "O you people! You have rights over your wives and your wives have rights over you. Treat your wives with kindness and love; verily you have taken them on the security of Allah."

Both husband and wife are a source of support, comfort and protection to each other. They are, therefore, expected to live together in peace and love, as the Quran says:

> "He created for you mates from among yourselves that you may dwell in tranquility with them and He has put love and mercy between your hearts."
>
> (30: 21)

Husbands are required to provide sustenance to their wives, clothe them and house them. They are required to live with them (wives) on a footing of kindness and equity.

A virtuous wife is bound to love her husband and prove to be a source of comfort to him. The Quran says:

> "Therefore, the righteous women are devoutedly obedient and guard in (the husband's) absence what Allah would have them guard." (4:34)

According to Abdullah Yusuf Ali, the meaning of the verse is that "the good wife is obedient and harmonious in her husband's presence, and in his absence guards his reputation and property and her own virtue as ordained by God,"

In this regard, the Holy Prophet (PBUH) said:

> "The best wife is one who pleases her husband when he looks at her; carries out his orders when he orders them; and who guards his property and her sanctity in his absence from home."

Relatives : Islam lays great stress on the rights of relatives. Allah has commanded us to do good and show kindness to our relatives, and the command to do so comes immediately after the command to do good to our parents. The Quran says:

> "Worship none but Allah and treat with kindness your parents and kindred and orphans and those in need." (2:83)

The Holy Prophet (PBUH) is reported to have said:

> "Giving of alms to relatives carries two rewards: one the reward of alms and the other is the reward of helping relatives."
>
> "A person who does not respect the rights of his relatives will not enter Paradise. "
>
> "One who breaks off his relations with his relatives shall not enter Paradise."

Neighbours : Verse 36 of Surah Nisa enjoins the doing of good to *"neighbours who are near, neighbours who are strangers."*

Verse 7 of Surah Maun condemns those who refuse (to supply) neighbourly needs.

It is reported the Holy Prophet (PBUH) laid so much emphasis on the rights of neighbours that some of his companions thought that neighbours might be included in the list of heirs.

There are a number of sayings of the Holy Prophet (pbuh) in connection with the rights of neighbours. He is reported to have said,

> "If you wish to become a perfect believer, you should treat your neighbour generously. "
>
> "The most virtuous of you all is he who gives the best treatment to his neighbours."
>
> "That person is not a perfect Muslim who eats his fill and leaves his neighbour hungry."
>
> "He who believes in one Allah and the life beyond, let him not injure his neighbour."

Orphans and the Needy : In many verses of the Holy Quran, the commandment regarding the needy and the poor and orphans are linked with those regarding parents and relatives. It says:

"And treat with kindness your parents and relatives and orphans and those in need." (2:83)

"Spend of your substance, out of love for Him, for your kin, for orphans, for the needy, for wayfarer." (2: 177)

"Say: Whatever you spend that is good is for parents and relatives and orphans and those in want." (2:215)

Apart from the command to do good and show kindness to them, emphasis is laid on the feeding of the poor. The Quran says:

"And they feed, for the love of Allah, the indigent, the orphan, and the captive." (76: 8)

"Have you seen the one who denies the Day of Judgement? Then such is the one who repulses the orphan, (with harshness) and urges not the feeding of the poor." (107: 1-3)

One of Holy Prophet's (PBUH) sayings about giving something to one who asks for help is, *"O Aishah! Do not turn the poor away, without giving them, if but half a date."*

About good treatment to orphans, the Holy Prophet (PBUH) said:

"The best Muslim house is that in which is an orphan who is well-treated and the worst Muslim house is that in which is an orphan ill-treated."

Islam's Invitation (Dawa)

Man is endowed with a lot of talents and potentials some of which he gains naturally through his physical and mental make up like eating, walking, sleeping and talking. In the intellectual field, he can acquire knowledge through environment, books and teachers. In these physical and mental fields, no Dawa is required because human experience, make up and intuition take care of these areas.

There are certain other areas, which he cannot learn anything about through science and observation only. For example:

1. Is there a Creator of this universe?
2. Is there life after death?
3. Is there a higher aim of life?
4. What is the place of morality in human life?
5. Are there any laws that Allah has prescribed for mankind and to which He demands complete obedience?

These areas can be explained only through Dawa. So Dawa means inviting ourselves and all others to obey Allah and His laws which were given to the mankind through a long chain of messengers and prophets. For this the Holy Quran enjoins upon us:

> "Let there arise out of you, a band of people, inviting to all that is good, enjoining what is right and forbidding what is wrong: They are the ones to attain felicity." (3:104)

It is for this purpose that Allah also said:

> "You are the best of peoples evolved for mankind, enjoining what is right, for bidding what is wrong, and believing in Allah." (3:110)

And also:

> "If a contingent from every expedition remained behind, they could devote themselves to studies in religion and admonish the people when they return to them that thus they (may learn) to guard themselves (against evil). (9:122)

Islam requires total surrender to Allah, in private as well as in public, inwardly as well as outwardly. This has two important and clear implications, one, as most of human life comprises of relationships with other people, living in surrender to Allah cannot be realized fully unless other people join us in our endeavour. Hence, inviting others to join in one venture, that is Dawa, is an essential part of being a Muslim. Two, Islam is a process, a life-long pursuit. Hence, we must continuously invite ourselves and everyone else to join in this pursuit: Thus, Dawa is integral to Islam. To be a Muslim means to continually strive to become a true Muslim, that means to do Dawa.

Dawa cannot be restricted to any race, colour, community or religion, Dawa has to be addressed to the 'self, to the individual and also to the society at large.

Dawa is the most important and significant Sunnah of the Prophet (PBUH) as the Holy Quran says:

> "O Messenger! proclaim the (message) which hath been sent to thee from thy Lord. If thou didst, not, thou wouldst not have fulfiled and proclaimed His mission." (5:67)

Allah has bestowed upon every human being the faculty to recognize and differentiate between good and evil. He has also put a yearning in them to adopt good and shun evil. This fact is inherent in His laws that human beings who follow His laws will be rewarded while those who reject His laws will be punished.

On the other hand, man has also been given free will so that in this life of endeavour and achievement, he may be free to work for and achieve what he likes. In pursuit of his goals a man may adopt ways and means which hinder his intuitive faculties to recognize. However man has been given more than just instincts and intuition by Allah, to save him from blunders and pitfalls. He virtually made it fool proof by sending a chain of prophets to clearly and openly, indicate right and wrong conduct, and to make the laws given by Allah clear to man by prophets own example. The Quran says:

> "Although there came to them our messengers with clear signs, yet, even after that, many of them continued to commit excesses in the land."
>
> (5:32)

And also:

> "O people of the book! Now hath come unto you, making (things) clear unto you, Our messenger, after the break in (the series of) Our messengers, lest ye should say: "There came unto us no bringer of glad tidings and no warner (from evil)"; But now hath come unto you a bringer of glad tidings and a warner (from evil)." (5:19)

All these prophets were human beings and they themselves put into practice what they were preaching. With the advent of the Holy Prophet (PBUH), Muslims were given the responsibility of being the models of right conduct for all mankind. According to the Quran:

> "Thus have We made of you an Ummah justly balanced, that ye might be witnesses over the nations."
>
> (2:143)

In the order of Dawa, the first thing is the belief in the fundamental concepts of:

(1) Tauhid-Unity of Allah.

(2) Risalat - Prophethood.

(3) Akhirat - Day of Judgement.

Thus, the starting point and the basic core of Dawa should be as the Quran makes very clear: total surrender to one Allah, obeying His messengers and belief in accountability in life after death.

It is to these beliefs that everyone should be invited but we should not start our invitation by repudiating what is wrong with others, but in the way the Quran says:

"Invite (all) to the way of thy Lord with wisdom and beautiful preaching and argue with them in ways that are best and most gracious." (16:125)

Dawa is the fulfilment of this command *"to invite all to the way of thy Lord."* Muslims should make the effort to invite other men to share and benefit from the religious truth which they have been given. Since this truth is not only theoretical, but also practical, the men of religion are urged to take it to others.

"Inviting" is not forcing; Allah has commanded:

"Let there be no compulsion in religion." (2:256)

The object of this invitation can be fulfiled only with the free consent of the invities that is why the Holy Quran has specified the means of persuasion to be used. If the non-Muslim remains unconvinced, the Muslim is to rest his case with God: The Holy Prophet (PBUH) allowed those Christians who were not convinced by his presentation of Islam to keep their faith and return home in peace.

From this, it follows that the order desired by Islam is one where men are free to present and argue their religious beliefs with one another. It is a kind of seminar where he who knows better is free to speak and to convince, and the others are free to listen and be convinced. Islam puts its trust in man's rational power to discriminate between the true and the false.

"He that receives guidance benefits his own soul: But he that strays injures his own soul." (39:41)

Islamic dawa is therefore, an invitation to think, to debate and to argue.

Muslim States vs the World

Islam is a religion of peace and no Muslim State can follow a policy of territorial expansion and unprovoked aggression. The foreign policy of a Muslim state should be such as to advance the cause of Islam and the moral, cultural and political objectives of its society and to preserve and protect its territorial integrity. The Quran and the Holy Prophet's (PBUH) Sunnah provide sufficient guidance to enable a Muslim state to frame its foreign policy.

In pre-Islamic days, international law had no independent existence; it was dependent on the will and pleasure of the head of the state. The first Muslim State in Medina was established and governed by the Holy Prophet (PBUH). It was a confederacy of villages inhabited by Muslims, Jews, Christians and pagan Arabs.

The rules of international conduct comprise not only internal legislation, but also treaties, relations and agreements with other states. The ambassador is considered to be immune from all violation, even if he brings an unpleasant message. He enjoys all liberty of creed and security as long as he stays in a Muslim state. Like other aspects of life in Islam, international relations of a Muslim state are based on Divine guidance given in the Quran. They are based on the following principles:

(1) Belief in the unity of mankind, in origin, in human status and in aims.

(2) Respect for other people's interests and rights to life, honour and property, as long as they do not encroach upon the rights of Muslims.

(3) Maintaining peaceful relations with the exchange of goodwill missions,

(4) Intolerance of encroachment in international relations. The Islamic state must defend itself and suppress all attempts to violate or disturb its peace, or endanger its security or exploit its peaceful policies.

The law of war and peace in Islam does not allow an aggressive war nor makes the killing of people and animals or the destruction of crops, homes and places of worship its objective. It does not allow the killing of women, children and aged people nor the torture of war prisoners or the imposition of its teachings on the conquered people. It is only a defensive measure justified as long as wrong, injustice and aggression exist in the world.

(5) Fulfilling the obligations undertaken by the Muslim state and honouring the treaties concluded between the Islamic State and other states. This is binding as long as the other parties remain faithful to their obligations and honour their treaties.

This state does not exist only for itself and its own subjects. It has a wide scope and an important mission in the international field. It has not only to strive for the prosperity and advancement of its own citizens but also make valuable contributions to humanity on an international level in education, economics, industry, politics and other fields.

Islam seeks to establish a world community, with complete equality among people without distinction of race, class or country. It seeks to convert by persuasion, allowing no compulsion in religions beliefs. According to Islam, it is the duty of every individual to make constant efforts for spreading good and preventing evil.

Law in Islam

Islamic law is based on submission to the Will of Allah. This is a fundamental principle of religion and since Islamic law is based upon Islam, it covers all aspects of life. It is a way or path guiding the Muslims. The law governing all matters is known as Shariah.

Islamic law or the *Shariah* is the law which binds Muslims into a single community. The word *Shariah* is derived from a root, meaning path or road. It is the path which leads to Allah, His law which guides Muslims to run their spiritual, moral, social and physical lives in accordance with Islamic principles.

The purpose of this law is to chalk out a system of duties which would enable the believers to live a righteous life in this world and prepare themselves for the next.

A Muslim is expected to live according to this law, both in his private and social life. It is, therefore, the guide to all human actions and embraces all aspects of human life. It guides man as to how he should conduct his life, deal with his neighbours, how he should eat and sleep, buy and sell and how he should pray and perform other acts of worship. It is through this law that the value of human actions in the sight of Allah is made known to human beings so that they can distinguish between the straight road and that which will lead them astray. The *Shariah* or the Islamic law provides for him the knowledge of right and wrong. It is by his freewill that man must decide which path to follow.

In essence, all of the *Shariah* is contained in the Quran. It contains the principles of all the laws, further explained in the *Hadith* and *Sunnah* which together constitute the second source of Islamic law. This was further understood with the help of the consensus of the Islamic community-Ijma. Finally, these three sources of Islamic law were complemented by human reasoning-Qiyas, where necessary.

Thus the *Shariah,* the source of all laws for the Muslims is revelation manifested through the Quran and explained through the *Sunnah* and then interpreted through *Ijma,* the agreed opinion of the jurists and finally *Qiyas* or human reasoning. These sources fall into two main categories; the primary sources which comprised the Quran and the *Sunnah* and the secondary or dependent sources which are *Ijma* or consensus and *Qiyas* or reasoning.

The supremacy of the Quran and Sunnah over the other sources can be illustrated from many incidents. For example, when the Holy Prophet (PBUH) appointed Muaz ibn Jabal as the Governor and judge in Yemen, he asked him:

"According to what will you judge?"

"According to the Book of Allah. "

"And if you find nothing therein?"

"According to the Sunnah of the Prophet (PBUH)."

"And if you find nothing therein?"

"Then I will exert myself to form my own judgement."

The Holy Prophet's (PBUH) response was:

"Praise be to Allah Who has guided the messenger of His Prophet to that which pleases His Prophet."

It follows from this tradition that the Quran and the Sunnah were the roots of the law, while the opinion of the jurists could be brought in by way of supplementation where the main sources were silent.

Discipline and Self-respect

Islam imposes strict discipline of good behaviour and conduct upon its followers. The maintenance of one's dignity and self-respect is an essential quality in a man. It is needed in every aspect of life and at every turn; without it, a feeling of inferiority exists, no one pays any attention to what such a person says. Others never respect a person who neither respects himself nor maintains discipline.

Islam expects Muslims to present the highest example of good morality and manners. As long as Muslims maintained firm faith and discipline, they did not lose their sense of self-respect.

The Quran says:

"You are the best of peoples, evolved for mankind, enjoining what is right, for bidding what is wrong...."

(3:110)

Self-respect is different from vanity. It is the name given

to the quality by which a person understands and learns to respect himself so that he does not stoop to anything low. When a self-respecting person comes across an evil, he passes by it untouched. The evil ones do not have the courage to even try to attract him.

To maintain one's self-respect, one has to be careful at all times and in every way. Such a person's behaviour must reflect his self-respect. Yet there must be no shadow of vanity or a sense of superiority about him. Dignified behaviour is the essence of self-respect. The Prophet (PBUH) said the following in the context of prayers:

> "When you hear the call for prayers, proceed calmly and with dignity and do not be in a hurry."

Beggary is strongly condemned in Islam as it is a negation of self-respect. It makes a man shameless. Even asking for help in everyday matters is not encouraged. The Prophet (PBUH) said that when a person must ask for help or assistance only the God-fearing should be approached. This command ensures that God-fearing persons will either comply, or if not in a position to help, will refuse politely. So the one who has asked for help will not lose his self-respect. A Muslim endowed with the values of Islam cares only for Allah; he does not bow down to anyone but Allah. As a Muslim, he knows that honour and respect are for Allah and His Prophet and through him for every Muslim. Thus, to maintain one's self-respect is to maintain the respect and honour of Islam.

Islam and Struggle (Jihad)

The Arabic word Jihad means to strive, to exert oneself. In religious terminology it expresses struggle against one's evil inclinations or exertion for the sake of Islam and the Muslim Ummah, for example, an armed struggle against the unbelievers if Islam is under threat, the spread of belief in Allah or to work for the moral betterment of the Islamic society.

Jurists have distinguished four different ways in which the believer may fulfil his Jihad obligation: by his heart, his tongue, his hands and by the sword. The first is concerned with defeating evil. This type of Jihad was so significant in the eyes of the Holy Prophet (PBUH) that he regarded it as the greater Jihad. The second and third are mainly fulfilled by supporting the right and correcting the wrong. The fourth is equivalent to the meaning of war and is concerned with fighting the unbelievers and the enemies of the faith. The believers are required to sacrifice their wealth and lives in the service of Allah.

Jihad is thus, the use of all our energies and resources to establish the Islamic system of life. In the first phase, a person learns to control his own bad desires and inclinations. This is Jihad or struggle within ourselves which is responsible for establishing Maroof-right, and removing Munkar-evil from our lives and from society. It demands the use of all our material and mental resources. Finally, we may be required to give up our life for the cause of Islam.

Jihad does not necessarily mean war or fighting since exertion in Allah's path may be achieved by peaceful means as well. In the early Surahs revealed in Mecca, the emphasis was on persuasion. The Holy Prophet (PBUH) in the discharge of his prophetic mission warned his people against idol - worship and invited them to worship Allah; as is evident from the following verse:

> "if any strive (with might and main), they do so for
> their own souls:" (29:6)

Which expressed Jihad in terms of the salvation of soul rather than a struggle for conversion to Islam. In the later revelations, Jihad is often expressed in terms of strife and there is no doubt that in certain verses, the concept of Jihad is synonymous with the words war and fighting.

In Mecca, the Muslims suffered for several years under the worst kind of punishments, were denied religious freedom, persecuted for the sake of their religion and terrorized with regard to property and personal safety. For all these reasons, they were compelled to leave their homes and migrate to Medina, patiently submitting to Allah's orders. Whenever they felt the urge to resist the oppression or to take revenge from the oppressors, the Prophet (PBUH) held them back, telling them to be patient.

"I have not been ordered to fight," he would say.

Then Allah revealed the first verses permitting war:

> "To those against whom war is made, permission is given (to fight), because they are wronged - and verily Allah is most powerful for their aid.
>
> (They are) those who have been expelled from their homes in defiance of right - (for no cause) except that they say, "Our lord is Allah. " Did not Allah check one set of people by means of another there would surely have been pulled down monasteries, churches, synagogues and mosques, in which the name of Allah is commemorated in abundant measure Allah will certainly aid those who aid his (cause)." (22:39-40)

This permission was motivated by the fact that the Muslims suffered injustice, and were forced to leave their homes and migrate without justification. These verses point out that God helps only those who fear Him and therefore do not use war as an instrument for destruction, for subjugating the weak and satisfying their own desires. On the contrary they obey Allah's orders and summon people to do what is right and abstain from wrong.

These verses are very clear and do not contain even the slightest evidence of religious compulsion. They are not only concerned with Muslims, but deal with non-Muslims as well when it is said: "there would surely have been pulled down monasteries, churches, synagogues and mosques."

Fighting between Muslims and non-Muslims has been dealt with comprehensively in many verses of the Holy Quran. These verses describe the causes which may lead to it, its aim, upon the attainment of which fighting must stop, the preparations for it by the Muslims and the necessary caution against its unexpected out-break.

The following verses caution Muslims against being the transgressors:

> "Fight in the cause of Allah those who fight you, but do not transgress limits. For Allah loveth not transgressors." (2:190)
>
> "And fight them on until there is no more tumult or oppression, and there prevail justice and faith in Allah; But if they cease, let there be no hostility except to those who practice oppression." (2:193)

These verses order the Muslims to fight in the way of Allah. They prohibit the provocation of hostility and this prohibition is reinforced by Allah's dislike of those who provoke hostility. They also define the aim upon the attainment of which war must end. This aim is achieved when there is no more persecution in matters of religion.

The principles explained in these verses can be found in the same or similar words, in many other Surahs for example, Surah Al-Nisa, Surah Al-Anfal and Surah Al-Taubah.

> "and fight the pagans all together as they fight you all together. But know that Allah is with those who restrain themselves." (9:36)

From these verses of the Holy Quran, it becomes clear that there is not a single verse in the Quran which could support the opinion that the aim of fighting in Islam is conversion. It also becomes clear that the reasons for fighting are: to stop aggression, to protect the mission of Islam and to defend religious freedom.

Poll-tax or Jizya is not a financial compensation for the granting of one's life or preservation of religion, but a symbol of submission and resistance from harmful acts and a contribution in carrying out the burdens of the state.

Although Jihad is considered to be very important, it is not included in the five pillars of Islam. The reason is that the five pillars are not necessarily to be enforced by the state; they must be observed by individuals. In other words, the basic articles are regarded as individual duties like prayer or fasting which each believer must perform and each is liable to punishment if he fails to perform the duty. Jihad, on the other hand, unless the Muslim community is subjected to a sudden attack and therefore all believers including women and children are under the obligation to fight, is regarded by all jurists as a collective obligation of the whole Muslim community. It is regarded as Farz-e-Kifaya which is binding upon the Muslims as a group not individually. If the duty is fulfiled by a part of the community, it ceases to be obligatory on others. The whole community, however, falls into error if the duty is not performed at all.

Jihad must be preceded by an invitation to Islam. The Prophet (PBUH) followed the rule, which he had himself laid down and his early successors seem to have followed their master's example. In the campaigns against the Byzantines and Persians, the Arab commanders addressed invitations to their enemies, inviting them first to accept Islam or pay the tribute, before they launched their offensive. In the early Muslim conquests, the commander often waited for three days after the invitation had been sent before actual fighting took place. During this period, the Muslims were ready to negotiate when the enemy demanded it. This often led to a peaceful settlement as in such cases as the surrender of a number of towns in Iraq and Syria.

In Islam, the objective of man is neither the achievement

of victory nor the acquisition of the enemy's property; it is rather the fulfilment of a duty-Jihad in Allah's way. The Muslims were advised to refrain from shedding blood or destroying property for the achievement of their objective. This general rule is based on Hadrat Abu Bakr's address to the expedition sent to Syria as well as to other similar utterances by succeeding Khalifas.

It is repeatedly stressed in the Holy Quran that the object of any fighting forced upon Muslims should be to put down aggression and persecution, for persecution is worse than killing. When the enemy stops fighting the Muslims should do likewise; when freedom from persecution is secured, fighting should be brought to an end.

If war becomes unavoidable, every effort must be made to limit its mischief and horror. It must be waged in such a way so as to cause the least possible amount of damage to life and property. All hostilities must be brought to an end as early as possible. Savage practices like disfiguring the dead enemy or torturing prisoners of war are prohibited in Islam.

Muslims' Relations with Non-Muslims

Islam is a religion of love, mercy and tolerance and it preaches freedom of belief and faith. It recognizes the rights of non-Muslims living in an Islamic State. They were called protected people or *zimmies* because they lived in peace and tranquility under the protection of the Islamic State.

The messenger of Allah practiced religious tolerance towards non-Muslims and did not use force to compel people of other religions to embrace Islam as it would have been against the commands of the Quran:

"Let there be no compulsion in religion." (2: 256)

Muslims are commanded here not to force Islam on people of other religions, because belief in any religion depends on faith, and faith cannot be induced by force. In Islam, religious tolerance is so highly recommended that there is no room for any compulsion to accept Islam; only argument and logic can be used to show others the guidance of Islam. The Quran advocates a just and kind treatment for non-Muslims. The Holy Prophet (PBUH) was command by Allah to grant asylum to any unbeliever who asked for it.

Muslims believe in all previous messengers and all of them are held in equal esteem. For a Muslim, Allah is none other than the God of Hadrat Musa and Hadrat Isa. The followers of these messengers are called the *'People of the Book'* in the Quran. The Holy Prophet (PBUH), therefore, gave them special consideration and status in the Islamic State of Medina and freedom to practice their religions. He showed immense goodwill and understanding towards them.

Their scriptures and places of worship were respected. They enjoyed complete security and protection of their lives, property and religion. No synagogue or church was destroyed. They were allowed to maintain and repair their places of worship and also to construct new ones. They were granted judicial antonomy. Their civil cases were decided according to their own laws and by their own courts. In addition, they were allowed to seek justice in a Muslim court, if they so desired. The Muslim authorities were not allowed to interfere with their personal laws.

In fact, in safeguarding the rights of non-Muslims, an Islamic state has gone to such extremes as to give them the liberty of maintaining even those practices which are entirely opposed to the teachings of Islam. For example, the consumption of alcohol is forbidden to Muslims, yet the non-Muslim inhabitants of the country have the liberty to use alcohol. They have special permission from the state to manufacture or import alcohol.

Islam insists on kind treatment of non-Muslims. The Holy Prophet (PBUH) said:

> "If anyone wrongs a man to whom, a treaty has been granted, or burdens him above his strength, I will advocate against him on the Day of Judgement,"

Hadrat Abu Bakr said:

> "If a province or people receive you, make an agreement with them and keep your promise. Let them be governed by their laws and established customs; and take tribute from them as is agreed between you. Leave them in their religion and their land."

Hadrat Umar treated non-Muslims very kindly and justly. While imposing taxes upon them, he was very careful that enough was left for their maintenance. Even on his deathbed, he left instructions that non-Muslims should be treated justly and not overburdened with taxes. Such were the injunctions of the Holy Prophet (PBUH) and his immediate successors about the rights of non-Muslims.

4

The True Faith

Basic Faiths : The fundamental beliefs, which serve as the foundation of a religion, are called its doctrines or articles of faith. All the prophets of Allah, in their attempts to reform mankind, concentrated mainly on transferring their beliefs to their followers. The Holy Prophet (PBUH), too, began propagating his message by focusing attention on these beliefs.

These beliefs are stated in Iman-e-Mufassal which says:

> "I believe in Allah, in His angels, in His books, in His messengers, in the Last Day and in the fact that everything, good or bad, is decided by Allah, the Almighty, and in life after Death."

The Holy Quran says:

> "O you who believe! Believe in Allah and His messenger and the scripture which He hath sent to His messenger and the scripture which He sent to those before (him). Any who denieth Allah, His angels, His books, His messengers and the Day of Judgement hath gone far, far astray. " (4:136)

And also:

"... It is righteousness to believe in Allah and the Last Day and the angels and the book and the messengers." (2:177)

The fundamental beliefs or articles of faith are:

1. Unity or Oneness of Allah
2. Angels
3. Revealed books
4. Prophets
5. Life after death.

Allah and Oneness

Belief in the Unity and Oneness of Allah - Tauhid is the first and main principle of the Islamic faith. It means that Allah is the Supreme Being, the Creator, Sustainer and Master of the universe, the highest authority and hence exclusively worthy of worship. The first Surah of the Holy Quran begins with the words:

"Praise be to Allah, the Cherisher and Sustainer of the worlds. " (1:2)

Tauhid is the belief in Allah with all His powers. Allah is All-knowing, All-wise, and All-powerful. He is and will always be. He has no beginning and no end. He is the First and the Last. He has no parents or son. He has no partners of any sort in His attributes, power, work and dominion. The Quran says:

" Say, praise be to Allah, Who begets no son and has no partner in (His) dominion ..." (17:11)

And also:

"No son has He begotten, nor has He a partner in His dominion..." (25:2)

The Quran has laid the greatest emphasis on Allah's absolute Unity and Oneness, The concept has been summed up in Surah Ikhlas of the Holy Quran, which says:

> "Say He is Allah, the One and Only Allah, the Eternal, the Absolute. He begetteth not, nor is He begotten. And there is none like unto Him. " (112:1-4)

At another place, we are told:

> "Allah! There is no god but He the Living, the Self-subsisting, Eternal." (2:255)

And again:

> "There is nothing whatever like unto Him and He is the One that hears and sees (all things)." (42:11)

Islam emphatically proclaims that Allah, the Creator is not bound by any of the limitations of human beings or of anything else He has created. He has no body, nor form, no physical attributes, nor characteristics. He is the Originator and Fashioner of the universe with its vast and perfect system, the One Who sustains it and keeps it functioning according to His laws and plans.

Allah is beyond anything which the mind or senses of man can grasp or comprehend or imagine. He is above having any similarity to any of His creations for He alone is the Creator and everything else is created by Him. He alone is Divine and no other human being or any other creature can share His Divinity or His unique attributes. Allah is always concerned and involved with every single part of His creation. All His creations exist and fulfil their functions by His command and will. For His concern is not only in creating, but also in sustaining and providing for His creatures, in guiding, regulating and maintaining them.

The vast universe with its flawless system clearly indicates that there is one Creator and one Controller. The sun, the moon, the galaxy and the whole universe obey the laws of the Supreme Authority. There is complete harmony and everything is set perfectly in the system. There is no flaw and no need for improvement in it. Had there been more than one Creator and Controller, there would have been chaos and confusion as the Quran says:

> "If there were in the heavens and the earth other gods besides Allah, there would have been confusion in both." (21:22)

But there is no conflict and disorder in the universe. This perfect order and combination is the proof of the presence of one powerful Creator and Regulator.

Allah has created everything in the earth and heavens for the service of mankind. When a person surrenders himself to Allah's commands, he gains superiority over all other creatures in the universe.

Tauhid shapes and regulates the entire course of a Muslim's life. A believer in Tauhid is sure that Allah knows and sees everything, so he is restrained from committing a sin either secretly or in the darkness of the night because of his firm conviction that Allah sees everything all the time.

A person who truly and whole heartedly believes that Allah alone is the Master of the universe, the sole Authority and Law-giver and he himself is a humble servant before Him, will not obey or give his devotion or allegiance to other deities besides Allah. He would reject them all and submit himself to Allah alone and strive with all his might and energies against serving any deities other than Allah.

Allah and His Angels

Allah conveyed His revelation to prophets including Hadrat Muhammad (PBUH) through an angel, Hadrat Jibbrail. In the Holy Quran, angels are spoken of as 'messengers' which denotes their spiritual function of Divine messengers.

The Quran says:

> "He doth send down His angels with inspiration of His command to such of His servants as He pleaseth ...." (16:2)

Because of this important role of angels as bringers of Divine revelation to prophets, the belief in them is so important as to form a fundamental article of faith in Islam.

Angels act as Allah's agents and serve Him in many ways. They are created of light and unlike jinn and men have not been endowed with a free will. They are absolutely obedient to Allah's commands and are engaged in worship and service to Him. They are sent to protect men, to administer Allah's punishments, to carry His messages and to perform various other functions.

Angels are heavenly beings not visible to ordinary mortals and thus, belong to the category of the unseen unless they appear in human form. They were sent by Allah to bring messages to Hadrat Zakriya and to Hadrat Maryam before whom the angels appeared in human form. Angels also appeared in human form before Hadrat Ibrahim to give him the glad tidings of the birth of a son. Hadrat Lut was also warned by angels in human form of the impending doom of his wicked people and told to leave the town that was going to be destroyed.

Angels are one of Allah's creation. They have been given the necessary qualities and powers to carry out their duties They are not His daughters nor are they objects of worship. They have no knowledge except what Allah has taught them, they obey Allah and act on His commands. They prostrated before Adam when Allah commanded them to do so. Angels glorify and praise Allah. They never get tired. They do not need sleep, nor do they require the things needed by human beings.

Angels have various functions and duties. They act as Allah's messengers but do not descend except by Allah's command. They strengthen the hearts of the righteous believers and are their protectors. At the Battle of Badr, they helped and strengthened the hearts of the believers and put terror into the hearts of the unbelievers. They implore forgiveness for the believers but they can offer no intercession for them. They send blessings on the Holy Prophet (PBUH) and the believers.

Angels are the guardians of Hell-fire. They will welcome in Heaven all those who obey Allah's commands and will throw the wrong doers into Hell.

Angels record man's words and deeds. Each human is attended by two angels who record all his deeds upto the moment of his death. This record will be presented to him on the Day of Judgement. They are called the 'respected recorders.' The Quran says:

> "But verily, over you (are appointed angels) to protect you kind and honourable, writing down (your deeds)."
> (82:10-11)

There are many angels, the prominent among them are:

(1) Hadrat Jibbrail who brought revelations from Allah to the prophets including Hadrat Muhammad (PBUH).

(2) Hadrat Israil, also called the angel of death is responsible for taking our souls upon death.

(3) Hadrat Israfil who will blow the trumpet at the time of the end of the world, that is, on the Day of Judgement.

Holy Books : Revealation : Human beings are the servants of Allah and His agents on earth who need guidance to carry out their various duties and responsibilities. This guidance is contained in the books of revelation sent to mankind through prophets and messengers. Belief in the reality of Allah's guidance to mankind in the form of revealed books is another basic article of faith in Islam.

Allah, who has created for man all things that are on the earth and has made subservient to him all that is in the heavens and on the earth, has provided everything for man's physical needs, has also provided him with spiritual guidance.

Revelation is the name given to the means of communication employed by Allah for conveying His command and messages to prophets and apostles. Revelation is not due to the prophet's own thoughts, intelligence or knowledge, it is not acquired through study or learning nor is it earned through labour but it is a special gift from Allah.

About the various methods employed by Allah for communicating His commandments to His apostles, the Quran says:

> "It is not fitting for a man that Allah should speak to him except by inspiration, or from behind a veil or by the sending of a messenger to reveal with Allah's permission what Allah wills: ...." (42:51)

The guidance sent by Allah from time to time to His messengers was basically the same. The principles of religion relating the unity of Allah, His attributes, prayer, belief in prophethood, the Day of Judgement and the concept of reward and punishment for one's deeds in the life Hereafter are common to all the revealed books. However, as the needs of the people differed in different periods, the details of the Shariat laws given in these books also varied.

Each of the previous apostles and prophets was sent to some particular nation, people or tribe and therefore, the revelation sent to each was intended for the guidance of his people. It was not intended to be universal because humanity had not yet reached the stage of readiness for such a comprehensive and final guidance from Allah. This is clear from what the Quran states concerning the messages given to various prophets.

Moreover, by the time of the advent of the Holy Prophet (PBUH), the books revealed upto that time had either been totally lost, or their original message distorted. The time had, therefore, come for Allah to send a final and complete revelation in the form of the Holy Quran.

The Holy Quran is the only revealed scripture, which has been preserved to the present time in its exact, original form and language. Although parts of the earlier revelations still survive, they are so intermixed with additions and alterations that it is very difficult to determine what part of them actually forms the original message sent by Allah. The Holy Quran does not mention all the prophets nor all the revealed books. It only mentions revelations sent to Hadrat Nuh, Hadrat Ibrahim, Hadrat Ismail, Hadrat Ishaq, Hadrat Daud, Hadrat Musa, Hadrat Isa and the Holy Prophet Muhammad (PBUH).

The revealed books mentioned by name in the Holy Quran are:

(1) Sahuf-e-Ibrahim

(2) Zabur, granted to Hadrat Daud.

(3) Taurat, revealed to Hadrat Musa. About it, the Quran says:

"And before this was the book of Moses as a guide and a mercy." (46:12)

Thus, according to the Holy Quran, the book that Allah revealed to Hadrat Musa contained guidance, Allah's commands and warnings for the Bani Israel who failed to act according to its teachings. They distorted and perverted Allah's word. No copy of the original Taurat is now available.

(4) Injeel, granted to Hadrat Isa. About this book, the Quran says:

"And in their footsteps we sent Jesus the son of Mary confirming the law that had come before him: we sent

> him the gospel therein was guidance and light, and confirmation of the law that had come before him: a guidance and an adomonition to those who fear Allah." (5:46)

The Injeel confirmed the Taurat and contained guidance and light for the Bani Israel. According to the Holy Quran, Allah took a covenant from those who call themselves Christians, but they forgot the message that was sent to them and failed to act according to its teachings.

(5) The Holy Quran is the last and the most comprehensive book revealed by Allah to His last messenger, Hadrat Muhammad (PBUH), through Hadrat Jibbrail. It was not sent down by Allah all at once. Its revelation to the Holy Prophet (PBUH) was spread over a period of twenty-three years. The Holy Quran confirms the previous revelations, and points out and corrects some of the errors that had crept into the earlier revealed books. Thus, the Holy Quran perfects and completes Divine Revelation.

The Quran speaks of the attributes of Allah and His power, of man's relationship and responsibility to Him, of the certainty of the coming of the Last Day and the life hereafter. It contains instructions about the principle of Islam and the method of worship and guides mankind to the right path. It lays down moral and ethical principles to govern all aspects of human life, both individual and collective. It narrates the stories of some of the earlier prophets and nations as an example and encouragement to the Prophet and his community and as a warning to those who deny Allah. Its main theme, repeated again and again is the reality of Allah's Supreme Power and man's position as His slave and vicegerent who is accountable to Him in everything. About the Holy Quran Allah says:

> "This is the Book; in it is guidance sure, without doubt, to those who fear Allah; who believe in the

Unseen, are steadfast in prayer and spend out of what we have provided for them; and who believe in the revelation sent to thee and sent before thy time, and (in their hearts) have the assurance of the Hereafter; They are on (true guidance) from their Lord, and it is these who will prosper." (2:2-5)

Quran is undoubtedly the only book in the world that remains in the same form today as it was fourteen hundred years ago. This is because Allah Himself promised to safeguard it from corruption and change. Allah says:

" We have, without doubt, sent down the message and We will assuredly guard it (from corruption)" (15:9)

The Holy Quran is a book for reading, reciting and learning in fact, prayers cannot be complete without the recitation of some parts of the Quran.

The Holy Prophet (PBUH) laid great emphasis on memorizing the Holy Quran. There is authentic proof to show that as soon as the Holy Prophet (PBUH) received a revelation, he would ask his scribes to write it down. The Quran was committed to memory as well as written down during the lifetime of the Holy Prophet (PBUH). The Quran was complete with the same arrangement of chapters and verses that we have now, at the time of the death of the Holy Prophet (PBUH).

The Quran is not only a blessed book, but also a complete code of life. We must, therefore, study it with the object of acting in all matters according to its teachings. We must mould our lives according to the guidance contained in the Holy Quran and abstain from whatever is against its teachings.The success of human beings on this earth and in the life after death depends on obedience to the Quranic teachings and principles which are as valid and binding today as at the time when they were revealed; for although the style and mode of human life have changed, the ultimate realities, the nature of good and evil and man's own nature are unalterable and permanent and are not affected by the passing of time or changes in the world.

***His Messengers* :** Since the beginning of creation, Allah has sent guidance for mankind through His selected people known as prophets or messengers. Belief in prophets forms the fourth ingredient of faith.

The Islamic concept of the role and function of prophethood is different from that of the other religions. In Islam, the word prophet - Nabi - denotes one who is very near to Allah through the total surrender of his entire being to Him and who receives revelation from Him which serve as a source of guidance for men. If the revelation is in the form of a scripture, the prophet is, in addition, a messenger -Rasool-as well.

Islam holds that a prophet possesses the following characteristics: he is absolutely truthful, he is free of all kinds of sins, he delivers the messages from Allah without any omission or concealment and he has the highest order of intelligence and mental ability.

According to the Quran, all the apostles and prophets sent by Allah were men, had wives and children and were mortal. All of them taught in the language of the people to whom they were sent. At the same time, the Quran tells us that they were good and truthful, Allah favoured them above all others, chose them and guided them and conferred His grace upon them. He gave them the Book and prophethood and sent them for the guidance of their people. The unbelievers scoffed at them and persecuted them but they bore it patiently. Some of them were endowed with more gifts than the others, but Muslims are asked to believe in all of them, to respect them and to make no distinction amongst them. The Quran says:

> "We make no distinction between one and another of His messengers." (2:285)

And also:

> "Those who deny Allah and His messengers and (those who) wish to separate Allah from His messengers, saying: "we believe in some but reject others": and (those who) wish to take a course midway - They are in truth (equally), unbelievers;" (4:150-151)

The Quran tells us that Allah always helped His apostles and prophets and punished and destroyed the wicked unbelievers. The apostles and prophets will be questioned on the Day of Judgement about the response of their people to their mission.

Allah sent prophets to mankind from amongst themselves for their guidance and reformation because a man can best serve as an example and a guide for his own race. The message could have been conveyed by the angels, but they belong to a different class of beings and cannot serve as models for men. The Quran says:

> "If there were settled on earth, angels walking about in peace and quiet, we should certainly have sent them down from the heavens an angel for a messenger." (17:95)

All the prophets who preceded Hadrat Muhammad (PBUH) were sent with a message of warning and guidance to a particular people. None of their messages was intended to be universal, until the last messenger, Hadrat Muhammad (PBUH) was entrusted with the final and complete guidance for the whole of humanity for all times to come.

The Quran says that Allah sent a warner and guide to every nation and it mentions the names of many of them. At the beginning of the line was Hadrat Adam, who was also the first human being. Allah bestowed prophethood on him and gave him guidance for himself and his descendants. The first human beings on earth were true believers in one Allah, who submitted to His guidance. But, gradually over a period of time, they became idolators, until Allah raised a new messenger from amongst them to recall them to the truth.

The Quran mentions Hadrat Nuh, who brought a message of warning to his peoples. They refused to listen and were destroyed by the flood. The next major prophet whose history is narrated in the Quran is Hadrat Ibrahim. Although he grew up among idolators, he surrendered himself to Allah with such total submission that Allah made him an example for people of all times. From Hadrat Ibrahim came a long line of prophets through his two sons - Hadrat Ismail and Hadrat Ishaq. From Hadrat Ishaq a number of prophets came which included Hadrat Yaqub, Hadrat Yusuf, Hadrat Musa, Hadrat Daud, Hadrat Sulaiman, Hadrat Yahya and Hadrat Isa. Hadrat Ismail was the ancestor of the Arabs and Hadrat Muhammad (PBUH) was among his descendants.

The Holy Quran proclaims that Hadrat Muhammad (PBUH) is the last messenger of Allah, 'The seal of the prophets.' He was born in Mecca, Arabia, nearly six hundred years after Hadrat Isa. It was the time when the Arabs practiced idolatory and the society was in a state of extreme corruption and decay.

When Hadrat Muhammad (PBUH) called people to Islam and to a noble and righteous path he was met with intense hostility. At first he was ridiculed and opposed and then with his small group of followers exposed to abuse, torture, boycott and ultimately the threat of assassination. But all of them remained firm and constant because they were sure of the truth of the message that was delivered to them. At last, after thirteen years of preaching and bearing patiently all the trials, the Holy Prophet (PBUH) with his followers migrated to Medina where he was able to establish the first Islamic state based upon the teachings of the Quran. Soon, the Muslim community although initially small in number and poorly equipped was able to subdue the unbelievers. The Holy Prophet (PBUH) then returned to the city of Mecca from where he had migrated several years ago. He forgave his bitterest enemies and thus, the conquest of Mecca was a peaceful one.

Prophet Muhammad (PBUH) died about a year later. He left behind for all times to come two permanent and unchangeable sources of guidance, the Holy Quran and his Sunnah - that is his own example and practice.

A complete and detailed account of the life of the Holy Prophet (PBUH) has been preserved by his followers. Hence the narrations preserved in the books of Hadith-sayings of the Holy Prophet (PBUH) deal with all aspects of life from the most personal matters to the conduct of war and affairs of the state. The Muslims have before them in every aspect of their lives the living example of the best of human beings as the Quran says:

> "We have indeed in the Messenger of Allah a beautiful pattern (of conduct) for anyone whose hope is in Allah and the Final Day, and who engages much in the praise of Allah." (33:21)

His wife, Aishah said about him that his conduct was the Quran. The Holy Prophet (PBUH) was very close to Allah, but he lived an extremely active and complete life. He was a devoted husband, father, a kind and responsible kinsman, a faithful and affectionate friend, a leader in worship as well as in battle and an excellent ruler and statesman. For the Muslims of his time as well as for the present and the future generations, he was and will always be the model, the teacher, the guide, the leader and the conveyor of Divine Guidance to mankind.

Post-death Life : Belief in life after death, the Day of Judgement, bodily resurrection and Heaven and Hell is one of the articles of faith in Islam. Death is an absolute certainty. According to the Holy Quran, every soul shall have a taste of death, and must pass away. A man's life on this earth ends with his death, after which another life begins. The Qiyamat-e-Sughra or lesser judgement takes place immediately after death. The word 'Barzakh' occurs in verse 100 of Surah al-Mominun:

> "Before them is a partition (Barzakh) till the day they are raised up." (23:100)

Abdullah Yusuf Ali has explained Barzakh: "Barzakh is the place or state in which people will be after death and before judgement. Behind them is the barrier of death and in front of them is the Barzakh, partition, a quiescent state until the judgement comes." Barzakh is therefore, the intermediate state in which the soul is placed after death till the resurrection.

The Holy Quran informs man of the reality of another life of infinite duration which will be very different from the life of this world. For Allah is easily able to transform His creatures from one state of being to another. The Quran speaks again and again of examples of such transformations: the coming to life again of the earth which lies dead and barren in winter or drought; the development of a sperm in the mother's womb into a human being with all the faculties of thinking and feeling. The Quran says:

> "And among His signs is this: thou seest the earth barren and desolate; but when We send down rain to it, it is stirred to life and yields increase. Truly, He who gives life to the (dead) earth can surely give life to (men) who are dead. For He has power over all things." (41:39)

Those who denied Allah and rejected His guidance and did evil deeds will be thrown into a fearsome and terrible abode, where they with their companions will be in a state of torment and agony. They will long to have another chance to return to the world to live their lives differently but it will be too late. For such people, the Quran says:

> "And on the day that the unbelievers will be placed before the fire (they will be asked) "Is this not the Truth?" they will say "Yea, by our Lord!" (One will say)
>
> "Then taste ye the penalty for that ye were wont to deny (Truth)!" (46:34)

And also :

> "The sinners will be in the punishment of hell, to dwell therein ..."
>
> Nowise shall We be unjust to them: But it is they who have been unjust themselves." (43:74, 76)

As for the people who believed in Allah, who obeyed and submitted to Him and lived their lives for His pleasure, and who died in a state of surrender to Him, the Holy Quran says:

> "My devotees! No fear shall be on you that Day; nor shall ye grieve - (Being those) who have believed in Our signs and bowed (their will to Ours) in Islam. Enter ye the garden, ye and your wives in (beauty and) rejoicing." (43:68-70)
>
> "Those who have faith and do righteous deeds - they are the best of creatures.
>
> Their reward is with Allah; gardens of Eternity, beneath which rivers flows; they will dwell therein for ever;...." (8:7-8)

The two states of Heaven and Hell are not spiritual. They will be experienced in physical forms by the new bodies with which Allah will raise men up. The Quran describes Hell as a state of intense, fearful burning and agony without respite, among the most horrifying surroundings and companions. For its inhabitants, it will be a temporary or permanent state of torture depending upon the nature and extent of their sins. The worst part of their suffering will be the awareness that they have brought about this punishment upon themselves by rejecting Allah and ignoring the guidance and the clear warnings which He had conveyed to them through His messengers. The Quran says:

> "Those who have earned evil will have a reward of like evil: ignominy will cover their (faces): No defender will they have from (the wrath of) Allah: ... they are companions of the fire: they will abide therein."
>
> (10:27)

The Quran tells us that the inhabitants of Heaven will experience happiness and joy that will far exceed anything one can imagine. The ultimate triumph and bliss for these people will be their nearness to Allah. The Quran says:

> "To those who do right is a goodly (reward) -yea, more (than in measure)! No darkness nor shame shall cover their faces! They are companions of the garden; they will abide therein." (10:26)

The Quran describes the outline of the events of the Last Day in a very clear and awe-inspiring language. It says that at a time which is known only to Allah, the hour of judgement will come all of a sudden; and it will be like the twinkling of an eye. When the first trumpet of Resurrection is sounded, the earth will be split apart, it will be shaken to its depths, it will be in violent commotion and become as a level stretch. The mountains will crumble to dust and will fly here and there like wool. The sun will be folded up, the moon will be in darkness, the stars will become dim and fall. The oceans will boil over and burst forth. Human souls will be dazed and lose all consciousness of time and place. The world will cease to be in the form which we see now and there will be a new heaven and a new earth. The Quran says:

"When the sky is rent asunder, and hearkens to (The command of) its Lord and it must needs (Do so) - and when the earth is flattened out, and casts forth what is within it and becomes (clean) empty." (84: 1-4)

On that day, the bodies of the dead will be rejoined with their souls, while those who are alive on earth at that time will die and be joined to this assembly. All men will stand before Allah, each one, alone and helpless, to give an account of their deeds. They will be given their book of deeds, which they will be asked to read. The good will be given their record in their right hands and the sinners in their left hands or from behind their backs. No injustice will be done on that day. People's hands, feet and tongues will bear witness against them. No one shall speak except by Allah's leave, no ransom or compensation will be accepted, there will be no bargaining or friendship and there will be no intercession except by Allah's permission. Parents, children, spouses and relatives will be of no avail.

The Quran says:

"Then he who is given his record in his right hand, soon will his account be taken by an easy reckoning, and he will turn to his people, rejoicing! But he who is given his record behind his back- soon will he cry for perdition, and he will enter a blazing fire." (84: 7-12)

And also:

"At length, when there comes the deafening noise - that Day shall a man flee from his own brother, and from his mother and his father, and from his wife and his children. Each one of them, that Day, will have enough concern (of his own) to make him indifferent to the others." (80:33-37)

Islam lays the greatest stress on the individual's accountability to Allah. The human being's life in this world is a trial, an examination period, during which he prepares himself, either for reward or punishment, for the next life which is ever lasting.

It is obvious that a person who has lived his life in submission to Allah is in an entirely different state from the one who has lived all his life in rebellion and ingratitude to Allah. Those who do not believe in a future life become immoral and irresponsible because, for them the short life on this earth is everything. On the other hand, those who have a firm belief in life after death fear Allah, follow the straight path, do good deeds and abstain from all evil deeds.

5

Compulsory Prayers

Allah and His Prophet

Meaning and Importance : The basis of the Islamic teaching and way of life are various obligatory acts of worship, Ibadat which are often referred to as the Five Pillars of Islam. These consist of:

a. Declaration that there is no god but Allah.

b. The prescribed prayers, five times a day.

c. Fasting, once a year in the month of Ramadan.

d. Zakat, helping the needy by giving alms.

e. Hajj, pilgrimage to Mecca, if and when circumstances permit.

Just as the pillars bear the burden of a building, these principles, according to the teachings of the Prophet (PBUH) are the basis of piety and of a virtuous worldly life; as the Prophet (PBUH) has taught that the only difference between individuals is the extent of their piety and not their colour or the social status that they enjoy in this world.

The purpose of the Islamic worship is to strengthen the Muslim faith and sense of submission to Allah, to discipline a Muslim for his role as Allah's faithful servant and vicegerent on earth, and to reinforce the ties of brotherhood and affection among Muslims. These acts of worship require the participation of all aspects of man's nature — his soul, his mind, his feelings, his body, his time, his energy and his possessions.

Thus, they demand the worship of Allah with all the faculties of an individual. For example, the declaration of faith is to be always present in the mind and heart of the Muslim and is to be uttered again and again with the tongue during his daily prayers. Prayers are to be performed five times daily, everyday of a man's life. Fasting is for a full month every year, while Zakat or "poor-due" is to be paid once yearly; and the pilgrimage is to be performed once in a lifetime, if possible.

These aspects of Islamic worship and the total involvement of human beings make them extremely unique. They are a complete expression of man's dependence and submission to His will, his humility before His Creator and his desire to serve and obey Him alone.

In these religious institutions, there is punctuality, regularity, orderliness, uniformity and an exhibition of complete equality.

Tauhid-Unity of Allah : The first part of the declaration that there is no god but Allah attests not only to the Oneness and Uniqueness of Allah, but it also signifies the Oneness of Lordship, the Sovereignty and the Authority in the universe and in this world. As there is no other Creator and Sustainer of the universe, there can likewise be no other Ruler, Law-giver and Supreme Authority for mankind. Allah is the Lord of all creation; He creates what He pleases, giving each of His creatures the nature, role and function which He desires for it; in this He is accountable to no one and all things are under His absolute control.

The primary emphasis of the Quran is upon the doctrine

of Tauhid. There are numerous verses in the Quran which highlight the concept of *Tauhid* which is the cardinal principle of Islam. In the very opening chapter of the Holy Quran, Surah Fatiha, it is said:

"Thee do we worship and thine aid we seek." (1:5)

Similarly, verse 36, it is said:

"Serve Allah, and join not any partners with Him." (4:36)

The most concise expression of this principle is to be found in Surah Ikhlas. This Quranic Surah as translated by Abdullah Yusuf Ali says:

"Say: He is Allah,
The One and Only;
Allah the Eternal, Absolute,
He Begetteth not,
Nor is He begotten;
And there is none
Like unto Him. (112:1-4)

True unity of Allah means that Allah is:

(a) *Unique in Person:* This signifies that Allah is only One and there is no plurality of gods. The Quran says:

Allan has said:

"Take not (for worship) two gods: for He is just one God." (16:51)

(b) *Unique in Attributes:* This signifies that no other being can be equal to Allah in attributes. For example, man may attain a degree of perfection in the attribute of kindness, but only Allah possesses the perfection of the attribute of kindness.

(c) *Unique in Action:* No one can do the works which Allah

has done or may do. All the messengers of Allah have conveyed the message of His unity:

> "O my people," said they, "Worship Allah. You have no other god but Him." (7: 59, 73, 85)

The role of the Prophet of Islam was to bring about the acceptance of this principle of religion by entire mankind. The Quran says:

> "Not a messenger did We send before thee without this inspiration sent by US to him: that there is no god but I; therefore, worship and serve Me." (21: 25)

The doctrine of *Tauhid* confers dignity on man who is otherwise a slave to every manifestation of power. Only Allah becomes his refuge, security and stability.

Associating partners with Allah is called Shirk. *Shirk* is not only the worship of idols, but also offering prayers and supplications to anyone, dead or living, believing that they hold the same attributes in a lesser degree than Him. Thus, the belief that Allah is not Sovereign or Independent and Sole Dispenser of affairs of the world and that other deities can intercede with Him and that any attempt to implore any other being besides Allah for the grant of any wishes of the believer or to answer his prayers is *Shirk*. The Quran considers *Shirk* to be an unpardonable sin. It says:

> "Allah forgives not that partners should be set up with Him; but He forgives anything else to whom He pleases; to set up partners with Allah is to devise a sin most heinous indeed." (4: 48)

Man has been created as lord of creation and everything in nature has been placed under his control. By worshipping other beings besides Allah man debases himself, the Quran says:

> "Shall I seek for you a god other than the (true) God,

when it is Allah Who hath endowed you with gifts above the nations." (7:140)

In Surah Luqman, ascribing partners to Allah is regarded as a tremendous wrong.

The Holy Prophet (PBUH) is reported to have said:

"Shirk is the greatest of all sins".

Meaning and Importance of Prophethood : The next basic requirement of Islam is belief and faith in all the prophets of Allah. This means that a Muslim believes that the prophets are devoted servants of Allah, selected and appointed by Him, to convey His Commands to mankind without any addition or deduction. Prophethood is a gift of Allah and only He can bestow this gift on whom He wishes.

Allah deputed prophets in different periods of time to communicate His guidance to human beings. They were raised from the nations to whom they were sent as messengers. They preached in the language of their nations, the Quran says:

"We sent not a messenger except (to teach) in the language of his (own) people, in order to make (things) clear to them." (14:4)

And again:

"And there never was a people without a warner having lived among them (in the past)." (35:24)

According to the Quran, all prophets sent by Allah were men, had human bodies and were mortal. At the same time, the Quran tells us that the prophets were Allah's chosen and selected. Allah chose them and guided them and gave them the Book and the prophethood.

They all received revelation from Allah and were sent for the guidance of their people. They all did good deeds and were truthful. The Holy Quran insists that the prophets were raised to be obeyed and followed. They called their followers to profess and follow the Divine code of rules to regulate their life. There are numerous verses in the Quran in which emphasis is laid on obedience to the prophets and following their example.

It says:

> "We sent not a messenger, but to be obeyed, in accordance with the will of Allah." (4:64)
>
> "He who obeys the messenger obeys Allah. "(4:80)
>
> "Say, (O Muhammad!), if you do love Allah, follow me; Allah will love you and forgive you your sins. " (3:31)

Many prophets came to this world. The last in the line of prophets is the Holy Prophet Muhammad (PBUH) who is termed as "the seal of the prophets."

The Quran says that the appearance of the Holy Prophet (PBUH) was foretold by previous prophets. His distinguishing feature was that he confirmed the truth of all the prophets that preceded him. He not only conveyed the message revealed to him, but also explained and acted upon it himself and after demonstration, urged the people to follow it for their own benefit.

The Prophethood of Hadrat Muhammad (PBUH) is distinguished in many ways:

1. It is universal which means that the Holy Prophet (PBUH) was not sent for any particular country or community but for the whole world and the entire mankind. Allah says in the Holy Quran:

> " We have not sent thee but as a universal (Messenger) to men, giving them glad tidings and warning them (against sin)." (34:28)

And the Holy Prophet (PBUH) also confirmed this:

"Every prophet who preceded me was sent especially to his own people but I have been sent as a Prophet for all mankind."

2. The Prophethood of the Holy Prophet (PBUH) is eternal. With him, the chain of revelation and Prophethood has come to an end. There will not be any other prophets.

"But he is the messenger of Allah and the Seal of the Prophets." (33:40)

The Holy Prophet (PBUH) said:

"With me the edifice of prophethood has been completed and with me the chain of prophethood has come to an end."

"No doubt, no prophet will come after me."

At another place, he said:

" When a prophet died, another prophet took his place; but there will be no prophet after me."

3. The religion and the Divine law which the Holy Prophet (PBUH) brought is perfect in all respects. This distinction was not enjoyed by any other religion. The Quran says:

"This day have I perfected your religion for you, completed my favour upon you, and have chosen for you Islam as your religion." (5:3)

Through the Holy Prophet (PBUH) a perfect law was given to suit the requirements of all ages and for all countries and this law that is, the Holy Quran was guarded against all corruptions. The life of the Holy Prophet (PBUH) is an explanation of the Holy Quran as confirmed by his wife Hadrat Aishah:

"His morals are the Quran."

It means that while the Holy Quran was the command, the Prophet's (PBUH) life was an example of the teachings of the Quran.

The Quran compares his personality to the sun, while the previous prophets were like lamps. Just as the light of the sun cannot be substituted by any other light and is universal, similarly, after the advent of the Holy Prophet (PBUH), no necessity is felt of any other prophet to follow him.

The Worship

Meaning and Importance : The importance of prayer in Islam is great as it is the foremost duty of the Muslims and the chief of the pillars on which the structure of Islam stands. It is the distinguishing feature between a Muslim and a non-Muslim. The Holy Prophet (PBUH) said:

> "What stands between a man and disbelief is the abandonment of salat."

And again:

> "Know that among your duties, prayer is the best."

A unique service that the Prophet (PBUH) rendered to humanity was that he made prayer to Allah not only the foundation stone of the individual development of a man but also the basis of a vast brotherhood of humanity.

The first revelations were in the following order:

> To read and write; to warn the people and declare the Greatness of Allah; and to pray to Allah not only during the daytime but also during night.

The Quran says:

> "Establish regular prayers - at the Sun's decline till the darkness of the night —And pray in the small watches of the morning —" (17: 78-79)

The object of prayer is to remember Allah. It is, therefore, the chief reason why prayer was dearest to the Prophet (PBUH), he said:

> "Prayer has been made a coolness for my eyes."

He declared prayers to be the pillar of Islam and said:

> "He who gives up prayer has indeed disbelieved."

The Quran mentions prayer many times and has laid the greatest emphasis on it; therefore, the sin of giving up prayer is great as also praying carelessly or with an absent mind.

> "So woe to the worshippers who are neglectful of their prayers. " (107: 4-5)

Observance of prayer five times a day is compulsory. Basically, it consists of recitations from the Holy Quran and glorification of Allah accompanied by various bodily postures, such as standing, bowing, prostrating and sitting. Through these postures, Muslims express submission, adoration and humility to Allah.

The self-discipline which is needed to perform salat regularly and at proper times, to perform the ablution which precedes prayer and to carry on these prayers in the early morning when sleep is so attractive, during the busy daylight hours when one is preoccupied with work and other activities, and at night when one is tired and wants to sleep reaffirms the human being's total dependence on his Creator and his position as His slave.

The Holy Prophet (PBUH) exhorted his followers to offer their prayers as if they were standing in front of Allah, looking at Him. In prayer, the Divine presence is to be felt as a reality:

> "You should worship Allah, as if you see Him; if you do not see Him, He surely sees you."

Prayer is further meant to seek help as well as guidance from Allah. This seeking of help and guidance is linked up in the daily prayer of the Muslims:

> "Thee do we worship and thine aid we seek. Show us the straight way." (1: 5-6)

In the Holy Quran, prayer is referred to as a sustenance for the human soul so that the man who does not pray to Allah must be regarded as spiritually dead.

Prayer protects one from sins and shameful deeds. Prayer purifies him and brings him closer to Allah. The Quran says:

> "Establish prayer, for prayer restrains from shameful and unjust deeds. "

This continuous reminder keeps the conscience alive, functioning in a proper manner. Without the regular performance of prayer, it is likely to become inactive and easily corrupted. It will be obvious that prayer once a week or even once or twice a day, does not fulfil this purpose and is only a partial and insufficient expression of the human being's relationship with his Sustainer, who in the words of the Quran is *"nearer to him than his jugular vein."*

The three conditions of the believers as given in the Holy Book are:

> "Those who believe in the unseen, are steadfast in prayer and spend out of what we have provided for them." (2:3)

It will be seen that belief in Allah, the Great Unseen, is immediately followed by the keeping up of prayer, thus showing that by means of prayer, belief is turned into a certainty of the Divine existence. This is again followed by spending out of what Allah has given to man, for the benefit of others, in charity. Thus, faith in Allah is translated into practice by prayer, which in turn, leads to the service of humanity. According to the Holy Prophet (PBUH), self development of a man depends upon prayer:

> "The believers must (eventually) win through— those who humble themselves in their prayers." (23: 1-2)

The Holy Prophet (PBUH) further explained what the Holy

Quran taught. On one occasion, he thus addressed his companions:

> "Tell me, if there is a stream at the door of one of you in which he washes himself five times a day, what do you say, will it leave any dirt on him?"

And on receiving the reply that it would not, he added,

> "This is the likeness of the five prayers with which Allah washes away all faults."

> " When one of you ", said the Prophet (PBUH), "says his prayers, he holds confidential intercourse with his Lord."

A Muslim is required to pray at the prescribed times wherever he may be. But it is preferable and meritorious to pray in congregation with his fellow Muslims if possible. This gathering of all Muslims living in the same locality five times daily, is a step towards the establishment of healthy social relations. In the daily service, these relations are limited to a narrow circle i.e., to members of the same neighbourhood. The circle becomes wider in the weekly Friday service which gathers together all Muslim members of a particular locality, and still more extensive in the two annual gatherings of Muslim festivals of Eid-ul-Fitr. Thus, prayer promotes social relations between different sections of the Muslim community.

Salat is the central point of the life of a Muslim, without which he would not be able to maintain a strong and vital link with his Lord or continue his inner struggle against wrong doing or temptation. Because of all these aspects, Salat is the principal means whereby the Muslim keeps in mind the limited and temporary nature of this world's life and the certainty of death and life to come. Thus, he is able to maintain a sense of balance and proportion between the needs and claims of this world and the Hereafter.

Cleanliness : A true Muslim must be pure and clean in

mind, body and heart. Islam enjoins strict cleanliness and purity on its followers. We are told in the Quran:

> "He loves those who keep themselves pure and clean."
> (2:222)

And again:

> "Allah loveth those who make themselves pure."
> (9:108)

The Holy Prophet (PBUH) is reported to have said:

> "Purification is the key to prayer," and also, 'Religion is built on cleanliness', and again, "Purification is one half of faith. "

In the light of the Quranic verses and traditions, it becomes clear that a person should be clean inwardly as well as outwardly at all times, especially at the time of saying prayers. Inward purification is to rid the mind of all corrupt ideas and evil thoughts. Outward purification is attained by taking a bath or performing ablution. If a man cleans himself five times a day, he would undoubtedly be in a constant state of physical purity.

There are certain conditions regarding cleanliness of body, clothes, place of worship, etc. that have to be fulfilled before a person can say his prayers. The Holy Prophet (PBUH) said:

> "Surely Allah does not accept prayers without purification."

Filth : Apart from waste products discharged from the body which are regarded as filth, other impurities recognized by Islam are semen, flowing blood, pus, swine and everything associated with it and wine. All these are included in the definition of Najasat Ghaleezah. If even the smallest quantity of Najasat Ghaleezah falls in any article of food or drink, the whole of it is polluted and becomes unclean and unfit for use by a Muslim. If some Najasat Ghaleezah falls on the clothes, they must be removed and washed thrice, squeezing the cloth each time.

Wudu or Ablution : Ablution or Wudu in the prescribed manner is necessary for a person who intends to say his prayers as the Quran says:

> "O you who believe! When you prepare for prayer, wash your faces and your hands to the elbows, rub your heads (with water) and (wash) your feet to the ankles." (5:6)

Ablution consists of some practices that are obligatory or Farz i.e., those specifically mentioned in the Quranic verses; others that are traditional i.e., the Holy Prophet's (PBUH) practice or sunnat, and others that are termed desirable or mustahab entitling a person to spiritual recompense or Sawab. The approved method of performing Wudu is as under:

> Making the intention or Niyyat, of Wudu, i.e. to say: 'I intend to perform the Wudu for securing Allah's good pleasure and in compliance with His command.' Then recite the following:
>
> In the name of Allah, the Beneficent, the Merciful.
>
> Allah! Forgive my sins."

If possible, one should sit facing the Qibla. The water to be used for Wudu should be absolutely clean.

First the right and then the left hand should be washed upto the wrists thrice. The wet fingers should be passed in between each other. If there are any bangles on the wrists or rings on the fingers, as in the case of females, they should be moved around so that the skin under them does not remain dry.

After this rinse the mouth thrice. Next, some water should be taken in the right hand and sniffed into the nostrils thrice and then blown out. The left hand should be used for cleaning the nose. Then the whole face should be washed with both hands, thrice from the forehead down to the lower portion of the chin and from the lobe of one ear to that of the other. No portion of the face should remain dry. For males, the wet fingers of the right hand should be passed through the hair of the beard. Thereafter, first the right arm and then the left arm upto the elbows should be washed thrice. After washing the arms wipe the head with wet hands from front to back, and pass the back of wet hands over the nape of the neck. Clear the inner side of ears with forefingers and outer with thumbs. Finally wash the feet, right and then left upto the ankles.

The Wudu should be a continuous process, each part being washed and cleaned in the prescribed order, without any break or interval. No part should be allowed to dry up before the other is washed. After the Wudu, the Kalima-e-Shahadat should be recited:

> "I bear witness that there is no god except Allah, who is One, Who has no partners, and I bear witness that there is no god except Allah, who is One, Who has no partners, and I bear witness that Muhammad is His servant and apostle.

And then the following prayer may be recited:

> "O Allah! Make me one of those who repent for their sins; and make me one of those who keep themselves pure; and make me one of Your righteous servants."

Wudu may be performed before every prayer. But the necessity for it arises only when a person has passed urine, stool or wind or if he has been fast asleep.

The items that are specifically mentioned in the Holy Quran i.e., Faraiz-e-Wudu are four in number. These are:

1. To wash the face from the top of the forehead to the chin and as far as each ear.

2. To wash the hands and the arms upto the elbow.
3. To wipe the head with wet hands.
4. To wash the feet upto the ankles.

The items established on the example of the Holy Prophet (PBUH) i.e., Sunan-e-Wudu are fourteen in number. They are:

1. To make the intention of Wudu.
2. To wash the hands upto the wrist.
3. To say one of the names of God at the commencement of the Wudu.
4. To brush the teeth.
5. To rinse the mouth three times.
6. To put water into the nostrils thrice.
7. To do all the above items in proper order.
8. To do all the above items without any delay between the various acts.
9. Each part is to be washed thrice.
10. The space between the fingers of one hand must be rubbed with the wet finger of the other.
11. The beard must be combed with the fingers.
12. The head must be wiped once.
13. The ears must be washed with the water remaining on the fingers after wiping the head.
14. To rub between the toes with the little finger of the left hand starting from the little toe of the right foot.

There are five Mustahab or desirable acts in Wudu. They are:

1. To begin from the right to the left.
2. To rub the neck.

3. To perform Wudu without the help of another person.
4. To face the Qiblah while performing Wudu.
5. To sit on a high and clean place while performing Wudu.

There are four Makruhat or undesirable acts in Wudu. They are:

1. To perform Wudu in an impure place.
2. To clean the nose with the right hand.
3. To talk about worldly affairs, while performing Wudu.
4. To perform against the rules and regulations laid down by the Holy Prophet (PBUH). A person's Wudu becomes ineffectual on becoming subject to the state of Hads-e-Asghar i.e., the state of impurity or uncleanliness which is brought about by answering the call of nature, by passing wind or by vomiting or Hads-e-Akbar i.e., the state of impurity or uncleanliness which is caused by sexual intercourse, menstruation or the period of childbirth. In addition to these, the following acts and circumstances also render the Wudu void:
    1. Discharge of intestinal worms or stone.
    2. Flowing of any impurity from any part of the body.
    3. Taking a nap, or going to sleep by resting the body against any object.
    4. Laughing loudly during prayers.
    5. Losing consciousness or fainting due to some illness.
    6. Becoming insane or mad.

Dry Ablution **:** Regarding Tayammum (Dry Ablution) the Holy Quran says:

"If ye are ill or on a journey And ye find no water, then take for your selves clean sand or earth and rub therewith your faces and hands. Allah doth not wish to place you in a difficulty, but to make you clean...."

(5: 6)

It will be seen from the above mentioned verse of the Holy Quran that permission for resorting to Tayammum is granted on the grounds of illness, travelling and the non-availability of water. It can be performed instead of Wudu or Ghusl (bath).

If one is suffering from a disease in which the use of water would be injurious and there are chances that the use of water would aggravate the illness; or if one cannot find water for *Wudu* or *Ghusl;* or if one is travelling in a place where there is no one to indicate where water could be found; or if there is a danger that the enemy might attack while one is performing ablution or taking a bath, then one can perform *Tayammum* instead of *Wudu* or *Ghusl.*

The approved, traditional method of Tayammum is as under: First to recite and then to make the following Niyyat: "I intend to make tayammum with the object of removing impurity and acquiring purity."

After this, both hands should be struck on some clean and pure earth or sand, the excessive dust blown off and both the hands rubbed on the face is such a way that no part of the face which has to be washed with water in *Wudu* is left out. In the case of males, it is desirable to pass the fingers through the beard. Again, both hands should be struck on the clean earth or sand, the excess dust blown off and first the right arm and then the left arm be rubbed upto the elbows. This completes the *Tayammum. A* dry stone free of dust, brick or an earthen pot may also be used for the purpose.

As in the case of *Wudu,* several prayers can be said with one *Tayammum.* The acts and circumstances which nullify *Wudu* also nullify *Tayammum.* If *Tayammum* is done because of the non-availability of water, then it would become ineffectual as soon as water is available. Similarly, if *Tayammum* was done on account of illness, then as soon as the disability to use water ceases, *Tayammum* will become void.

The Bath : The Holy Quran says:

> "O you who believe! Do not approach prayers in a state of ceremonial impurity (except when travelling on the road) until after washing your whole body. "
>
> (4: 43)

The Arabic word for bath is *Ghusl* derived from *Ghasl* which means to wash. In religious terminology, it is the act of washing the whole body after Hads-e-Akbar or greater impurity which is caused by sexual intercourse, menstruation or the period of childbirth. Other occasions of taking a bath founded on the practice of the Holy Prophet (PBUH) are upon the admission of a convert to Islam; before Friday prayers and on festivals and after washing the dead.

The approved, traditional method of *Ghusl* is as follows:

1. Make the Niyyat i.e., to say: "I intend to take a bath for seeking purification;"
2. Both hands including the wrists should be washed;
3. Any impurity that there may be on any part of the body should be removed.
4. *Wudu* should be performed in the prescribed manner taking special care about gargling and ensuring that water reaches the throat; but if one is fasting, care must be taken to see that water does not enter the throat while cleaning the nose.
5. Water should be poured thrice on the entire body from the head to the feet, first on the right-hand side and then on the left, taking care to rub the body well.

No portion of the body should remain dry and water should reach even the roots of the hair. In case of females, care should be taken about bangles and rings. There are three faraiz in a bath. They are:

1. Gargling.
2. Putting the water into the nostrils.
3. Pouring of water over the entire body, at last once in such a way that not even a hair's breadth of the body remains dry.

The acts in a bath established on the example of the Holy Prophet (PBUH) are:

1. To wash both hands upto the wrists.
2. To wash those parts of the body where impurity is found.
3. To make the intention of removing the impurity.
4. To perform *Wudu.*
5. To wash the whole body thrice with water.

The *Wudu* performed while taking a bath is sufficient for saying prayers.

Call to Prayers : Every prayer with the exception of the two Eid prayers and funeral prayers is preceded by a call or Adaan. When it is time for a particular prayer, the *Adaan* is called out. *The Muazzin* i.e., the person who calls out *the Adaan* should be a Muslim, male, adult. It is preferred that he should perform the *Wudu* before calling the *Adaan* and stand on a raised platform with his face towards the Qibla. Inserting the tips of his forefingers in his ears, he should give the *Adaan* in a loud and clear voice pronouncing the words correctly and distinctly. The words of the *Adaan* are as under:

1. "Allah is Great." (4 times)
2. "I do bear witness that there is no god except Allah." (Twice)
3. "I do bear witness that Muhammad is the Apostle of Allah" (Twice)

4. "Come to prayer." (Twice; turning the face to the right)
5. "Come to success. " (Twice; turning face to the left)
6. "Allah is Great." (Twice)
7. "There is no god except Allah." (Once)

In the Adaan for the Fajr prayers, after saying item no 5, the following words are included:

8. "Prayer is better than sleep." (Twice)

Except When : A person is saying his prayers; The Imam is delivering the Khutba; A person is answering the call of nature; it is compulsory on all those who hear the *Adaan,* to repeat in a low voice, the words of the *Muazzin.* When he hears and the listener should say:

"The strength to shun evil and to do good deeds is only from Allah." When he hears he should say:

"You have spoken the truth and said a good thing."

When the Adaan is over, the listener should pray in the following words:-

"O Allah! Lord of this perfect call and the prayer to be offered presently, grant Muhammad the way of approach unto Thee and also eminence and raise him unto the glorious station Thou hast promised him and bestow his intercession on us on the Day of Judgement. Verily Thou never go back on Thy word."

The words of the *Adaan* in the order in which they are pronounced have come down to us unchanged from A.H. I., when the *Adaan* was said for the first time in the presence of the Holy Prophet (PBUH).

Iqamat - Announcement for Congregational Service

When the congregational prayers are about to start, people stand up and form rows and the Muazzin recites the *Iqamat.* The words of the *Iqamat* are the same as those *of Adaan,* but the person reciting the *Iqamat* does not insert the tips of his fingers in his ears nor does he turn his face to the right or the left while reciting:

After which he says:

"Prayer has indeed begun." (Twice) after which the people present in the mosque say:

"May Allah make the prayer well-established and permanent."

Names and Times of Prayers : The names of the five obligatory prayers are:

1. *Fajr:* This is an early morning prayer.

   The time of this prayer commences after the break of dawn and ends just before sunrise. It is makruh or undesirable to say prayers when the sun is rising. No nafil prayer is to be said till the sun has risen well.

2. *Zuhr:* (Early afternoon)

   The time of this prayer commences when the sun begins to decline and the shadows of things cease to decrease. It ends when the shadow of everything becomes equal to twice the shadow of a thing at noon or mid-day.

   No prayer is to be said or the Quran recited at the time of the decline of the sun.

3. *Asr:* (Late afternoon)

   The time of this prayer commences after the end of the time for Zuhr prayers and ends before sunset.

4. *Maghrib:* (Evening)

   The time of this prayer commences immediately after sunset and ends on the fading of twilight.

   No prayer is to be said or the Quran recited at the time of the setting of the sun.

5. *Isha:* (Early night)

The time of this prayer commences after the fading of twilight and ends before dawn but it is desirable to say this prayer before midnight.

Number of Rakat in the Five Daily Prayers The five daily prayers consist of:

(a) Farz or obligatory
(b) Sunnat (traditional) i.e., the Holy Prophet's (PBUH) practice.
(c) Wajib
(d) Nafal

The Sunnat is again divided into Sunnat Muakkadah and Sunnat Ghair Muakkadah.

By Sunnat Muakkadah is meant an act which the Holy Prophet (PBUH) always did except for some valid reason. The *Rakat* which are *Sunnat Muakkadah* must be offered.

By Sunnat Ghair Muakkadah is meant an act which the Holy Prophet (PBUH) did but which he sometimes did not do without any valid reason. The offering of *Rakat* which are *Sunnat Ghair Muakkadah* entitles a person to spiritual reward.

1. *Fajr:*	2	Pre-Farz Sunnat (Muakkadah)
	2	Farz
Total =	4	Rakat
2. *Zuhr:*	4	Pre-Farz Sunnat (Muakkadah)
	4	Farz
	2	Post-Farz Sunnat (Muakkadah)
	2	Nafil
Total =	12	Rakat

3. *Asr:*	4	Pre-Farz Sunnat (Ghair Muakkadah)
	4	Farz
Total=	8	Rakat
4. *Maghrib:*	3	Farz
	2	Post-Farz Sunnat (Muakkadah)
	2	Nafil
Total =	7	Rakat
5. *Isha:*	4	Pre-Farz Sunnat (Ghair Muakkadah)
	4	Farz
	2	Post-Farz Sunnat (Muakkadah)
	2	Nafil
	3	Witr-Wajib
	2	Nafil
Total =	17	Rakat

Components of Salat (Arkan) : Each Rakat consists of:

a. Six items which are Farz:

(1) Takbir Tahrima, (2) Qiyam, (3) Qirat, (4) Ruku, (5) Sajda, (6) Qaada Akhira.

If any item (Ruku) is left out, the Salat shall have to be repeated.

b. Thirteen items which are Wajib.

If any item is left out then Sajda Sahw (Prostration due to forgetfulness) becomes necessary and this shall remove the defect.

c. Twenty items which are *Sunnat.*

If any item classified as *Sunnat* is left out due to mistake, no *Sajda Sahw* is necessary and the *Salat* does not become void.

d. *Mustahab.*

Conditions of Salat : Before a person can say his regular prayers, the following conditions must be fulfilled; otherwise the prayers would be void:

a. The body of the person must be clean.

b. The clothes worn must be clean and free from all impurities.

c. The place where the prayers are to be said must be clean and free from all impurities.

d. The 'Satar' (those parts of the body which should be kept covered) must be properly covered. For a male, the *Satar* consists of the portion of the body from the navel to the knees. For a female, her entire body with the exception of her face, hands and feet is *Satar.*

e. It must be the time for the particular prayer to be offered.

f. The *Qiblah* must be faced while saying the prayers.

g. Intention or *Niyyat* must be declared for saying the kind of prayer i.e., *Farz, Sunnat* etc., of the particular prayer time i.e., Fajr, Zuhr etc. that one is offering.

Method of Salat : The approved traditional method of *Salat* is as follows:-

1. Standing erect with the face towards the *Qibla* i.e., the Kaaba in Mecca, with both hands hanging down the sides of the body and with feet nearly four inches apart. The Niyyat should be made in the following words:

"I intend to offer two/three/four Rakat of prayer Farz/Sunnat/Nafal of Fajr/ Maghrib/Isha (as the case may be) for Allah the Most High and I am facing the Holy Kaaba."

2. Eyes should be kept at the spot where the forehead will touch the ground while doing the *Sajda*. This is a *Mustahab.*
3. Raising both hands, with the palms and the fingers open and facing the *Qibla,* as far as the ears in such a way that the thumbs of both hands are in line with the lobes of the ears. Females may raise their hands upto the shoulders, but the hands
4. With hands still raised, *Takbir Tahrima* i.e." God *is Great"* is to be said once. If a person is Munfarid, i.e., praying alone, the Takbir may be said in a fairly loud voice; but if he is a Muqtadi, i.e. saying the farz prayer in congregation under the leadership of an Imam, who shall say all the Takbirs in a loud voice, the *Takbir Tahrima* should be said in a low voice inaudible to the other members of the congregation.
5. While saying the *Takbir Tahrima,* both hands should be brought down and folded on the navel in such a way that the palm of the right hand sets on the back of the palm of the left hand with the thumb and the little finger of the right hand making a circle and holding the wrist of the left hand, and the remaining three fingers of the right hand resting on the left forearm. Females are to fold their hands on their breasts. This is called Qiyam. The eyes should be kept at the spot where the forehead will touch the ground while doing the *Sajda,*
6. While standing in the position of *Qiyam* the *Sana* is to be recited which is as follows:-

"Glory to Thee O Allah; and Thine is the Praise and Blessed is Thy name and Exalted is Thy Majesty; and there is no one worthy of worship except (Thee)."

7. Then the Tawwuz i.e..

"I betake myself to Allah for refuge from the accursed Shaitan, is to be recited."

8. After the Tawwuz, the Tasmiyah i.e.,

"In the name of Allah, the Beneficent, the Merciful" is to be recited.

Serial Numbers: 6, 7 and 8 are Sunnat.

If a person is Munfarid all three-Sana, Tawwuz and Tasmiyah are to be recited; but if he is a Muqtadi, only Sana should be recited. The Imam shall recite all the three in a low voice, not audible to the congregation.

9. After the Tasmiyah, Surah Fatiha is to be recited:-

"Praise be to Allah, the Cherisher and Sustainer of the worlds. Most Gracious, Most Merciful. Master of the Day of Judgement. Thee do we worship and Thine aid we seek. Show us the straight way. The way of those on whom Thou hast bestowed Thy Grace, those whose (portion) is not wrath, and who go not astray."

After the last word of Surah Fatiha, (amen) is to be said in a low voice. This is *Sunnat*.

If a person is *Muqtadi*, he is not to recite *Surah Fatiha*. The Imam shall recite it in a loud voice and the congregation should hear the recitation of the Imam with attention and shall only say at the end.

10. Immediately after the *Surah Fatiha*, some other *Surah* is recited. The voice should neither be too loud nor too low. If a person is *Muqtadi*, he is not to recite any Surah but should hear the Imam's recitation. This is called Qirat.

11. After the *Qirat* is over, *"God is Great"* is said. While doing so, hands are unfolded and the Ruku performed. *Ruku* is to bow down, hold the knees with the open fingers of the two hands, keeping the back straight and

in line with the head. The arms should be kept away from the ribs and the legs should be kept straight. In this position, the Tasbih Ruku, viz.

"Glory to my Lord, the Great " is said three times. This is Sunnat. The Imam, Muqtadi and Munfarid shall all say the Tasbih Ruku in a low voice.

12. After saying the *Tasbih Ruku,* and standing erect, the *Tasmiyah* is recited viz:

    "Allah listens to him who gives praise."

    This is Sunnat.

13. After the Tasmiyah, the Tahmid viz:

    "O our Lord! All praise is due to Thee alone" is recited.

This is *Sunnat.*

If it is a congregational prayer, the Imam shall say the *Tasmiyah* in a loud voice and the members of the congregation-the *Muqtadis* shall say the *Tahmid,* in a low voice. But if a person is *Munfarid,* he should say both the *Tasmiyah* and the *Tahmid* while rising from the Ruku and standing straight. This is *Sunnat.* Standing straight for a short while after Ruku is called Qaumah.

This is *Wajib.*

14. After the *Tahmid,* the Takbir i.e., *"God is Great "* is said once. The Imam shall say the *Takbir* in a loud voice, and the *Muqtadis* in a low voice.
15. While saying the *Takbir,* the prostration or *Sajda* is performed. For this, both knees, then both hands, then the nose and lastly the forehead are placed on the ground. The face should be between both palms and the two thumbs should be in line with the two ears. The fingers of the hands should be kept close to one another, but not closed; the finger tips should face the *Qibla.* The elbows should be kept away from the ribs and the stomach away from the legs. The elbows should not be

put on the ground. Females are to perform the *Sajda* in such a way that they do not raise the rear portion of their body, but rest it on their calves. They are allowed to put their elbows on the ground.

16. While doing the *Sajda,* the Tasbih Sajda i.e., *"Glory to my Lord, the Most High"* is to be recited thrice, in a low voice. This is *Sunnat.*
17. After the *Tasbih Sajda,* first the forehead, then the nose and finally the hands are to be raised and the *Takbir viz: "God is Great "* is to be recited once.

This is *Sunnat.*

Next is to sit straight by folding the left foot and sitting on it and keeping the right foot erect, with the toes of the right foot facing the *Qibla.* The hands should be kept on the thighs close to the knees. Females should keep both feet on the right side and sit on their buttocks. This short sitting between two Sajdas is called Jalsa.

This is *Wajib.*

The eyes should be kept on the back of the hands. This is mustahab.

18. Then the *Takbir "God is Great"* is to be said once and the second *Sajda* performed in the same manner as the first *Sajda* reciting the Tasbih Sajda again at least thrice.
19. The *Takbir* is to be recited while rising from the second *Sajda.*
20. Next is to stand straight and repeat the whole procedure from S. No 5 till S. No. 19.
21. Then the next position is to sit erect as explained in S. No 17. If *the Niyyat was* for two *Rakat,* this will be called Qaada Akhira which is Farz, but if the *Niyyat* was for three or four *Rakat,* this sitting will be called Qaada Ula.

This is *Wajib.*

22. In the Qaada Ula, first the Tahiyya

"All prayers and worship rendered through words, actions and wealth are due to Allah alone. Peace be on you, O Prophet, and the mercy of Allah and His blessings. Peace be on us and the righteous servants of Allah." And then the Tashhaud viz:

"I bear witness that none deserves to be worshipped except Allah; and I bear witness that Muhammad is His servant and apostle." —are to be recited.

Both these items are *Wajib.*

While reciting the *Tashhaud, a circle* with the thumb and the middle finger of the right hand should be made and the third and the little finger of the same hand should be closed. While uttering the words, the forefinger of the right hand should be raised and while saying, it should be lowered. The position of the circle should be retained till the end of the Qaada Ula or Qaada Akhira, as the case may be. The tips of the fingers of both hands should face the *Qibla.*

23. If the *Niyyat* was for three or four *Rakat,* after reciting the *Tashhaud, Takbir* viz *"God is Great"* is to be said once and the person is to rise from the Qaada Ula for the Qiyam of the third *Rakat.*

The third and fourth *Rakat* are to be completed in the same manner as the second *Rakat.*

After the second *Sajda* of the fourth *Rakat,* is the *Qaada Akhira,* in which first the *Tahiyya,* then *Tashhaud* and finally the Darood viz:-

"O Allah! Exalt Muhammad and the true followers of Muhammad as Thou exalted Ibrahim and the true followers of Ibrahim, for surely Thou art praised and magnified. O Allah! Bless Muhammad and the true followers of Muhammad as Thou blessed Ibrahim and the true followers of Ibrahim, for surely Thou art praised and magnified "is to be recited. This is Sunnat.

24. After the *Darood,* the following prayer is to be recited:-

"O my Lord! Make me one who establishes regular prayers and also among my progeny. O Our Lord! Accept my prayer. O One Lord! Cover (me) with your forgiveness - me, my parents and believers on the Day of Judgement."

25. After this prayer, the *Salat* is to be ended with *Salam.* For this the face is first turned to the right. Looking over the right shoulder

"Peace be upon you and the mercy of Allah" - is to be said. Then turning the face to the left and looking over the left shoulder, the same words are to be repeated.

Delayed Prayer : The believers are enjoined to offer their prayers at the appointed times. Failing to do so is a sin unless there is a reasonable excuse for delay. With the exception of prayers missed by women in child birth or menstruation and any Muslim who is insane or is unconscious for some time, every Muslim must offer the delayed obligatory prayer. These prayers have to be offered as soon as possible except at times when prostration is forbidden. In the *Niyyat,* the word Qaza should be added.

If several prayers have been missed in a day, then the *Qaza* should be offered in proper order. For example if prayers have been missed beginning from Fajr then Fajr Qaza should be offered first, then Zuhr and Asr and so on. If the missed prayers are too numerous to remember or if the time available is not enough for both missed and present prayers, then the present prayer should be offered first. The missed prayer should be offered later.

Qaza can be offered for only the Farz and Witr prayers. Except for the pre-farz *Sunnats* of *Fajr* for which Qaza may be offered before sunset the same day, no Qaza of other Sunnats is to be offered.

If Zuhr, Asr or Isha prayers become Qaza while travelling, one should, when he returns home, offer the Qaza of these as if he was still a traveller that is, two Rakat each. If however, the prayers become Qaza before a journey and one offers the Qaza during the journey, he should offer the full four Rakat of the three prayers.

If a person is unable to offer his missed prayers before death, he should make a will to pay compensation which is 1¾ kilos of wheat per prayer out of the property he leaves behind. The compensation for the missed Farz of the five daily prayer and the Witr of Isha comes to 10½ kilos per day.

Friday Prayer : Friday is a day of special importance for Muslims. The following verses of the Holy Quran relate to congregational prayers on Friday:-

> "O ye who believe! When the call is proclaimed to prayer on Friday (The day of assembly) hasten earnestly to the remembrance of Allah, and leave off business (and traffic) that is best for you if ye but knew! And when the prayer is finished, then may ye disperse through the land and seek of bounty of Allah."
>
> (62: 9,10)

The Friday prayer is therefore of special importance for Muslims as established by the above verses of the Holy Quran and the sayings of the Holy Prophet (PBUH).

Friday prayers take the place of the Zuhr prayers on that day, and may not be offered qaza, therefore whoever misses it, cannot make up for it. Instead, he has to offer the Zuhr prayer. Friday prayer must be offered in congregation.

Friday prayer are obligatory on all adult males of sound mind, who are healthy and are residents. Those exempted from attending the mosque for Friday prayer are minors, slaves, the sick, travellers and women. These people are to offer Zuhr prayers in their homes. All normal work is allowed on Friday. The Muslims can carry on with their usual duties and activities provided they come to the congregational service on time. After the service is over, they may return to their business and other worldly activities. It is traditional to take a bath on Friday and to wear clean clothes.

Muslims are required to leave their business and go to the mosque as soon as they hear the Adaan for Friday prayers. On reaching the mosque, one should first offer the Tahayyat-ul-Masjid prayers and then the four pre-farz *Sunnats.* The second Adaan is called before the *Khutba.* After the Adaan the Imam stands up and facing the audience, delivers the Khutba or the sermon, which is an essential part of the Friday service.

The Khutba is obligatory and listening to it is Wajib. While the Khutba is being delivered, no conversation is allowed. Even praying, reading the Quran or reciting durud is forbidden. Everyone should be seated and listen to the Khutba quietly till the end. The Khutba consists of two parts, each of which begins with praising Allah and asking blessings for the Holy Prophet (PBUH). In the first part, some Quranic passages are recited and explained. After this, the Imam sits down for a short rest and then stands up to deliver the second part of the sermon. In this part especially, the imam prays for the general welfare of the Muslims.

After the Khutba, *Iqamat* is called and people arrange themselves in rows. Two obligatory Rakat are offered under the leadership of the Imam who recites the *Sana, Tawwuz* and *Tasmiya* in the first Rakat in a low voice. Then the Imam recites *Surah Fatiha* and some other passages from the Quran in a loud voice in both Rakat. The *Muqtadis* should listen to the Imam's recitation and say Ameen in a low voice. When this is done, the prayer is complete.

The Muqtadis may now offer individually four sunnat, followed by two more sunnat and two *nafal.*

Eid Prayer : The two main festivals in Islam are Eid-ul-Fitr and Eid-ul-Adha. Eid means recurring happiness or festival. Eid-ul-Fitr is celebrated on the 1st of Shawwal which follows Ramadan or the month of Fasting. Eid-ul-Adha falls on the tenth day of Zil Hajja and follows the completion of Hajj.

Eid is a day of thanksgiving during which Muslims assemble in a brotherly and joyful atmosphere to offer their thanks to Allah for helping them to fulfil their spiritual obligations. The Eid days start with congregational prayers in the morning. During the prayer the Muslims remember and glorify Allah's name, offer thanks to Allah for Ramadan and ask for His forgiveness and for strength of faith.

The method of prayer for Eid-ul-Fitr and Eid-ul-Adha is the same. Eid prayers are Wajib on all those persons on whom Friday prayers are obligatory. These are congregational prayers and cannot be said individually. Eid prayers are not a substitute for the obligatory Fajr prayer and there is no Qaza for Eid prayer. The time for Eid prayer is anytime after sunrise but before noon. Usually, Eid-ul-Adha prayers are held a little earlier than the Eid-ul-Fitr prayers. No Adaan or Iqamat is required. The prayer consists of two Rakat with the Imam reciting in each Surah Fatiha and another passage from the Quran in an audible voice.

The intention for prayer is in these words:

> "I intend to offer two Rakat Wajib of Eid-ul-Fitr / Eid-ul-Adha (as the case may be) with six additional Takbirs, behind this Imam and I am facing the Holy Kaaba."

When the Imam recites Takbir-e-Tahrima, Allah-o- Akbar in a loud voice, the Muqtadis should also say the Takbir in a low voice, and fold their hands below their navel as in other prayers. Both the Imam and the Muqtadis now recite the Sana in a low voice. After reciting Sana, the Imam raises both hands upto the ears and says Allah-o- Akbar in a loud voice. The Muqtadis also raise their hands upto the ears and say the Takbir in a low voice.

The Imam and the Muqtadis should then lower their hands and keep them hanging by their sides. They should repeat this, that is, saying of Takbir and raising and lowering of hands twice. After the third Takbir, the hands are to be folded in the usual manner. The Imam shall now recite Tasmiyah, Surah Fatiha and some other Surah. The Muqtadis should listen attentively and not recite anything. They should only say 'Ameen' in a low voice after Surah Fatiha. After this, the first Rakat should be completed in the usual manner.

In the second Rakat, the Imam recites Tasmiyah, Surah Fatiha and some other Surah. The Muqtadis should only listen attentively and just say Ameen after Surah Fatiha. After this, the Imam raises his hands and recites the Takbir in a loud voice. The Muqtadis also raise their hands and say the Takbir in a low voice. They should now bring their hands down and keep them hanging by their sides. The hands should be raised and lowered and the Takbir said two more times. Both the Imam and the Muqtadis now say one more Takbir without raising their hands and bow down for Ruku. The second Rakat should be completed in the usual manner.

After the two Rakat of prayer are over, the Imam delivers the Khutba in two parts, with a short break in between. The Khutba is Sunnat and should be heard attentively.

In the sermon of Eid-ul-Fitr, the Imam must draw the attention of the audience to Sadaqat-ul-Fitr. This is a charity, which is obligatory on every Muslim who can afford it. This charity is more rewarding and preferable if it is distributed before the prayers, so that the poor may also be able to celebrate the day in a festive and cheerful spirit.

In the sermon of Eid-ul-Adha , the Imam should draw attention to the duty of sacrifice, which is to be observed by every Muslim with means. It is preferable to slaughter the animal of sacrifice on Eid day after prayers. The sacrifice of an animal on second on third day of Eid is also acceptable.

Private Prayer Dua : Allah created man to be His vicegerent on earth and bestowed upon him the ability to distinguish between right and wrong. He can achieve nothing but what he strives for. It is stated in the Holy Quran that with every difficulty, there is relief. According to Abdullah Yusuf Ali:

> "Whatever difficulties or troubles are encountered by men, God always provides a solution, a way out, a relief, a way to lead to ease and happiness, if we follow His path and show our faith by patience and well-doing."

Along with honest endeavour and effort man needs the help of his Creator in order to achieve his worldly goals. As such man turns to Allah, Who is the solver of all difficulties and asks for His help. Such supplication and invocation is called *Dua*. The Holy Prophet (PBUH) is reported to have called *Dua* the kernel of worship and the weapon of a believer. According to Tirmidhi, the Holy Prophet (PBUH) said that only Dua can change Allah's' decree.

> According to the Holy Quran, "And He (Allah) giveth you of that ye ask for." (14:34)

Abdullah Yusuf Ali says:

> "Sincere and true prayer in faith is answered by God. Thus He gives us everything which a wise and Benevolent Providence can give."

The Holy Prophet (PBUH) is reported to have said:

> "Verily your Lord is ashamed (i.e., shy) of His servants when they raise up their hand to Him in supplication to return them empty."

The Holy Quran, the final and complete revelation from Allah for the guidance of the whole of mankind and for all time, contains guidance for every stage of man's life. It teaches man how to pray and the way to ask for Allah's help, guidance, forgiveness and protection. The Holy Quran says:

> "When My servants ask thee (i.e., the Holy Prophet) concerning Me, I am indeed close (to them): I listen to the prayer of every suppliant when he calleth on Me: Let them also, with a will, listen to My call, and believe in Me, that they may walk in the right way."
> (2: 186)

A commentator of the Holy Quran says:

> "The God of Islam, never distant or remote, is the constant companion of His servants, their unfailing support, and infallible prop to those in need and distress. Prayer is the strongest and most visible acknowledgement of God's sovereignty and man's utter dependence on Him."

And also:

> " Prayer is the highest medium in Islam, whereby man can enter into communion with God."

In verse 60 of Surah Momin Allah says:

> "And your Lord says: Call on Me: I will answer (your prayer)." (40: 60)

The two verses of the Holy Quran quoted above teach us that Allah is close to us and listens to our prayers and answers them. Our prayers should, therefore, be made to Allah with the fullest faith. They should be addressed only to Allah Who alone is able to respond to all prayer and invocations.

The Quran says: "For Him (alone) is prayer. "
(13: 14)

Invoking the assistance of angels, prophets or saints is strictly forbidden. We must call upon Allah with sincerity and humility. The Holy Prophet (PBUH) is reported to have urged his followers to pray to Allah with full confidence in the acceptance of their supplications. Allah undoubtedly accepts one's prayer and grants it in his own time in the manner or form that He considers best.

The Holy Quran says:

> "When We bestow favours on man, he turns away and gets himself remote on his side (instead of coming to us); and when evil seizes him (he comes) full of prolonged prayer. " (41: 51)

In explanation of this verse Abdullah Yusuf Ali has pointed out:

> "If they receive good they go further away from God, instead of coming nearer to Him. If they suffer ill, they call on God and offer prolonged prayers, but it is not sincere devotion and therefore worthless."

Allah is Samad that is, Independent and Absolute and as such does not need our prayers. It is we who stand in need of Allah's help, protection and guidance. The Holy Quran says:

> "My Lord is not uneasy because of you if ye call not on Him ..." (25; 77)

According to Abdullah Yusuf Ali:

> "God needs no praise, for He is above all praise; He needs no petition for He knows our needs better than we do ourselves; and His bounties are open without

> asking, to the righteous and the sinner alike. Prayer is for our own spiritual education, consolation and confirmation."

The best of all the prayers contained in the Holy Quran is its first Chapter- Surah Fatiha. Marmaduke Pickthall says: "This Surah has been called the Lord's prayer of the Muslims: It is an essential part of all Muslim worship, public and private."

The Holy Prophet (PBUH) is reported to have said:

> "No prayer is complete without the recitation of the Fatihatul Kitab (Surah Fatiha)."

Abdullah Yusuf Ali has observed:

> "It (Surah Fatiha) sums up our faith, our hope and our aspiration in things that matter. We think in devotion of God's name and His nature; we praise Him for His creation and His cherishing care; we call to mind the realities seen and unseen; we offer Him worship and ask for His guidance and we know the straight from the crooked path by the light of His grace that illumines the righteous."

According to Encyclopaedia Brittanica, Surah Fatiha is 'a vigorous hymn of praise to God... The thoughts are so simple as to need no explanation, and yet the prayer is full of meaning.'

Mosque - Masjid : The objective of the Muslims, according to several verses of the Holy Quran is to establish prayer and to enjoin good upon the people and to refrain from committing wrong. These verses also sum up the duties and responsibilities of the believers. In order to fulfil these obligations, the Muslims are required to establish a state based on equality, liberty, brotherhood and justice. The institution of mosque played an important role in the practical realization of this state.

It is a characteristic of the Islamic state that religion and politics go together. In the early days of Islam the head of the state was the ruler and chief administrator as well as the religious head. The mosque, was the central place of worship and state administration.

The mosque may not be a consecrated institution as in other religions, yet the Quranic injunction is to establish prayers in a particular place called *Masjid* or Mosque. As such, prayers are offered in congregation, under the leadership of the head of the state or his representative in the various mosques of the state.

The congregational prayer serves as a strong force in uniting the believers. The gathering of all people living in a locality five times daily in the mosque, helps in the establishment of healthy social relations between different sections of the Muslim community. This gathering becomes larger in the weekly Friday service and still larger in the two Eid gatherings. The largest gathering of Muslims occurs on the occasion of the annual pilgrimage or Hajj when Muslims from all parts of the world assemble together.

Congregational prayer levels social differences and promotes an atmosphere of equality and brotherhood. In the mosque a king may stand shoulder to shoulder with his poorest subject and the white man will stand with the black. The congregation prayer leads to a realization among the worshippers that all men are equal before Allah. Differences of rank, wealth and colour vanish, and all bow before Allah.

The mosque is the religious as well as a cultural centre for the Muslim community. The Friday sermon addresses religious, moral and welfare issues of the community. In the time of the Holy Prophet (PBUH) and his successors all matters relating to war and peace, administration and community welfare were addressed and discussed in the mosques. All important announcements were also made from the mosques. In fact during the early years of Islam, mosque was the centre of Muslim activities.

The Holy Prophet's (PBUH) mosque and later many other mosques became centres of education. The Prophet's (PBUH) mosque had arrangements to house people who came there to acquire knowledge. These people were lodged in rooms call Suffa, attached to the mosque. People who were trained as missionaries for the spread of Islam, were also given lodgings at the mosque. In later times, libraries were established in mosques, some containing more than 100,000 books.

The mosque also served as the council hall of the Muslims. In the time of Hadrat Umar two councils were appointed to advise the Khalifa, these councils met in the mosques. The meetings of the Shura used to take place in the mosque and all the administrative affairs of the Khilafat used to be carried on from the mosque during the rule of the first four Khalifas. Deputations from Muslim as well as non- Muslim tribes were received in the mosque, and some of the more important deputations were also lodged there. Judicial affairs were also settled in the mosque. Thus, from the earliest times till today, the mosque has been serving not only as a religious and cultural centre for the Muslims but also as an educational, social and political centre.

The mosque is regarded as the house of Allah and therefore one should enter a mosque with respect. Clothes should be clean and footwear must be removed. Talking loudly, indulging in idle talk or gossip or reading worldly books in a mosque is forbidden. Buying or selling is also not allowed inside a mosque.

Observing Fasts

The Importance : Fasting is one of the five pillars on which the structure of Islam rests. Fasting was made obligatory for Muslims in 2 A.H. It is next in importance to prayers. It is prescribed for the Muslims in the form of a month long abstinence from food and drink accompanied by intense devotional activity. The month of fasting is the month of Ramadan, the ninth month of the lunar calendar, in which the first revelation of the Quran came to the Holy Prophet (PBUH). In this connection Allah says:

> "Ramadan is the (month) in which was sent down the Quran as a guide to man kind .... So everyone of you who is present (at his home) during that month should spend it in fasting, but if any one is ill, or on a journey, the prescribed period (should be made up) by days later. " (2: 185)

Ramadan is the month of purity in which virtue flourishes and evil is suppressed. The Prophet (PBUH) is reported to have said:

> "When the month of Ramadan comes, the doors of Heavens are opened and the doors of Hell are closed."

and

> "If a person does not abstain from telling lies or doing wrong when he is observing fast, let it be known to him that Allah does not want that he should stop taking his food."

At another place, he said:

> "Allah says, fasting is for Me and I shall certainly compensate it. Fasting is a shield; so when the fasting of anyone of you come up, he shall not utter foul words. If then anyone rebukes him or fights with him, let him say, I am a man observing fast."

Fasting, like prayer, is a universal religious institution and has been a part of the law brought by previous prophets. All the religions of the world and all the great religious personalities adopted fasting as the principal method of controlling one's desires. The Jews observe an annual fast on the occasion of the descent of Hadrat Musa from mount Sinai. Jesus Christ fasted for forty days in the desert and commanded his followers to fast. Thus, the institution of fasting is universal and existed in some form or the other even before Islam. According to the Holy Quran:

> "O you who believe! Fasting is prescribed to you as it was prescribed to those before you so that you may (learn) self-restraint." (2: 183)

But the Muslim fast is different in all respects from the fasts observed by the followers of other religions. It is not meant as a punishment or self-torture. The verse quoted above informs us that by prescribing a month's fasts, Àllah wishes to teach us self-restraint and to make us righteous and God-fearing.

The instincts of hunger and sex are strong in both animals and human beings. Temporary restraint from these directs attention to higher and spiritual things.

Islam developed a higher significance of fasting, 'that you may guard against evil'. The keynote of fasting is self-discipline and self-control. It is an institution for the improvement of the moral and spiritual condition of man. It makes a Muslim disciplined and steadfast in his habits. It also makes him capable of enduring hardships. It gives rise to a sense of compassion and humanism and removes barriers between the rich and the poor. By fasting, the rich undergo an experience which makes them aware of the condition of the poor and hungry and instills in them a desire to help the poor. It enables the rich to thank Allah for the bounties bestowed on them.

Thus, on the material side, fasting involves total abstinence from food, drink and sex and on the spiritual side abstinence from falsehood, speaking ill of others, quarrelling or wrong behaviour.

Method and Conditions : According to the Shariah, Saum or fasting means abstinence from food, drink and sex with the Niyyat or intention of worship from dawn till sunset. If a person does not eat or drink during the prescribed time, but he has not made the Niyyat for a fast, then in the terminology of Shariat or Islamic law, it will not be a fast.

Fasting during the month of Ramadan is obligatory on all Muslim adults, male and female. However, females who are in a state of menstruation or period of childbirth are not to keep the fast as long as such condition lasts; but they have to fast for an equal number of days after the purification bath has been taken.

A person who is ill may postpone the fast of Ramadan, if his physician fears that the illness would increase or be prolonged. Likewise, a woman who is pregnant or suckling her baby may also postpone it. Postponement of fast during a journey is also allowed. These fasts should be kept as soon as possible, after the end of Ramadan and in any case, before the next Ramadan. A person who is so old and weak that he is unable to fast is not obliged to fast. But such a person must feed a needy person twice a day for each missed fast, or give grain or cash equal to Sadaqah-e-Fitr.

Before keeping a fast, it is desirable to take Sehri which can be eaten till dawn. The intention for the fast should then be made for which the following words may be used:

"I intend to keep tomorrow's fast of Ramadan."

Now the person is subject to all restrictions and prohibitions associated with a fast till the setting of the sun. Eating, drinking, smoking, taking of medicine by mouth and sexual intercourse are forbidden during fast. Swallowing something which is not used as food or drink, or as a medicine, injecting liquid medicine, voluntary vomiting, smoking, the entering of water in the throat while gargling are things for which only a Qaza fast is necessary i.e., the person shall have to keep a fast after Ramadan instead of the one that was broken. But if the breaking of the fast through eating, drinking and sexual act was intentional, then in addition to the *Qaza* fast, the person shall have to pay the Kaffara that is, for every fast thus broken, he shall have to fast for continuous sixty days. Even if a single day's fast is missed, he shall have to start all over again to complete the number of sixty days at a stretch. If it is a female, then the period of her menstruation shall not be treated as a break. If the person cannot fast for continuous sixty days, he may, for each broken fast, feed sixty poor people twice a day; or he may give grain or cash equal to Sadaqah-e-Fitr to sixty persons.

While fasting, the use of toothbrush, hair oil and perfume is allowed. If paste or tooth-powder is used, care must be taken that it does not enter the throat. Injecting medicine directly into the stomach or the brain shall make the fast void. Eating or drinking by mistake does not break the fast and the fast should be completed in the prescribed manner. No *Qaza* or *Kaffara* is due in such a case.

If there is a fear that the person may die of thirst, or he has become so weak that there is a danger to his life, then the fast may be broken. In such cases, only *Qaza* is necessary.

Immediately, after the setting of the sun, the fast is to be broken, after reciting the following prayer:

"O Allah! I fasted for Thee and 1 believe in Thee and
I put my trust in Thee and with the sustenance Thou
hast given me, I now break the fast. "

Fasting is forbidden on the days of *Eid-ul-Fitr and Eid-ul-Adha* and on the 11th, 12th and 13th of Zil Hajja.

Tarawih : Tarawih are those prayers which are performed in the nights of the month of Ramadan. These prayers are *Sunnat Muakkadah* for both men and women. Men should preferably offer them in congregation in a mosque.

The *Tarawih* prayers start after the four *Farz* and the two *Sunnat Muakkadah* of Isha prayers. Twenty Rakat are to be performed each evening; intention is to be made for two *Rakat* at a time. The *Muqtadis* recite only the *Sana* in the first *Rakat* of each two *Rakat* after which they have to listen to the Imam's recitation of *Tawwuz, Tasmiyah* and *Surah Fatiha.* The *Muqtadis* says the *Takbir, Tasbih Ruku, Tahmid, Tasbih Sajda, Tahiyya, Tashhaud, Durud* and the *Salam* after every two Rakat. There is a short pause in which the following *Tasbih Tarawih* is recited:-

> "Glory to Him to Whom belongs all honour and all greatness; to Whom is due all respect and all awe; to Whom belongs all power and dignity; and Who is Irrestible. Glory to the Everliving Eternal, Sovereign; Who never sleeps and Who will never die. He is full of the greatest glory and is Most Holy; Who is our Lord and the Lord of the angels and the spirit. There is no other god except Allah. We pray for His forgiveness and for entry in the garden of paradise and for protection from the fire of hell."

Those who are unable to go to the mosque for the Tarawih prayers may offer them in their homes.

Alms Giving

Meaning : The Arabic word Zakat (Alms) has been derived from 'Zakat' which means, to purify. By giving charity, the giver's heart is purified from the love of wealth as Allah has said in Surah Taubah that those who prize gold and silver to the extent of hoarding and do not spend out of it in the name of Allah will be branded with fiery hot gold and silver. The Holy Quran contains severe warnings to those who pile up wealth and withhold *Zakat.* There are also several warnings of the Prophet (PBUH) to those who do not pay *Zakat,* about the penalty of the Hereafter and the destruction of the property on which *Zakat* has not been paid.

The Holy Prophet (PBUH) described *Zakat* as wealth taken from the rich and given to the poor. *Zakat,* also called poor rate or poor-tax is really a welfare tax. It is the backbone of the economic system of Islam. Its aim is to improve the condition of the poor and give them economic security and to prevent the accumulation of wealth in a few hands. *Zakat* is a blessing for the giver and a blessing for the receiver and it increases the wealth of the nation.

> "That which ye lay out for charity, seeking the Countenance of Allah, it is these who will get a recompense multiplied." (30:39)
>
> "The parable of those who spend their substance in the way of Allah is that of a grain of corn: it grows seven ears and each ear has a hundred grains. Allah gives manifold increase to whom He pleases.".
> (2:261)

Just as maintaining regular prayers is the sign of Iman that is, faith, the regular payment of Zakat is an attribute of a true believer. On the other hand, one of the signs of non-believers is that they deny the Hereafter and do not pay *Zakat.* Hadrat Abu Bakr, the first Khalifa said that there was no difference between *Salat* and *Zakat.* In fact, he sent an armed force against a group of people who refused to pay *Zakat* while observing *Salat* and professing to be Muslims.

Importance : Zakat was made compulsory in the second year of the Hijrat. It is the second of the two most important pillars of Islam, the first being *Salat* or prayer. By offering regular prayers, a Muslim discharges his obligation towards Allah. By regularly paying the obligatory *charity-Zakat,* he performs his duty and discharges his obligation towards poor Muslims. The importance *of Zakat* may be judged from the fact that the word *Zakat* occurs thirty-two times in the Holy Quran. With the exception of a few verses, it is always mentioned with Salat. The Quran says:

"Those who believe and do deeds of righteousness, and establish regular prayers and regular charity, will have their reward with their Lord. " (2:277)

" So establish regular prayer give regular charity and holdfast to Allah. " (22:78)

The other three pillars of Islam - Prayers, Fasting and Hajj are acts of worship which benefit no one but the person who performs them, but *Zakat* which is an act of worship, performed through giving away of a portion of one's wealth as commanded by Allah, benefits mankind.

The Quran has ordered the payment of *Zakat* several times. It says:

"Those who (in charity) spend of their goods by night and by day, in secret and in public, have their reward with their Lord: on them shall be no fear, Nor shall they grieve." (2:274)

"O ye who believe! Give of the good things which ye have (honourably) earned, And of the fruits of the earth which we have produced for you." (2:267)

The Holy Quran speaks of charity as next to prayer and says that prayer without charity is useless:

"So woe to the worshippers who are neglectful of their prayers, those who (want but) to be seen, (of men) but refuse (to supply even) neighbourly needs." (107: 4-7)

Apart from the verses regarding *Zakat,* the Holy Quran contains repeated instructions about spending in the way of Allah. In the definition of righteousness contained in the Quran, we are told that the righteous spend for the love of Allah. Verse 92 of Surah Imran tells us:

"By no means shall you attain righteousness unless you give (freely) of that which you love."

The same Surah says:

"They ask you (Holy Prophet), how much they are to spend. Say what is beyond your needs."

Rate of Zakat : The amount of payment and distribution of *Zakat* was defined at Medina in the second year of the *Hijrat*.

The payment of *Zakat* is compulsory on every adult, free Muslim who owns property to the extent of the prescribed rate called Nisab, provided such property has remained in his ownership and possession uninterruptedly for full one year. Zakat is payable not only on cash but also on gold and silver, jewelry, crops, animals, minerals, agricultural lands and all kinds of commercial goods.

1. *On Cash, Gold and Silver:* Zakat is paid at a rate of 2 ½%. A person who possesses 52½ tolas of silver or 7½ tolas of gold is liable to pay *Zakat*.
2. *Produce from Mines:* Owners of mines have to pay one-fifth of the produce of mines. This is called *Khums*.
3. *Land Tax:* The basis of this compulsory tax on the produce of agricultural lands called *Ushr* is to be found in the Quran. It is levied at the rate of one-tenth of the agricultural produce of land benefiting by rain or some natural spring; and one-twentieth of the produce of artificially irrigated lands.
4. On all articles of trade exceeding 200 dirhams.
5. *On Sheep and Goats:* For every forty sheep or goats- one goat; from 121 to 200 sheep or goats-two sheep or two goats; and over, that for every hundred sheep or goats, one sheep or goat is to be received by the state.
6. *Bulls, Cows and Buffaloes:* On thirty to forty cattle, one calf of one year; on every forty cattle, a two year old calf.

7. *On Camels:* On every five camels, one goat or sheep; from ten to fourteen camels, three goats; and from twenty-five to thirty-five camels, a female camel and so on.

***Sadaqatul-Fitr*:** This obligatory charity is an act of worship on the completion of the month of Ramadan. It is obligatory on all Muslims on whom *Zakat* is compulsory.

***Distribution of Zakat* :** The Holy Quran tell us how the *Zakat* money is to be distributed. It says:

> "Alms are for the poor and the needy and those employed to administer the (funds); for those whose hearts have been (recently) reconciled (to Truth); for those in bondage and in debt; in the cause of Allah; and for the wayfarer..." (9:60)

1. People who are poor and do not possess wealth equal to Nisab.
2. People who are extremely needy to the extent that they are forced to beg for their daily food.
3. Those people who are appointed by an Islamic Head of State or government to collect Zakat. It is not necessary that they be needy persons.
4. Those people who have recently accepted Islam and are in need of basic necessities of life.
5. Slaves who work for remuneration and who have an agreement with their masters to purchase their freedom on payment of fixed amount.
6. People in debt who do not possess wealth with which to repay loans. It is conditional that the debt is not due to any un-Islamic purpose.
7. Those people who have to fulfil an obligation, but are unable to do so due to poverty.

8. Those travellers who maybe well-to-do at home, but during their journey do not possess basic necessities, can be given *Zakat* in order to fulfil their travel needs and to return home.

It is unlawful to give *Zakat* to the descendants of the Holy Prophet (PBUH), to one's parents or to one's children, It cannot be given to non-Muslims neither can it be given to a person as remuneration for services.

Journey to Mecca and Medina

The pilgrimage to Mecca in Saudi Arabia constitutes the fifth and last of the acts of worship prescribed by Islam. The Quran says:

> "Pilgrimage thereto is a duty men owe to Allah - those who can afford the journey." (3: 97)

To make the meaning of this verse clear, it is necessary to read the previous verse also:

> "The first house of worship appointed for men was that at Mecca; full of blessing and of guidance, For all kinds of beings: In it are signs evident whoever enters it attains security; pilgrimage thereto is a duty men owe to Allah-those who can afford the journey." (3: 96-97)

The literal meaning of the word Hajj is the will and desire to visit, but in the terminology of the Shariah, it means the will to visit the Holy Kaaba which was the first structure built by Hadrat Adam for the worship of Allah. Then, about 4,500 years ago, Hadrat Ibrahim and Hadrat Ismail rebuilt it at the command of Allah. The story of the rebuilding of the Kaaba is thus related in the Holy Quran:

> "And remember, Ibrahim and Ismail raised the foundations of the House (with this prayer):
>
> "Our Lord, Accept (this service) from us:

> Our Lord! make of us Muslims, bowing to thy (will) and of our progeny a people Muslim, bowing to thy (will); And show us our places for the celebration of (due) rites." (2: 127-128)

From the words of this prayer, the purpose for which the Kaaba was built, becomes clear and we come to know that its completion was ordained at the hands of the children of Hadrat Ismail who settled at this spot and from them, the Holy Prophet (PBUH) was raised for the perfection of this purpose.

Pilgrimage to the Sacred House is not an obligation. It is compulsory only on those who are sound of mind, adults and have the provisions of travel. All those persons who fulfil these obligations and yet abstain from performing Hajj once in their lifetime give a lie to their being Muslims. A *Hadith* of the Holy Prophet (PBUH) states:

> "If a person is not hampered by any disease, real necessities or a tyrannical ruler and yet does not perform Hajj, his death and the death of a Jew or a Christian are the same."

Hajj constitutes a form of worship with the entire being of a Muslim, with his mind, body and soul, with his time, money and the sacrifice of all comforts of life to assume for a few days, the condition of a pilgrim totally at Allah's disposal.

Hajj is the only pillar among the fundamental pillars of Islam which requires both physical and financial sacrifices. Prayer and fasting are only physical worships and nothing is spent in their performance. *Zakat* is only financial worship, it does not require any physical labour. But in performing *Hajj* both physical and financial sacrifices are required.

The rites of Hajj centre on complete submission and devotion to Allah. At the same time, they serve as an example of total submission and obedience of Prophet Ibrahim, especially his willingness to sacrifice what he loved most in the world, his son Ismail, at Allah's Command.

Pilgrims come for Hajj from all parts of the globe. As they approach Mecca, they enter into the state of *Ihram*, which means divesting oneself of all marks of status to assume the humble dress and conditions of a pilgrim devoted wholly to Allah. The pilgrims are to abstain from marital relations, quarrelling or from using bad language. They are also prohibited to harm any living thing in the boundary of Mecca.

Hajj is one of the fundamental religious institutions of Islam. It is the greatest of all acts of worship; it is in fact, the culmination of worship. It is an exhibition of brotherhood, equality, punctuality and discipline. It affords an opportunity to Muslims from various countries of the world to become acquainted with one another and of discussing common problems facing the Muslim community.

According to Abu Hurrayrah, the Holy Prophet (PBUH) said that anyone who visits the House of Allah, does not indulge in foul language and avoids the disobedience of Allah, will become as pure and free from sins as a child.

At another place, the Holy Prophet (PBUH) said:

> "Hajj which is free from sins and defects is rewarded with Paradise."

The importance of *Hajj* has been well described by Imam Abu Hanifa who said that *Hajj* is the greatest of all worship, Ibadat, enjoined in Islam. Its chief importance lies in the fact that it strengthens one's faith in Islam.

Method : Hajj is an annual congregational worship which is performed in the twelfth month of the Muslim calendar, that is Zil-Hajja. The main stages of *Hajj* are as follows:

Ihram : The pilgrim puts on the Ihram, two white sheets of unsewn cloth. One sheet is used for covering the lower portion of the body (from the navel downwards) and the other is to be used for covering the upper portion of the body. The head remains uncovered.

The *Ihram* for women is their everyday ordinary clothes. It is compulsory for women to cover their heads, but no cloth should touch their faces.

Before putting on the *Ihram,* the intending pilgrim should first take a full bath, and clean the body thoroughly. He may now put on the *Ihram,* and cover his head with some unsewn piece of cloth and offer two Rakats of *Nafal* prayers.

Immediately afterwards, he should remove the cloth from his head and with his face towards the Kaaba, make the *Niyyat* of offering the *Hajj.* After this, he should recite the Talbiah in a loud voice:

> "Here I am at Thy service, O Allah! Here I am at Thy service. There is no partner with Thee. Here I am at Thy Service. All praise and all blessings and favours belong to Thee, and all sovereignty is Thine. Thou hast no partner."

The pilgrim has now formally entered the state or condition of *Ihram* and is subject to all the prohibitions and restrictions *of Ihram* which are as follows:

1. Wearing sewn clothes (by males).
2. Wearing of shoes which cover the raised bone of the feet.
3. Putting on a bandage on the head or face.
4. Covering the head or face. Women are required to cover their heads only.
5. Shaving, cutting or trimming of hair.
6. Cutting of nails.
7. Using perfumed hair oil, or any kind of perfume.

8. Using abusive or foul language, or quarrelling.

The following are the undesirable acts *of Ihram:*

1. Rubbing the body for removing dirt or dust.
2. Using perfumed soap for washing the body or face. Bathing with water is permitted.
3. Combing the hair, or passing the fingers through the hair or scratching the head, as these acts may cause the hair to fall, or may kill the lice in the hair.
4. Smelling perfume or some sweet-smelling grass.
5. Using a pin or needle for holding the sheets of the *Ihram.*
6. Using spices in food such as cardamom, clove or cinnamon or using perfumed tobacco.

The following are the permitted acts of *Ihram:*

1. Use of tooth brush or miswak.
2. Harmful insects may be killed.
3. Halal animals, but not hunted, may be eaten.
4. The use of blanket for covering the body, but not the head or face is allowed.

Ihram is the first and foremost *Farz* of *Hajj* and *Umrah.* It is a declaration of one's intention *or Niyyat to* perform *Hajj* or *Umrah. Ihram* is the visible indication or symbol of the pilgrim's renouncing all the vanities of the world to devote himself to the worship of Allah. *Ihram* is a time of forbearance and patience. It symbolises purity, renunciation and the equality and brotherhood of all believers.

After completing Ihram the pilgrim enters Haram, the sacred area around Mecca. Kaaba, the holiest and most sacred place for Muslims is in Mecca and there are strict rules for the preservation of its sanctity. For this purpose, several circles have been drawn around the Kaaba. The first and innermost circle is called Masjid-e-Haram. The second circle is called Mecca Mukaramma, the city of Mecca, forbidden to non-Muslims, within which living things are protected from violence. It is a place of peace and security. If anyone seeks an asylum in Mecca, he cannot be captured or killed; the hunting or killing of any bird or animal is prohibited, even the cutting of its trees is forbidden.

Haram : The third circle is called *Haram,* the boundaries of which were fixed by Allah's command first by Adam and then by Ibrahim. The Holy Prophet (PBUH) got pillars erected to indicate the boundaries *of Haram.*

Mawaqit : The fourth circle is called Mawaqit. These are the places beyond which no one proceeding to Mecca for *Hajj* and *Umra* can advance without putting on the *Ihram,* otherwise he shall have to offer a sacrifice as penalty.

Kaaba or the House of Allah, according to old tradition, was constructed on the earth by angels nearly two thousand years before the creation of Adam. When Adam was sent down on earth, the angels indicated to him the exact location where this House had been constructed by them and Adam built the Kaaba.

The House of Allah disappeared on account of the Flood during Hadrat Nuh's time. It was then re-constructed by Ibrahim and his son Ismail. At one place in the Holy Quran, Allah has called it 'My House' and at another place He has called himself Rabb of this House. There are twenty-four gates through which this House may be entered, but it is best for the pilgrim to enter through the Bab-as-Salam.

Mounted in silver and set in the south-eastern corner of the Kaaba is the sacred Black Stone, Hajr-e-Aswad received by Hadrat Ismail from the angel Jibbrail during the re-building of the Ancient House. According to tradition, this stone was milky white; it has become black because of the sins of people. This holy stone was touched or kissed by Hadrat Ibrahim and by the Holy Prophet (PBUH). Its kissing is symbolic of pure love of Allah and our resolve to obey Him in all matters.

Standing apart from the Kaaba but within the area which encompasses the ancient House are:

a. *Well of Zam Zam:* This well is in the south-eastern side of Masjid-e-Haram. The spring that feeds this well sprang up from under the feet of Ismail, when his mother Hajra, was searching for water for her infant son between the Safa and Marwa hills. From that time till the present day, millions of people have drunk the water of this well.

b. *Maqam-e-Ibrahim:* The place of Ibrahim. This is a stone on which Hadrat Ibrahim stood while constructing the Kaaba.

c. *Hatim:* This is a small area, between Rukn-e-Shami, the corner facing Syria and Rukn-e-Yamani, the south-western corner of the Kaaba but was not included in the covered enclosure. The offering of prayers in the *Hatim* is held to be like offering prayers inside the Kaaba.

Tawaf: The pilgrim enters the Great Mosque and walks seven times around the Kaaba. This is called Tawaf. Each of the seven circuits is called Shaut. Traditionally, *Tawaf is* begun by touching or kissing the Black Stone.

There are several kinds of *Tawaf:*

a. *Tawaf-e-Ziyrat also called Tawaf-e-Ifadah or Tawaf-e-Rukn:* It is a Rukn or obligatory component of Hajj and must be performed between the dawn of 10th and 12th of Zil-Hajj.

b. *Tawaf-e-Qudum:* It is *Sunnat* and is performed on entering Masjid-e-Haram.

c. *Tawaf-e-Sadr or Tawaf-e-Wida:* This is performed at the time of departure and is Wajib for all those living outside the Mawaqit.

d. *Tawaf-e-Umra:* It is obligatory or *Farz* for those performing *Umra.*

e. *Tawaf-e-Nafal:* Any *Tawaf* other than the preceding four categories is called Tawaf-e-Nafal. There is no restriction as to the time or number of such Tawaf, but they must be performed after wudu and Niyyat and in the prescribed manner.

After completing the seven circuits, the pilgrim goes to the Al-Multazim or the place of Holding and prays to Allah for forgiveness. This is a portion of the wall of the Kaaba between its door and the Hajr-e-Aswad.

Sayi : The pilgrim then performs the Sayi which is running seven times between the Safa and Marwah hills. These two hills are close to the well of Zam Zam. Safa is to the south-east, from which the *Sayi* is commenced and Marwa is to the north-east where the *Sayi* ends. It was between these two hills that Hadrat Hajra, wife of Hadrat Ibrahim, ran several times in search of water for her infant son, Ismail. It is in memory of this that *Sayi* is performed. This ritual expresses respect for maternal love and gratitude to Allah, who made the sacred spring of Zam Zam appear for Hadrat Hajra's relief.

The commandment about *Sayi* is contained in the Quran:

> "Behold! Safa and Marwa are among the symbols of Allah. So if those who visit the House in the season or at other times, should compass them round."
>
> (2: 158)

The pilgrim should first climb on the Safa hill. It is not necessary to climb the hill fully. He should climb to such a height only as would afford a view of the Kaaba. After descending from Safa, the pilgrim should move towards Marwa and thereafter; walk briskly between the two hills.

Journey to Mina: After the *Sayi,* on the morning of 8th Zil-Hajja, the pilgrim journeys to Mina, a plain which lies between Arafat and Mecca, about four miles east of Mecca. The pathway into this plain passes through a hill called Aqaba which is famous in the history of Islam as the place where the Holy Prophet (PBUH) took the two pledges from the Ansars of Medina. The pilgrims must reach this place before noon, so that the Zuhr prayers may be performed there. On the way to Mina and in Mina, the pilgrim should continue to recite Talbiah, Darood and Kalma Tauhid.

It is desirable to offer the *Zuhr, Asr, Maghrib,* and *Isha* prayers of the 8th Zil-Hajja and the *Fajr* prayers of the 9th Zil-Hajja in Mina.

Wuquf-e-Arafat: On the next day, that is, on the 9th of Zil-Hajja which is called Yaum-e-Arafat, the pilgrim should leave Mina after the *Fajr prayers* and move on to the plain of Arafat.

This plain is situated at a distance of nine miles from Mecca and about six miles from Mina. According to tradition, it was in this plain that Adam and his wife were reunited after years of wanderings. It was in this plain that the Holy Prophet (PBUH) delivered his Khutba Hajjat-ul-Wida and where he received the final revelation about the completion of Islam:

> "This day have I perfected your religion for you, completed My favour upon you and have chosen for you Islam as your religion." (5: 3)

The stay in the plain of Arafat is called Wuquf-e-Arafat. The best form of Wuquf, deserving the highest spiritual reward is to remain standing, facing the Qibla, while reciting *Talbiah, Istighfar, Kalma Tauhid* and praying to Allah. The assembly at Arafat is the most important part of the *Hajj,* without which

Hajj would be incomplete. The stay at Arafat is the supreme experience of *Hajj.*

The Zuhr and Asr prayers on the 9th of Zil-Hajja are to be offered together in this plain.

Journey to Muzdalifah: Immediately after sunset, without offering Maghrib prayers, the pilgrim should leave Arafat for Muzdalifah, a plain between Mina and Arafat about six miles from Mecca and three miles from Mina. In the Holy Quran, this place is called the Sacred Monument and the Muslims are especially asked to remember Allah at this place:

> "Then when you hasten from. Arafat remember Allah near the Holy Monument." (2: 198)

At *Muzdalifah* the Maghrib and Isha prayers are offered together at one time. The whole night at *Muzdalifah* is to be spent in prayer and remembrance of Allah. After saying the Fajr prayer on the 10th of Zil-Hajja before sunrise, the pilgrim should leave for Mina. Pebbles for throwing at the devil (shaitan) are picked up from here.

Rami of Jamarat-ul-Uqba: The pilgrim now proceeds to Mina just before daybreak. Here he spends three nights stoning the three stone pillars called Jamarat, That which is nearest to Mecca is called Jamarat al-Uqba, the second which is near the mosque of Mina is called Jamarat-ul-Wusta. At a little distance from this place is the Jamarat-al-Sughra or the smallest Jamarat.

It is reported that Satan (shaitan) tried to deceive and mislead Hadrat Ibrahim at these three places and Hadrat Ibrahim stoned the devil. It is in memory of this, that Rami the symbolic ceremony of stoning the devil (shaitan) is held at Mina. It is to show that we reject the devil and obey no one but Allah.

On the 10th of Zil-Hajja, the pilgrim must cast seven of the forty-nine pebbles collected at Muzdalifah at *Jamarat-al-Uqba* only. The approved method of doing Rami is to stand about five or six feet from the stone pillar, hold the pebble with the thumb and forefinger of the right hand and throw each pebble, one after the other and while doing so, the following is to be recited:

> The pebbles should fall as close to the pillar as possible. Immediately after the Rami on the 10th, the Talbiah is to be stopped.

Sacrifice: Returning from the site of Jamarat-al-Uqba, the pilgrims offer a sacrifice in memory of Hadrat Ibrahim who was willing to sacrifice his son Hadrat Ismail at the Command of Allah. This sacrifice is also part of world wide celebration which unites Muslims everywhere in the common rite of Eid-ul-Adha. Both the sacrifice and the throwing of stones are only outward acts. The real thing is the spirit of piety and submission to Allah which these acts express.

After the sacrifice, the male pilgrim should shave his head. The female pilgrim may clip a lock of hair only. Now the pilgrim is no longer in *Ihram* and the robes can be put off. The pilgrim may now cut nails, take a bath and wear ordinary clothes. However the prohibitions of *Tawaf* are not yet lifted.

Tawaf-e-Ziyarat: The pilgrim should now try to reach Mecca as quickly as possible for the *Tawaf-e-Ziyarat* which is the second most important item of Hajj, the first being Wuquf-e-Arafat. If *Tawaf-e-Ziyarat* is not performed, the Hajj shall be void. If *Tawaf-e-Ziyarat* is performed after the 12th of Zil-Hajja of the year in which the Hajj is performed, sacrifice shall have to be offered as penalty.

After *Tawaf-e-Ziyarat,* the pilgrim should return to Mina to pass the night there.

Rami on 11th and 12th: On 11th and 12th of Zil-Hajja the prescribed time for Rami is after declining of the sun before the *Maghrib.* On both these days, the seven pebbles shall have to be thrown, one after the other, in the prescribed manner, at each of the three stone pillars in this order:

1. Jamarat-ul-Sughra, which is the first of the three pillars while proceeding from Mina to Mecca;
2. Jamrat-ul-Wusta, which comes next; and
3. Jamarat-ul-Uqba which comes last.

Tawaf-e-Wida: On his return to Mecca from Mina, the pilgrim should per form the *Tawaf-e-wida.* This *Tawaf* should be performed before leaving Mecca.

Before departure from Mecca, the pilgrim should go to Al-Multazim, offer two Rakat prayers at Maqam-e-Ibrahim, kiss the *Black Stone* and drink water from the *Zam Zam.*

Faraiz or Obligatory Acts of Hajj:

1. Putting on the *Ihram* and making the *Niyyat* of *Hajj* and reciting the Talbiah.
2. Wuquf-e-Arafat i.e. staying in the plain of Arafat between the declining of the sun on the 9th of Zil-Hajja upto the dawn of the 10th Zil-Hajja.
3. Tawaf-e-Ziyarat on the 10th, 11th or 12th of Zil-Hajja after the shaving of the head or the shortening of the hair.

These three obligatory duties are to be performed in the prescribed order and in the prescribed manner. If any of these three *faraiz* is left out, there can be no *Hajj* and the mistake cannot be set right by sacrifice.

Secondary Imperatives or Wajibat of Hajj:

1. Stay at Muzdalifah,
2. Sayi between Safa and Marwah,
3. Stoning the devil,
4. Sacrifice,

5. Shaving the head (males) or shortening the hair (females),
6. Tawaf-e-Wida.

If any of these items is left out, the *Hajj* shall not become void; but the pilgrim shall have to pay the penalty either in the form of sacrifice or sadaqah.

Sunnats of Hajj:

1. Tawaf-e-Qudum;
2. Spending the night of the 9th Zil-Hajja in Mina;
3. Leaving Mina after sunrise on the 9th for Arafat;
4. Leaving Arafat after the departure of Imam;
5. Staying the night at *Muzdalifah* on the return from Arafat;
6. Taking a bath in Arafat.

If any of these *sunnats* cannot be performed, there is no penalty.

***Umra* :** The word *Umra is* usually translated as minor pilgrimage and it is commonly translated as *Hajj-e-Asghar.* Although many acts of worship performed in *Umra* are the same as those performed during *Hajj,* there are certain fundamental differences between the two. While *Hajj* is obligatory, *Umra* is not. *Hajj* can only be performed on the prescribed dates, but no date or time has been fixed for *Umra.* There is no *Wuquf-e-Arafat,* no *Wuquf-e-Muzdalifah,* no stoning of the devil, no combining of prayers, no *Tawaf-e-Qudum,* no *Tawaf-e-Wida* and no sacrifice of animals in *Umra.*

The *Ihram* is an essential condition for *Umra. Tawaf, Sayi,* shaving of the head or shortening of the hair are components or *Arkan of Umra.*

In *Umra,* the *Talbiah* is stopped at the beginning of the *Tawaf.* It is undesirable to perform *Umra* between the 9th and the 13th of Zil-Hajja.

Pilgrim Road

In the Name of God be the course and the mooring.
Prayer of Nuh as he launched the ark,
and of pilgrims as they set out for Mecca.

Quran: Sura II: 41 *Hud*

I come with many sins
From a far land ...
O God ! this Sanctuary is Thy Sacred Place.
Prayer on entering the gates of Mecca

Once at least in a lifetime, every Muslim capable of doing so is supposed to pack his bag, leave his home and take the road for Mecca; Mecca, to which his thoughts have turned every day since in childhood he learned to pray.

Over a million people go there each year, most of them during the month of piigrimage. In 1980, the total had risen to 1,900,000 and about half of these came from outside Saudi Arabia. The Saudi government keeps a register of pilgrims from other countries. In 1968 these were 318,507; in 1969, 406,895. In 1974, out of a total of 1,484,975, the number from outside Arabia was 918,777.

Much of this human torrent flows through Jadda, with its modern airport and deep-water harbour. More and more come by air: 5 3 2,000 in 1979, 571,000 in 1980. This involves handling up to 50,000 arrivals a day during the short and hectic period just before the Hajj. To meet this challenge Jadda's immense airport, dedicated in April 1981, includes a special Hajj Terminal, imaginatively constructed like a huge tent. Here the pilgrims can enter, wait to meet their guides, and find transport by road on the final stage of their journey to Mecca.

Every contrast of colour and costume, class and race is to be seen, but to enter Mecca all are dressed alike in two sheets of unsewn white cloth. External trappings and all things superficial are laid aside. King and peasant, descendant of the

Prophet and newest African convert, all are equal in this demonstration of brotherhood – and sisterhood. Women, never veiled on pilgrimage, take full part.

The King moves from Riyadh to lead the pilgrimage and entertain rulers and ambassadors of Muslim states. Informal discussions on policy and action are an important element. The Saudi Arabian government moves its headquarters to Mecca, and a considerable part of the oil wealth of the country has gone into modernising the arrangements for the reception of so vast a crowd.

Health precautions have turned what used to be a hazardous journey into a still rigorous but comparatively safe undertaking. Strict quarantine regulations, hospitals and mobile clinics, water supplies, drinking taps by roads along which almost a million must walk in a day: all these help the health record, and there have been no serious epidemics in recent years.

In the 1970's, a programme of building completed the expansion of the Great Mosque itself, so that 300,000 pilgrims can gather in its court at one time, each with a clear view of the square-built, black-draped building at its centre, the Kaaba. Tradition dates the worship of God here back to the days of Ibrahim.

No non-Muslim may enter Mecca. Soon after the day when the Prophet re-entered the city and cleansed the sanctuary of its idols -and before his own Pilgrimage of Farewell - it was closed to any but followers of Islam.

Father Ibrahim : The pilgrimage rites recall two events: the story of Ibrahim and the Farewell Pilgrimage made by the Prophet shortly before his death.

The Patriarch and Prophet Ibrahim travelled the desert caravan routes linking the centres of early civilisation: the same routes along which, through the past fourteen centuries, millions of pilgrims have passed - destination Mecca. More important, he travelled the road from the worship of many gods to that of the One Creator. The stories of his family, of his break with idols and his finding faith in the God, Allah, are told in the Quran.

Muhammad regarded himself as the restorer of the pure faith in One God first pioneered by Ibrahim, the spiritual father of the three great monotheistic faiths, as well as the ancestor of the Jews and of many Arabs; cousins whose destiny has been closely linked in history ever since.

According to Meccan tradition, the sanctuary there was first built by Ibrahim and his son Ismail. To reach Mecca from Damascus took later pilgrim caravans forty days. Hebron, where Ibrahim settled and where his tomb is venerated by Muslim, Jew and Christian alike, is nearer still. The journey to Mecca would not be a long one for such a traveller.

There, it is said, he took Hagar when she was turned out by Sarah. Her frenzied search for water was rewarded by the bubbling up of a spring, Zam Zam, from which every pilgrim drinks. Her desperate wanderings are recalled in the running to and fro of pilgrims between the two hillsides of Marwa and Safa. The climax of the Pilgrimage is the Feast of Sacrifice *(Eid-ul-Adha)*. This is in honour of Ibrahim's willingness to sacrifice his son. If they can afford it, Muslim families all over the world kill a sheep or other animal at this time, and give part of the meat to the poor.

Significance of Hajj : The Arabic word *Hajj* means "to set out for a definite purpose". Specifically, it refers to the pilgrimage to the city of Mecca. A *Haji* is one who has performed the Pilgrimage. An Islamic Correspondence Course, edited by Haji Riadh El-Drouble and issued by Minaret House, London, devotes one unit to the Hajj. The story of Ibrahim and his readiness to sacrifice his son is quoted from the Quran. Many, but not all, Muslim commentators think that the son in the story is Ismail, but the text might refer either to him or to Ishaq.

The spirit of Hajj is the spirit of total sacrifice: sacrifice of personal comforts, worldly pleasures, acquisition of wealth, companionship of relatives and friends, vanities of dress and personal appearance, pride relating to birth, national origin, accomplishments, work or social status.

This sacrifice of self was attained to the highest degree by the Prophet Ibrahim (peace be on him) who is known as "The Friend of God" *(Khalil Allah).* The story of his sacrifice is narrated in the Quran in the following manner:

(Ibrahim said) "O my Lord! Grant me a righteous (son)." So We gave him the good news of a boy ready to suffer and forbear.

Then, when the son reached (the age of serious) work with him, he said, "O my son! I see in vision that I offer you in sacrifice: now see what is your view."

The son said: "O my father! Do as you are commanded. You will find me, if God so wills, one practising patience and constancy."

So when they had both submitted their wills (to God), and he (Ibrahim) had laid him (Ismail) prostrate on his forehead (for sacrifice), We called out to him: "O Ibrahim! You have already fulfilled the vision."

> Thus indeed do We reward those who do right. For this was obviously a trial. And We ransomed him with a great sacrifice. And We left (this blessing) for him among generations (to come) in later times: "Peace and salutation to Ibrahim!"
>
> Quran: Sura 37: 100-109 *The Ranks*

Although the events to which this narrative refers occurred many centuries ago ... the spirit of submission to God cannot be illustrated for us in any clearer manner.

"Hajj" also signifies the brotherhood of all Muslims,

demonstrated in this greatest of all international assemblies ... (It) reminds Muslims of the forthcoming assembly on the Day of Judgement ... and also of the birth, rise and expansion of Islam, the overthrow of idolatry, the establishment of the worship of one God, and the difficulties and accomplishments of the Prophet Muhammad (peace be on him) and the early Muslims.

Motives for the Pilgrimage : Since 1960 the number of pilgrims from outside Arabia has more than trebled. Modern means of transport facilitate but cannot fully explain this increase.

What draws the pilgrims? Here are answers from a number of Muslims.

The leader of twenty thousand Iranian pilgrims: Abul Fazl Hazeghi, educator and parliamentarian:

> The purpose of the Pilgrimage is to clean the heart. A pilgrim has to set right anything wrong between him and another person, to make his will and to pay his debts. When he leaves home he should be free of debt, hate, bitterness, resentment, impurity.

Personally, I had three times the honour to take about twenty thousand pilgrims from Iran to Mecca. I have seen many people getting a new direction of life - completely different; some of them paying a large part of their wealth to be used for people's welfare, for the building of mosques, hospitals, clinics, etc. I was witness to many restorations between man and man, sect and sect, removing all kinds of misunderstanding and creating new friendships.

A professor:

> I have been several times to Mecca. I went with one idea, and came back with another. I looked forward to seeing the places where the Prophet lived and

> worked. I found more than that: the vast concourse of people from many lands, all the same, all equal; and their yearning for God, as all move round the Kaaba, hundreds of thousands of us together.

A former prime minister:

> I have been three times - twice for the Hajj. The simplicity of it is inspiring. But Muslims miss something of what it could be. It could be a conference at which everything of importance to Muslims is dealt with. The Prophet used it in this way. At his last pilgrimage, he made a great speech which is a charter for all Muslims.

An Egyptian lady:

> It is like a rehearsal for Resurrection Day - everybody equal, all kinds of people together, the whole of humanity before God.

An article addressed to London students faces the difficulties encountered by pilgrims. Mecca has its dust and flies, its colds and coughs, its taxi-drivers and water sellers who are cynics. "Hajj does need preparation and training," says the writer. He urges an imaginative use of television and radio to introduce different groups of Muslims to each other — in place of the sometimes incongruous mingling of sermons and western dance music. He concludes:

> Hajj has maintained the capacity to lift man from the jumble of his preoccupations and out of the mechanical framework within which he lives. Never is prayer offered with a greater feeling. In the unending flow of worshippers around the Kaaba throughout the day and throughout the night, there is satisfaction to the heart, joy to the eye, and mystery to the soul...

The scorched and barren landscape synchronises perfectly with these feelings of the pilgrim and even helps to produce them. It could never have done so were it cool and green and luscious. Yet there is no debasement, but ardour and grandeur.

The days of the Hajj are indeed unique days. Would that its great possibilities are realised!

Mecca Airlift : During the pilgrimage season hundreds of planes are chartered to bring pilgrims from every continent. Typical is one that started from Britain, in February 1968.

In the bitter cold of London's wintry dockland, the party gathers at the East London Mosque. It is an illustration both of the breadth of the Muslim world, and of the variety of Britain's multiracial society. Pakistanis and Indians are in the majority. A number of Iranians move together. Somali land, Zanzibar, Kenya and Nigeria are represented among the Africans.

Gayest note on a grey day is the emerald head-scarf of a Nigerian woman. She is one of a party of Nigerian students. Her husband says:

> Few months ago nothing was farther from my mind than the Hajj.

I had lost all faith and grip on life. But my brother's son never stopped coming to see me, and in the end he helped me to make a fresh start.

I am going home in a few months. I began to think, "I cannot take home the bad ways I have learned here," and I decided to clean up my life. Now my mother is coming from Lagos, and we shall meet in Mecca and make the pilgrimage together.

Among the party is an exiled ruler. An old man from Guyana is seen off by his son and daughter-in-law, immigrants to Britain. He has stayed with them for two weeks on his way. It is his first journey and he is nervous, as is an elderly Turk whose womenfolk are comforting him. The wife of the caretaker of the mosque encourages the lonely, and sees that everyone has the necessary documents. She is Welsh. She became a Muslim twenty-seven years ago and has, she says, prayed the regular five times a day ever since. Her warm heart, common sense, box of medicines and knowledge of Mecca will stand the others in good stead. Youngest of the party is a fifteen-year-old schoolgirl, travelling with her mother and her father, who has a business in Lancashire.

The women wait in a room above the mosque. Five coaches are at the door. Before they leave, the Call to Prayer is sounded, sheets are rapidly laid on the floor, and all pray. One woman starts to sing -reciting the verses of the Quran which her Urdu pilgrimage book recommends.

Bags and people are piled into the coaches, and they are away. Tomorrow morning they will be in Jadda, the next day in Mecca.

Discipline of Hajj : In a talk to would-be pilgrims in London, it was said, "There is no beauty in the Holy Land. You go to please God, not yourself." While the hardship is now lessened, the Pilgrimage remains a severe physical ordeal. The lunar months of the Muslim calendar come round at different seasons of the year, and the Hajj often takes place in intense summer heat. Any loss of temper or any altercation destroys its value.

There are many books designed to help pilgrims find their way through the month they spend in Arabia. A recent one comes from Dr Hassan Hathout, Egyptian doctor. It is a commonsense document, combining advice on health and diet with spiritual background. Dr Hathout stresses the permanent gain in tolerance and self-restraint.

The journey of Hajj is not easy. It is a taxing process and I do not speak in terms of the distance you cover from Home to Hajj. Coming together with a few hundred thousand people within a limited span of time and space, having to perform the same rites, entailing mass movements in a limited time from one place to another, is an ordeal. Yet the main cause of difficulty is the human one.

These people have many different backgrounds and customs, do not speak the same language, and yet they are gathered into this colossal human mass. One can imagine that endless situations would arise all loaded with nervous tension and intolerance. Yet strong "brakes" are placed on any tendency to nervousness or intolerance - it is a criterion of pilgrimage to be pure and tolerant. The Quran says: "The Hajj season comprises the specified months. He who proposes to do Hajj in them must abstain from obscenity, wickedness and ill-tempered disputes during Hajj."

However provoked, you should remain gentle and tolerant. This attitude of peace and forgiveness is imposed by your own self - and you do not pretend to be tolerant, but you feel you really are. This is indeed a great exercise in self-restraint and self-exploration - for you will sometimes be surprised to discover your tremendous faculties for love and patience, thus unearthing treasures you can count on in your future life.

Some of us who are highly sophisticated, especially those with western upbringing, do time and again ... voice many complaints ... (but) it seems to me that one of the aims of Hajj is to put the one Nation together in the one pot and make them mix and mingle ... The privileged cast away their arrogance and pride because they know it is a sin to be harsh to your brother or be scornful of him ... It is democracy in practice - and it is democracy in love - under God . It is true that some Muslims live in circumstances precluding them from attaining the standard that would please. Instead of being angry with them we should be angry for them.

Prophet's Farewell Pilgrimage : One of the great events of

Islamic history took place during Muhammad's last pilgrimage, shortly before his death. He addressed his followers in a speech that was the climax of his mission. This speech, made in dialogue with his hearers, has come down as a summary of his message. Every biographer of the Prophet describes the event, and every pilgrim recalls it as he follows the course of the Hajj in the Prophet's footsteps.

The crowd, an estimated one hundred thousand, gathered at Arafat, a few miles outside Mecca, as it does today. Muhammad rode the same favourite camel, Al Kaswa, that had carried him as a fugitive from Mecca to Medina ten years earlier. By his side was Bilal, the negro ex-slave whose great voice had won the honour of giving the first call to prayer on behalf of the Prophet. His voice, picked up by others through the crowd, was the relay-system by which the words of Muhammad reached the whole assembly.

Then came the last verse of the Quran to be revealed:

> This day have I perfected your religion for you, completed My favour upon you, and have chosen for you Islam as your religion.
>
> Quran: Sura 5: 4 *The Table*

In the course of this address, the Prophet called for the wiping out of vendettas- starting with a blood-feud in his own family as an example. This may be compared with Moses' farewell speech to the men and women of the Exodus, when he said, "Vengeance is mine, saith the Lord, I will repay."

(Deuteronomy 32:35)

Among many summaries of this speech, here is one designed for teaching children and students. It comes from *An Easy History of the Prophet of Islam*, published in Lahore.

1. All the customs and practices of the pagan age are abolished.

2. All compensation for bloodshed of the old days is abolished: and on behalf of my family I declare illegal the indemnity for the blood of Ibn Rabia ibn Harith [murdered cousin of the Prophet].
3. All usuries of the past are wiped out.
4. Fear God in respect of women. You, men, have your rights over your wives and they have their rights over you.
5. As regards your slaves, be fair to them. Give them to eat what you eat and to wear what you wear.
6. Your blood and your properties are as sacred for one another as are this day, this month and this place.
7. Each Muslim is a brother of another. All Muslims form one brotherhood.
8. An Arab has no superiority over a non-Arab, nor has a non-Arab over an Arab. You are all born of Adam, and Adam was made out of clay.
9. Whoever is entrusted with a thing belonging to another must deliver his trust to its owner.
10. The debtors must pay their debts.
11. I leave behind one thing, and you will never go astray if you hold it fast, and that is the Book of God.

Three Holy Cities: Mecca, Medina and Al-Quds (Jerusalem): Mecca, Medina and Jerusalem are all holy places to the Muslim. Almost every pilgrim to Mecca also visits Medina (2,25 miles northwest of Mecca), where the Prophet Muhammad lived for ten years and was buried.

Through the centuries, pilgrims to Mecca have regarded a visit to Jerusalem as a completion of their pilgrimage. The city is known in Arabic as Baitul-Maqdis (the Holy House), or Al-Quds.

There Muslim and Christian pilgrims have sought the same

holy places. When the end of the Hajj has coincided with Easter, large numbers of pilgrims of both faiths have often mingled in the streets. The writer was among them in 1966, the year before the Six Day War.

The Christian shrines were visited by the Muslim pilgrims. One party from Iraq were heard in disappointed argument because a service prevented them from entering the cave in the Church of the Nativity in Baitulaham where by tradition Jesus was born. They had just been to Hebron, to the ancient mosque which marks the tomb of Ibrahim. From some countries, there were pilgrim parties of both faiths: from Nigeria, for instance, and Yugoslavia. The parked coaches from the latter country might carry either Christians or Muslims.

The streets of the Old City were brightly lit, the shops open all night. Many homes had been opened to house the thousands from Syria and Egypt who, with the Cypriots, formed the mass of Christian pilgrims. Alongside these Christian homes were those with gay pictures chalked on the doors to welcome home Hajis. *Hajj mabrur wa dhanab maghfur.* "Pilgrimage made and sins forgiven." Less edifying were the second-hand clothes markets outside Herod's Gate and at the coach park, where Europe's old coats were finding their way to remote villages and Bedouin camps.

For the Muslims, all these things were incidental to the visit to Al-Masjid al-Aqsa, the Farthest Mosque, revered by the Prophet; the place towards which his prayers were first directed, and the starting point of his great mystical experience, the journey into heaven, during which he received the revelation about the five daily times of prayer. This event is known as the "Night of Ascent", and is said to have inspired Dante.

About one fifth of the area of the Old City is taken up with the courts of the Noble Sanctuary, Al-Haram al-Sharif, with its large congregational Mosque, Al-Aqsa, to the south, and in the centre the marvel of the Dome of the Rock. In 1966, repairs and restoration had just been completed. The fresh gold on the dome dominated the landscape and the city. A tall crane still stood by its side, and the little Dome of the Chain awaited repair, its condition a measure of the extent of the work done on the larger structure.

Every Muslim child knows the story of the Arab capture of Jerusalem. In AD 638 the Patriarch in the beleaguered city offered to surrender it, but only to the Caliph 'Umar in person. 'Umar, simply dressed, entered the city and said his prayers not in, but near, the Church of the Holy Sepulchre, so that his followers might not be tempted to take it over. The treaty he made is regarded as a model of tolerance. This and the parallel story of the reconquest of the city by Saladin (Salah ad-din) after a century of Christian occupation are viewed in sharp contrast with the bloodshed and slaughter associated with the Frankish armies in 1099 when the Crusaders took the city.

The Dome of the Rock, first of the great architectural achievements of Islam, was finished by the ninth caliph, Abdul Malik, in the year AD 691. In its thirteen centuries of life, it has been fortunate in its restorations. Each, including the most recent, has kept to the character of the building and has enhanced its beauty. As with other great works of art, it has a perfection which is, in its own sphere, unsurpassed.

The care of Al-Aqsa and the Noble Sanctuary is the trust of a group of families whose tenure goes back eight hundred years, though many were exiled after 1967. They were installed by Saladin after he recaptured Jerusalem from the Crusaders in AD 1189. Khatibs, Hussainis and Nashashibis have lived in the houses overlooking the Noble Sanctuary ever since, and generation has followed generation in its service. Some have been there longer still. Khalidis - the family of the great general Khalid ibn Walid have resided in the city since AD 638. More recent comers are Shihabis, who arrived from Lebanon three centuries ago. To them are entrusted the Prophet's cloak and pen, precious relics which are shown to the faithful each year on the Night of Ascent, Muhammad's mystical journey to heaven.

In the Dome of the Rock, human skill and artistry surround something unique in its rugged simplicity. The stretch of bare rock beneath the dome is a stark reminder of a Greatness no image can evoke, which commands the total submission of man's every gift and talent.

The rock is linked with Ibrahim. Centuries after his time, David bought it, and Solomon built his temple here. In these courts Jesus walked and taught. No place on earth has been the focus of so much faith and so much hope. It is central to all three of the great monotheistic faiths. They have a basic kinship stemming from Father Ibrahim. Cooperation between Jews, Christians and Muslims was the hope of the Prophet Muhammad. He was disappointed, but his respect for others who believe and obey God is deeply rooted in the Muslim mind.

6

The Foundations

The Reasoning (Ijtihad)

The Holy Quran is the fundamental source of the Shariah. It is the last and final revelation therefore its teachings shall always remains the source of Shariah for all times.

The Sunnah of the Holy Prophet (PBUH) comes next which sometimes elaborates and explains what has been mentioned in the Holy Quran and sometimes adds something to its commandments. In the latter case, it becomes the basis for legislation in Islam. The Quran and the Sunnah are thus the eternal sources of law for Muslims and the basic principles of legislation in Islam. However when sometimes the Quran and the Sunnah are silent about a matter, then it is a clear indication by the Supreme Law giver that the matter should be decided by the people concerned, in accordance with the needs of time and place. In all such matters, there is no alternative for a Muslim but to resort to Ijtihad which is the process of reasoning based on the Quran and the Sunnah. The Muslims are free to strive and endeavour to find solutions by using their own independent judgement Ijtihad in the light of the Quran and the Sunnah.

The main purpose of Ijtihad is to find ways and means to

preserve and safeguard the principles of Islam in an ever changing and developing human society and to find solutions to new problems which have not been directly or clearly discussed or decided by the Quran and the Sunnah. The literal meaning of the word 'Ijtihad' is effort and it comes from a Hadith of the Prophet (PBUH) in which the Holy Prophet (PBUH) asked Muaz whom he had appointed governor of Yemen, by what criteria would he govern the regions assigned to him. 'According to the book of Allah', he answered. "And if you find nothing therein", the Prophet (PBUH) asked. Muaz answered, "According to the Sunnah of the Prophet (PBUH)." "And if you find nothing therein?" the Prophet (PBUH) asked again. "Then I will exert myself to form my own judgement", Muaz answered. And this the Prophet (PBUH) approved. Umar bin Aas was told by the Holy Prophet (PBUH) that if by exercising Ijtihad, he took a correct decision, he would get the reward of ten good deeds and if he took a wrong decision, he would get the reward of one good deed.

The most outstanding contributions in the field of Ijtihad have been made by Hadrat Umar. Less than twelve years after the Holy Prophet's (PBUH) death, he found it necessary to exercise Ijtihad. His first Ijtihad was with regard to the interpretation of the word 'thief in the Quranic verse:

> "As to the thief, male or female, cut off his or her hands. " (5:38)

He excluded from the definition of thief all those who stole because of hunger or during famine.

Hadrat Umar also exercised Ijtihad in awarding punishments for theft. For example, the hands of a slave who had stolen a mirror from his master's wife were not cut on the ground that he himself, being the property of the master, could not be considered to have stolen. Similarly, he acquitted a man who had stolen from Bait-ul-Mal. Once, during Ramadan, he broke his fast on a cloudy day in the mistaken belief that dusk had fallen. But soon the sun started shining. Hadrat Umar said:

> "It does not matter. We pondered over the matter according to our lights."

A well-known incident is his interpretation of verse 60 of Surah Taubah regarding charity. It says:

> "Alms are for those whose hearts have been (recently) reconciled (to the truth)." (9:60)

Among others, who received a share from both Zakat and war booty were the Quraish chiefs like Abu Sufyan and Safwan bin Umayyah. They used to get one hundred camels each. Hadrat Abu Bakr gave them additional authority for land grants. But Hadrat Abu Bakr passed away before the grants could be awarded. When the chiefs approached Hadrat Umar for implementation of the grants he not only tore those orders, but also stopped giving them the hundred camels which they used to get. His reason was that such a grant was a political necessity, when Islam was weak. But since Islam had become powerful during the time of Hadrat Umar, the old practice was no longer justified.

In the early centuries of Islam, there were jurists who developed and advocated Ijtihad. But in the later centuries, with the influence of different schools of law that had evolved and developed, this faculty of Ijtihad gave way to Taqlid that is, an acceptance of what the great scholars of fiqh have held in the past.

There are many problems facing Muslim society today in political, economic and social spheres - that can only be solved by Ijtihad, specially, in those matters where no distinct and direct command is found either in the Quran or the Sunnah. Some of these problems are, the current commercial transactions including insurance, the right of private ownership, nationalisation, tax system, the method of election to assemblies and election of the Head of the State, and the problems concerning international law particularly on the points of nationality and domicile, in different Muslim countries in the context of the concept of Dar-ul-Harb.

Ijtihad is concerned with matters, relating to human actions. It has no concern with one's faith, beliefs or religious convictions. The reason for this distinction is that in worldly matters we may ourselves discover the right way by using our intelligence. But intelligence alone cannot guide us in the field of religion.

Furthermore, Ijtihad should not be against any command or principle of the Holy Quran. People qualified for Ijtihad must not only possess vast religious knowledge, but must also be men of Taqwa that is, piety who can rise above their own personal ambitions and weaknesses. Although Islam does not believe in priesthood yet it does not give the right to everyone to undertake the difficult task of ijtihad. This right is limited to those only who fulfil all the basic and essential conditions of Ijtihad, in both religious knowledge and piety.

Ijtihad is meant to make the legal system of Islam dynamic and effective it should encourage a steady growth and development in Islam according to the needs and social circumstances of different times and places which will make Islam forceful and vigorous and prevent stagnation and decay.

It is only through the use of Ijtihad that we will be able to meet the challenges of modern civilization. It will contribute immensely to the intellectual revival of Islam in modern times and give a new force and vitality to Muslim society. It will also help to bring the Muslims all over the world close to one another.

The Consensus of Opinion (Ijma)

Ijma is the third source of Islamic law. Literally, Ijma means agreeing upon or uniting in opinion. It means the consensus of the Islamic community on some point of law. It can operate only where the Quran and the *Hadith* have not clarified a certain aspect of the law. It is a gradual process through which the community over a period of time comes to a consensus over a question of law. The view of Muslims over the centuries has been that giving opinion on problems of law should be the function of Ulama who alone are well-versed in the science of law which is very complex and requires deep study before we can claim to be an authority over them.

The laws of the Quran and the *Sunnah* were, no doubt, supreme but there was no bar to making laws according to the needs of the people as long as they did not go against the spirit of the revealed law and the *Sunnah.* These laws were, however, to be made in consultation. It is reported from the Holy Prophet (PBUH):

> "If anything comes to you for decision, decide according to the Book of Allah. If anything comes to you which is not in the Book of Allah, then look to the Sunnah of the Prophet (PBUH). If anything comes to you which is not in the Sunnah of the Prophet (PBUH) then look to what people unanimously agree upon. "

In reply to Hadrat Ali as to how to proceed in cases where there was no definite direction in the Holy Quran or the *Sunnah,* the Prophet (PBUH) is reported to have said:

> "Gather together the righteous from among my community and decide the matter by their counsel and do not decide it by any man's opinion ."(Abu Daud).

And again:

> "My nation will not agree unanimously in error."

Counsel was freely resorted to by the Prophet (PBUH) himself in all important matters. Medina was attacked thrice by the Quraish, and every time the Prophet (PBUH) held consultations with his followers about the best way to repel the enemy. On one of these occasions, he acted upon the opinion of the majority and marched out of Medina to meet the enemy, although his own opinion was that the Muslim army should not leave the town.

The Holy Prophet (PBUH) has said:

> "Whatever the Muslims hold to be good is good before Allah. It is incumbent upon you to follow the most numerous body. Whoever separates himself from the main body will go to Hell. If you yourselves do not know, then question those who do."

These traditions of the Holy Prophet (PBUH) are a sanction of *Ijma.*

Ijma is of three types:

1. *Ijma* or consensus of the Companions of the Holy Prophet (PBUH) which is also universally accepted and binding and is therefore, unchangeable.
2. *Ijma* of the jurists.
3. *Ijma of* the people, i.e., general body of the Muslim community.

As regards the last two, the jurists, particularly Imam Abu Hanifa, are of the view that they cannot be confined or limited to any particular age or country, and therefore, *Ijma* of one age can be modified by *Ijma* of the same or subsequent age.

Holy Quran, basis of Faith

The first source of Islamic law is the Holy Quran which is the revelation of Allah and the Book in which His Message to mankind is contained. It is the word of Allah revealed to Prophet Muhammad (PBUH) through the angel Jibbrail. It is the foundation of Islamic Law and a Book of exalted power.

The Quran contains a set of moral and juridical injunctions

which are the basis of Islamic law and which concern the life of human beings in every detail.

The early revelations received in Mecca deal largely with questions of beliefs and morals. It was later, after the Prophet's (PBUH) migration to Medina when Muslims lived in an organised society that the principles regarding contracts, succession, crime, constitutional law and international law were revealed. Many of these revelations were very short. The principle contained in a simple sentence could be the foundation on which a whole structure of law could be built, for example:

> "Give full measure when you measure and weigh with a balance that is straight." (17: 35)
>
> "Those who unjustly eat up the property of orphans eat up afire into their own bodies." (4: 10)

The place of the Holy Quran as a source of law is due to its being a source of guidance not only to the spiritual good of the Hereafter but also towards the spiritual, physical and social good attainable in this world. It attends to minimum details for the refinement of the individual or for peaceful and congenial relations among human beings. It calls for lowering the voice when talking and modesty in walking. In order not to accumulate wealth in a few hands and to avoid disputes and quarrels, a fair plan is provided for the distribution of wealth left behind by a deceased person. Human dignity is to be respected, injustice even to an enemy is prohibited and the rights and properties of others are to be protected. Parents are instructed to inculcate in their children Islamic virtues and good manners. Children have to treat their parents with reverence, obedience and tenderness. A ruler is to be aware of his duties and responsibilities. He is to be obeyed for the smooth running of the State and for peace and tranquillity.

The Quranic law is everlasting and perpetual. It does not change with the passage of time. It should be studied with the object of acting in accordance with its teachings and moulding our lives accordingly.

The Quran is addressed to the entire humanity, above all barriers and limitations of race, religion and time. It contains directives for the head of the state as well as a common person, for the rich as well as the poor, for peace as well as for war, for spiritual as well as material prosperity. Its laws guide human beings to perfection. It appeals to the reason of man and invites him to exercise his purpose in life.

Compilation of Quran : The task of recording the revelations received by the Holy Prophet (PBUH) was undertaken during his lifetime. He entrusted the duty of recording the Quran in writing to a number of his companions particularly the four Khalifas and Zaid bin Sabit, Khalid bin Walid, Sabit bin Qais etc. Whenever a chapter or a verse was revealed, it was written down. The Holy Prophet (PBUH) also indicated the proper place of a verse in a relevant chapter. One of his companions had reported: One day I was sitting in the company of the Holy Prophet (PBUH). During my presence, the Holy Prophet (PBUH) raised his eyes to the sky and then lowering them said:

> "Jibbrail had come to inform me of the proper place of the verse. "

The arrangement of the chapters was done by the prophet himself, under Divine guidance. In this way the Quran was recorded in scriptural form and learnt by heart during the lifetime of the Holy Prophet (PBUH).

The Quran was written on thin and flat tablets of stone, wood, branches of palm trees, bones of camels and goats and on pieces of leather. It was not compiled in a book form during the lifetime of the Holy Prophet (PBUH). According to the scribe Zaid bin Sabit:

> "The Holy Prophet (PBUH) departed from this world and the Quran had not been collected and compiled on anything so far."

The work of recording the text of the Quran in writing was, therefore, completed during the Prophet's (PBUH) lifetime but not its compilation. After the death of the Holy Prophet (PBUH) his companions felt the necessity to collect and compile the text of the Quran. Hadrat Abu Bakr, the first Khalifa in consultation with Hadrat Umar undertook this noble task, which was completed during his rule and under his supervision. A large number of people who had learnt the Quran by heart had died in the battle of Yamama. Hadrat Umar therefore pointed out to Hadrat Abu Bakr that if more people who had memorised Quran died in future battles, Muslims would be deprived of a great part of the Quran. He suggested that the Quran should be compiled. Hadrat Abu Bakr however, hesitated and said that he would not do the job left undone by the Holy Prophet (PBUH). Hadrat Umar argued that under the circumstances the compilation of the Quran had become an absolute necessity. According to Hadrat Abu Bakr:

> "Umar went on persuading me to accept his suggestion till I was convinced that he was right so I accepted his suggestion."

Hadrat Abu Bakr then directed Zaid bin Sabit to collect the Quranic verses from every part of the Islamic Empire and compile them into book form. Zaid expressed his feelings in these words:

> "By Allah, if I had been asked to uproot a mountain and put it in another place it would not have been so hard a task for me as the compilation of the Holy Quran. I objected why Abu Bakr and Umar wanted a thing done, which was left undone by the Holy Prophet (PBUH). But Abu Bakr insisted that getting the Quran compiled was necessary. He persuaded me every now and then till my opinion also changed and became identical with that of Abu Bakr and Umar. I started the work and traced out and collected the

Quran from every corner and every person who was in possession of any part of it. I collected it from palm leaves, white stones, small pieces of wood and people who had committed it to memory."

Zaid bin Sabit was not content just finding a written piece of the Quran. He also verified it from those people who had heard it from the Holy Prophet (PBUH) and committed it to memory. Though Zaid himself was a Hafiz of the Quran, he always tried to find a verse in writing before including it in his manuscript, so that the version of the Quran he recorded was the one heard from and written under the supervision of the Holy Prophet (PBUH).

The script prepared by Zaid remained with the first Khalifa and after his death was transferred to the custody of Hadrat Umar. After the death of Hadrat Umar, this script was transferred to Hadrat Hafsa.

Imam Bukhari has narrated on the authority of Anas that after the conquest of Syria and Iraq, the people of these countries recited the Quran in different ways. This disturbed Hadrat Anas who went to Hadrat Uthman and requested him to take immediate action for the removal of these differences, otherwise it might create rifts among the Muslims.

Accordingly, Hadrat Uthman acquired the copy of the Quran prepared by Hadrat Zaid bin Sabit, from Hadrat Hafsa and appointed scribes to make copies of it. Copies of the Quran were prepared and sent to the capital city of every province of the Muslim state. Hadrat Uthman also ordered that all existing copies of the Quran with the exception of the authentic ones be burnt. Thus, the Quran that is being read now is the same as in the time of Hadrat Abu Bakr. Nothing has been deleted or added to it. The arrangement of the chapters and verses is the same as ordered by the Holy Prophet (PBUH), in accordance with instructions received from Hadrat Jibbrail.

The fact that the Holy Prophet (PBUH) used to recite the

Quran by this very arrangement has been established by traditions reported from him through different people. It also stands established by the opinion of the companions that the present form of compilation and arrangement of the Quran is the same as that ordered by the Holy Prophet (PBUH) under Divine guidance.

The Guide

> It is no new tale of fiction, but a confirmation of previous scriptures, and an explanation of all things, and a guidance and mercy to those who believe.
>
> (Quran: Sura 12: III Joseph)

Three voices God Loves:

The voice of the cock
The voice of one reading the Quran
The voice of one seeking pardon in the early morning.
Tradition of the Prophet Muhammad

Quoted by Al-Ghazzali:

The guide on the road of life is the Holy Quran.

The revelations that came to the Prophet Muhammad were written down by his Companions, put in order under his instructions, and finally compiled by the third Caliph 'Uthman, less than ten years after the Prophet's death. The text is exactly the same now as it was then.

In one book it ranges the whole of life: the worship of God, the nature of man, and the way he should live. It gives both a portrait of creation and instructions by which the individual, the family and the community should conduct their affairs.

The western reader, faced with an English "interpretation", finds himself at a disadvantage. The transition from the original has stripped away its beauty. The unsurpassed music of its language is gone - and the Quran is meant to be *heard*. The vivid word pictures it paints raise no such response as they do in the mind of an Arab reader. Moreover, while it is divided into chapter *(sura)* and verse, it does not provide a sequence easy to read or to tabulate. It calls for an effort of imagination and study which is difficult to make. The orthodox view that the Quran cannot be translated becomes quickly understandable to anyone who tries to enter into the truth and the experience it conveys.

Nevertheless, from early times the effort at interpretation has been essential for Muslims whose language is other than Arabic. It is the duty of every Muslim to read, and to the best of his ability to understand, the Holy Book. For example, a manuscript centuries old, in the library of Aligarh Muslim University, shows a Persian commentary painstakingly written under the Arabic text in Mughal times. In Istanbul, the "Book Market" has numbers of editions on sale - some of them having the original Arabic transliterated into the modern Turkish script, with a version in Turkish alongside. Translations are appearing in languages ranging from Swahili to Russian and Chinese, including the European languages, with the aim of bringing the Quran to believer and unbeliever alike.

Language of the Quran : The language of the Quran, with its dignity, its rhythm, its range and the depth of its meaning, is to the Muslim a part of the miracle of its revelation.

In the remote deserts and tribal communities of Arabia, a rich linguistic vehicle developed, ready to carry a prophetic message to millions and to become the means of expression of a great civilisation.

The Arabic language is built on simple three-letter "roots" which each convey a basic idea and which are developed into an intricate pattern of words covering many shades of meaning. There are only about a thousand of these roots. Human personality enters into each original concept: acting, demanding, cooperating, suffering, seeking and being sought, intense or relaxed. The result is a structure that gives infinite flexibility.

Many of these roots are common to all the Semitic languages. Before Muhammad's day they had already served mankind well, as the linguistic basis of the early Mesopotamian civilisation, and as the means of expressing the grandeur of Old Testament prophecy. In Arabia the development of language was far richer and more complex. Pre-Islamic poetry used words that convey heroism, joy and sorrow, deep feelings and high ideals — words that were there prepared and ready to carry the inspiration of the Prophet of Arabia to the world.

The dynamic of Arabic is still active. The same original roots are being used to serve the needs of modern science and technology. And while colloquial speech diverges, the classical Arabic - simplified, but in essence the language of the Quran- is heard and understood all over the Arab World. It is the vehicle of radio, television and cinema, and is read in newspapers that may be bought on the streets of any world capital.

What the Quran means to a practising Muslim is explained here by two scholars, one a political scientist and the other a sociologist.

Muslim Lives by the Quran : "The Muslim lives by the Quran," says Professor Yusuf K. Ibish, Professor of Islamic Political Theory and Institutions in the American University of Beirut. He comes from Damascus, has a Harvard Ph.D., and is a trusted authority on Sufism.

I have not yet come across a western man who understands what the Quran is. It is not a book in the ordinary sense, nor is it comparable to the Bible, either the Old or New Testaments. It is an expression of Divine Will. If you want to compare it with anything in Christianity, you must compare it with Christ

Himself. Christ was the expression of the Divine among men, the revelation of the Divine Will. That is what the Quran is. If you want a comparison for the role of Muhammad, the better one in that particular respect would be Mary. Muhammad was the vehicle of the Divine, as she was the vehicle. His illiteracy was comparable with her virginity, symbolic of purity.

There are western orientalists who have devoted their life to the study of the Quran, its text, the analysis of its words, discovering that this word is Abyssinian, that word is Greek by origin. The Bible and other literary works have also been subjected to this treatment. But all this is immaterial. The Quran was divinely inspired, then it was compiled, and what we have now is the expression of God's Will among men. That is the important point.

One has to make an effort to understand. Like the bride behind the veil the Holy Quran does not lend itself easily to the seeker. You can read it as you would read any book, and you will gather certain things from it. But to grasp its message truly, you have to penetrate from the external appearance to the inner reality, from the exoteric to the esoteric meaning. It is a two-level process, and of course one needs the guidance of those who know.

The Muslim lives by the Quran. From the first rituals of birth to the principal events of life and death, marriage, inheritance, business contracts: all are based on the Quran. A man can live and die decently if he seeks inspiration from the Quran. Most people from outside look on it as a small book containing limited instruction about conduct and life. This is not so. There are guiding principles, and you can unfold any number of valid interpretations.

Professor Yusuf Ibish, Beirut

Motivator of Thought : Dr Ali Issa Uthman is one of a Palestinian family coming from a village near Jerusalem, one of those divided by the armistice-line of 1948. He was educated in Chicago, where he took a Doctorate in Sociology. He was for some years Adviser to UNRWA on Education, and in particular on social studies. His book, *The Concept of Man in Islam, in the writings of Al-Ghazzali*, was published in Cairo in 1960. He says:

> The Quran is organic in ideas - not in structure. Get away from the idea of a book that starts and develops. When you have read it all, then you have everything. You can pick it up and start reading it anywhere.

It appeals to common people as well as scholars. My mother is illiterate and she has an enjoyment of the Quran that I perhaps do not have the music of it. My understanding can get in the way. She and my father always used to pray. They were disturbed if they could not get their ablutions done in time to pray the evening prayer before the sun set, or if ever they slept after the sun had risen. As a child, I used to open my eyes every morning in our Palestine village and see them at prayer. The younger generation who have been to school know and understand the words, but miss the feeling my parents had.

We cannot see Muslim thought in the right perspective unless we appreciate and understand the Quran as a motivator of thought and an end of knowledge. Without such understanding, the student of Muslim thought must continue to work in the dark. It is in the direct impact of the Quran on the Muslim mind that we may discover those unwritten, but perhaps most important and fundamental, orientations towards truth and human ends. In these orientations lie the Muslims' general sense of history and change, their peculiar sense of time, and their peculiar sense of purpose in seeking knowledge.

Truth in itself and outside man's knowledge does not have a biography of development. Only the individual's understanding of it has. Thus there is permanence in truth and change in understanding. The history of Muslim thought in general cannot be fully understood by an "evolutionary" approach to the history of ideas. The truth which is essential for happiness is supposed by Muslims to be all there and complete - in the Quran and the *Sunna,* (the tradition and practice of the Prophet).

Dr Ali Issa Uthman, Palestine and Beirut

Towards Understanding the Quran : One of the most influential Twentieth Century commentaries on the Quran is that by Sayyid Abul Ala Mawdudi (1903-1979). Written in Urdu, this massive work of scholarship was produced in the midst of the struggles for independence and the early years of Pakistan. It is entitled *Tafhim Al-Quran* (Towards Understanding the Quran). He undertook the task in 1941 and completed it in 1973, six volumes and thirty years later, strenuous years of leadership and controversy. A full English translation is appearing.

The following extracts from Mawdudi's Preface are taken from *Translations from The Quran,* made on the basis of Mawdudi's work by Altaf Gauhar, author and Editor-in-Chief of *South* magazine and *Third World Quarterly,* published from London. "These translations were undertaken at a time when the only book to which I had access was the Quran," he says.

Tafhim al-Quran is not a literal translation of the original text. It is an attempt to present the meanings of the Quran in plain language keeping the historical perspective in view. The Quran speaks to you in the language of life, vividly and melodiously: by comparison the language of translation is a poor echo of the glorious original one is left cold and begins to wonder whether this is indeed the Book which has no equal.

The Quran is great literature as it is great instruction. Its words go straight to the heart and it is this quality which, like a crack of lightning, shook the length and breadth of Arabia.

The Quran presents an arrangement which is completely contrary to our expectations. We find beliefs, precepts, orders, criticisms, warnings, promises, arguments, evidence, historical illustrations and references to natural phenomena following one another in rapid succession without any apparent regard for logic ... It talks of the origin of man, the structure of the earth and the heavens ... It recalls the beliefs and criticizes the conduct of different nations, analyses metaphysical problems and refers to many other things. The object however is not to give lessons in metaphysics, philosophy, history or any other science, but to remove misunderstandings about reality ... to acquaint (man) with the result of actions which conflict with its underlying principles.

Whether one is a believer or not, as a rational person one must read this book *by* taking into account the fundamental assumptions made in the book itself, and by the Prophet who presented it to the world.

Holy Quran and the Prophets : No less than eight chapter headings in the Quran recall figures in the Old and New Testaments. Moses and Jesus, founders of Judaism and Christianity, are prophets like Muhammad with the title of *Rasool* (apostle), greater than *nabi* (announcer).

In the course of the Quran, David and Solomon receive no less than thirty-three mentions, and Nuh appears some thirty times, as well as heading a chapter. The Sura of Joseph is the longest narrative given. Jonah, "the Man of the Fish", and Sheba, whose famous Queen visits Solomon, are both names of Suras.

Many of the stories are allusive rather than narratory. Evidently the facts were well known to the hearers, and the commentators fill in the details. Some of the information given is found in Jewish sources other than the Old Testament, and in the case of Jesus in the Apocryphal Gospels. The lives of the prophets were current knowledge in Muhammad's day, as they have continued to be throughout the Muslim world.

In one chapter of the Quran (Sura *6: 83-86 Cattle)* eighteen prophets are named. The authoritative modern commentary by Abdullah Yusuf Ali analyses these in four groups. They cover, he says, the great teachers accepted among the three religions based on Moses, Jesus and Muhammad. First come Ibrahim, Ishaq and Jacob. Then follow those who "led active lives and are called 'doers of good'."

These are Nuh, David and Solomon, Job and Joseph, Moses and Aaron. In contrast, the next group were not men of action but preachers of truth who led solitary lives. They include Zachariah and his son John (the Baptist), Jesus and Elias (Elijah), and their designation is "the righteous". Finally come four who were concerned in the clash of nations, and who through conflict and personal misfortune kept to the path of God: Ismail, Elisha, Jonah and Lot.

The chapter headed *The Prophets* (Sura 21) has a similar passage. Elsewhere over and over again the historic sequence is repeated - a warning, followed by either repentance or destruction, as God sends His messengers to one nation after another. The view of history in the Muslim mind is a prophetic one.

According to the Quran, the succession of prophets has been completed — sealed — by the mission of Muhammad. The truth necessary for man to live by has been revealed. There is no need for more. But if men do not presume to claim the stature of the prophets, there is still plenty of scope for humbly following their example. Muhammad's own constant emphasis that he was only a man like other men lays stress on the responsibility carried by all believers.

Here is one of many passages which show the heritage of prophetic inspiration common to Muslim, Jew and Christian.

We inspire thee [Muhammad] as We inspired Nuh and the prophets after him, as We inspired Ibrahim and Ismail and Ishaq and Jacob and the tribes, and Jesus and Job and Jonah and Aaron and Solomon, and as We imparted unto David the Psalms; And messengers We have mentioned unto thee before, and messengers We have not mentioned unto thee; and Allah spake direct unto Moses;

> Messengers of good cheer and of warning, in order that mankind might have no argument against Allah after the messengers. Allah was ever Mighty, Wise.
> (Quran: Sura 4: 163-165)

The Analogy (Qiyas)

The fourth source of Islamic law is Qiyas which, literally, means "judging or comparing with a thing." Qiyas means essentially to use human reasoning to compare an existing situation with one for which legislation already exists. If the Quran has banned wine, it means that by reasoning, it has also banned all forms of alcoholic drinks, whose effect is like wine or something that causes intoxication.

The death of Prophet Muhammad (PBUH) deprived the Muslim community of the means of obtaining revelation and at the same time of his guidance in political and religious matters. The expansion of the Muslim Empire and the spread of Islam outside Arabia raised questions previously unknown, the answers to which could not be found in the Quran or the *Sunnah*. Thus, they found themselves forced to take decisions or to regulate their conduct from their own opinion and reasoning.

Such resort to reasoning is often traced back to the conversation between the Prophet (PBUH) and Muaz ibn Jabal, the Governor of Yemen. When the Prophet (PBUH) appointed

Muaz ibn Jabal as Governor and Judge in Yemen, the Prophet (PBUH) asked him:

"According to what will you judge?"
"According to the book of Allah."
"And if you find nothing therein ? "
"According to the Sunnah of the Prophet (PBUH)."
"And if you find nothing therein?"
"Then I will exert myself to form my own judgement."
ibn Jabal replied.

According to another *Hadith,* the Prophet (PBUH) is reported to have told Abu Musa Ashari:

"Judge upon the Book of Allah. If you do not find in it what you need, upon the Sunnah of the Prophet (PBUH) and if you do not find in that also, then use your personal opinion."

Imam Abu Hanifa, one of the four great Imams was the first to give prominence to the doctrine of *Qiyas,* although as a principle of law, it was in practice even before him.

The Tradition (Sunnah)

The Prophet (PBUH) as the founder of Islam and the messenger of Allah's revelation to mankind is the best interpreter of the Book of Allah and his Hadith and the Sunnah; his sayings and actions are, after the Quran, the most important source of Islamic law.

The word *Sunnah* means literally a manner of acting, a rule of conduct, a mode of life. Applied to the life of the Prophet (PBUH), this meant, therefore, a rule deduced from the sayings or conduct of the Prophet. Such sayings and conduct could take the form of an utterance of the Prophet (PBUH) an action or practice of the Prophet (PBUH), or the approval by the Prophet (PBUH) of the action or practice of someone else.

The Holy Quran being the word of Allah, treats major

issues and often deals with subjects in brief terms, leaving the details to be explained by the Holy Prophet (PBUH) of Allah. It says:

> "—-and We have sent down unto thee the Message: that thou mayest explain clearly to men what is sent for them." (16:44)

In the Quran we are commanded to pray and pay *Zakat*, but there is no explanation of the frequency of prayers or the number of Rakat in each prayer. Neither is there an explanation given as to the amount on which the duty of *Zakat* applies or the percentage which has to be paid. All these details were learnt either from the Prophet's deeds or words or from both. The Holy Quran commands that we should be good to our neighbour; a number of *Ahadith* further stress this duty. The same applies to many other situations; hence the vital connection between the Quran and the practice and sayings of the Prophet (PBUH).

Many verses of the Holy Quran deal with questions of law but not all the injunctions of the Shariah are clearly stated in it. There are many statements which needed further explanations before they could become guides for human actions. This explanation and clarification was provided by the Holy Prophet (PBUH) who himself participated in the formation of the Shariah.

When the Islamic commonwealth was founded in Medina in 622 A.D., the Prophet was not only the spiritual leader but also the supreme judge of the Islamic community. Cases would be referred by his followers to the Prophet (PBUH) for his judgement. The underlying principle applied was the word of Allah from the Quran; but if the Quran was silent, or needed interpretation, the Prophet (PBUH), as the messenger of Allah would be the authority for reaching a decision.

The Holy Quran itself commands that the Prophet's (PBUH) teachings should be obeyed. It says:

"So take what the Messenger assigns to you, and deny yourselves that which he withholds from you." (59:7)

It also says:

"He who obeys the Messenger obeys Allah."(4: 80)

The Quran frequently commands:

"O ye who believe ! obey Allah and obey the Messenger. " (4: 59)

"Obey Allah and obey His Messenger. " (3: 32, 5: 92, 64: 12)

Thus, after the Quran, the Prophet's (PBUH) *Sunnah* and *Hadith* are the most precious sources of guidance which Islamic society possesses and along with the Quran, they are the fountainhead of all Islamic laws and thought.

The Prophet (PBUH) was a *Nabi* and a *Rasool* who brought the cycle of Prophecy to an end. So, after him there will be no new *Shariah* or Divine Law brought into the world until the end of time.

Compilation of Hadith : Tradition in Arabic means Sunnah or Hadith. The difference between the two is that while Sunnah indicates the doings of the Holy Prophet (PBUH), Ahadith indicates his sayings.

The word *Hadith* is derived from 'Tahdis' which means to inform. There is another finding by the researchers of the word *Hadith.* According to them, this word is derived from a root which means to be new or modern, the opposite of which is ancient. Thus, by ancient is meant the Holy Quran and by new or modern is meant the *Hadith* of the Holy Prophet (PBUH). It is reported by Abdullah bin Masud that the Holy Prophet (PBUH) had said:

"Only two things carry importance, one is speech and the other is the method of action. So the words of

Allah are the best of speech and the best method is the deeds of the Holy Prophet (PBUH)."

From the beginning of the birth of Islam, Muslims were interested in what the Holy Prophet (PBUH) said and did. After his death, when Islam had spread widely, new converts wanted to hear about him from his Companions and close associates. These people were the best authority for a knowledge of *Hadith* as they had listened to the Prophet (PBUH) and witnessed his actions. Thousands of Companions adhered to the Prophet's commandment:

> "Preach what you hear me say. Also let those who see and hear me, take upon themselves to communicate my words to others and preach to their children, relatives and friends."

The Companions therefore considered it their duty to preach the Traditions of the Prophet (PBUH) to those who had not seen and listened to him. After their death, Muslims had to rely on the communications of the successors, people of the first generation after Prophet Muhammad (PBUH) who had received their information from the Companions, and in the following generations, with the accounts of the "successors of the successors", that is, people of the second generation who had been associated with the successors and so on.

In those days, to recite and to memorize the Traditions was considered to be a great privilege. They were preserved in writing as well. In due course of time, a great amount of *Hadith* literature was collected.

Some writers headed by William Muir and Goldzhier put forth the argument that the collection and compilation *of Ahadith* was started some ninety years after the death of the Holy Prophet (PBUH). However, there is ample testimony to the fact that such records existed much earlier. During the time of the Holy Prophet (PBUH) and his Companions, more than ten thousand *Ahadith* were collected out of which 5,374 were attributed to Abu Hurrayrah.

It has been verified from different sources that Abu Hurrayrah used to write down what he heard from the Holy Prophet (PBUH). Another Companion, Hadrat Abdullah bin Umar, on the order of the Holy Prophet (PBUH) used to write down every word of the Prophet's (PBUH) speech. This compilation was known as Sadiqa. These Companions persuaded their children and relatives to follow their instance. For example, Hadrat Anas used to stress upon his children:

> "O my children, write down the text of Hadith."

Hadrat Ali used to keep a booklet with him which contained many traditions mainly concerning the orders and instructions issued from time to time by the Holy Prophet (PBUH).

Imam Zohri, who was born in a Quraish family had preserved the Prophet's (PBUH) utterances in such detail that historians have remarked :

> "Zohri would go to any soul in Medina and record from him or her about the Prophet's life events."

Soon after the death of the Prophet (PBUH), the need for some authoritative guidance in Quranic interpretation was felt. The need was felt all the more because of the political and religious divisions. Also because of the expansion of Islam from a small community in Central Arabia to a mighty empire due to which Muslim rulers faced all kinds of political, economic, legal and social problems quite unknown during the days of the Prophet (PBUH). The problem was to apply the Prophet's (PBUH) teachings and way of life to conditions which were never thought of before. It was solved by recording and placing in the appropriate context a large number of sayings and practices of the Holy Prophet (PBUH).

Numerous collections of *Hadith* were prepared by many

scholars from various angles, and different methods were adopted in the arrangement of the material. Two models were mainly adopted. In the first category, *Hadith* traced to each Companion was put together under his name, no matter what their theme might be. Such a collection is called Musnad. Therefore, the titles of the chapters are Musnad of Abu Bakr, Musnad of Abu Hurrayrah, Musnad of Aishah, etc.

The most famous compilation in this category is Musnad of Imam Ahmad bin Hanbal, founder of the fourth school of law. It contains 40,000 Ahadith of which 10,000 have occurred more than once.

The second category of *Ahadith* are grouped into chapters and sub-chapters according to their theme. For instance we find chapters on *purity, prayers, fasting, Zakat, pilgrimage, marriage,* so on. The best known work of this type is Al-Muwatta which contains 1,720 *Ahadith* compiled by Imam Malik bin Anas, founder of the Maliki school of law. Another compilation of this category is Al-Musannaf of Imam Abd Al-Razzaq Al-Sanani (126-211 A.H.) which has been published in eleven volumes. It contains 11,033 *Ahadith.*

Hadith compilers introduced each *Hadith* with its own Isnad which means the series of authorities who may be called narrators or transmitters or Muhaddis. These authorities can be as few as two. Imam Malik, for example, in some *Ahadith* related from his teacher Nafi, who related from his teacher Abdullah bin Umar, a distinguished Companion of the Holy Prophet (PBUH). Yet the number could be three, four, five and even six, depending on how far the compiler's time was from the time of the Prophet.

The early authorities of *Hadith* who scrutinized each *Hadith,* both the text and the *isnad,* included in their compilations only those which they believed to be genuine, and rejected those which they suspected as fabricated. Yet, they graded each Hadith in terms of the degree of reliability. A *Hadith* could be authentic, Sahih, or less than authentic, although it was not false or a fabrication but a weak or Zaeef Hadith which resulted from some weakness in the text or in the *Isnad.*

The authorities on *Hadith* said that the text should have no conflict with the Quran or with a more reliable *Hadith.* The *Isnad* must be full and unbroken and each narrator mentioned in it must be known for his knowledge, piety and memory.

Upto the beginning of the third century of Islam, compilations of *Hadith* did not discriminate between authentic *Hadith* and others lesser than authentic so the *Ahadith* were mixed up.

Imam Muhammad ibn Ismail-al-Bukhari (194-256 A.H.), was the first to conceive the idea of compiling the authentic *Ahadith* and therefore, he called his compilations as Sahih, "the authentic compilations". It took him sixteen years to compile this work which contains 7,397 *Ahadith* including four thousand repeated ones. He selected these *Ahadith* from amongst 600,000 *Ahadith* which he gathered in long and repeated journeys around the capitals of the world of Islam. On account of the strict conditions that he laid down for accepting a *Hadith* as *Sahih,* his work was acknowledged as one of the most authentic books on *Hadith* literature.

The example of Imam Bukhari was also followed by a number of other leading scholars. Eminent among them was Imam Muslim ibn Hajjaj (202-261 A.H.), whose compilation contains 12,000 *Ahadith* including 4,000 repetitions. The collections by *Bukhari* and *Muslim* are held in high esteem and are known as the two Sahihs i.e., the two collections recognized as authentic. Only those traditions which are recognized as absolutely correct are included in these works.

Among some others authors who followed them were Abu Daud (205-275 A.H.), author of *Al-Sunan; Al-Tirmidhi* (210-279

A.H.), author of *Al-Jami; Al-Nasai* (215-303 A.H.), author of *Kitab al-Sunnah;* and *Ibn Majah,* author of Kitab al-Sunnah. These four works along with those of *Bukhari* and *Muslim* became widely recognized in the Muslim world as the six leading Books *Al-Kutub al-Sitta* or *the six Sahihs,* i.e., *the sound, correct and reliable collections.*

At a later period, new collections were compiled by many scholars. In these works, contents were taken from the 'Six Books' and arranged in different ways until about the end of the fourth century of the age of Islam it was felt that all *Ahadith* circulating orally had been reduced to writing. Therefore, *Hadith* literature became exceedingly rich, and we as Muslims are very fortunate to have for our benefit such a great intellectual and religious wealth from which guidance can be derived.

7

Islamic Morality

Ethics in Islam

Mankind, according to the Prophet, are a fold, every member of which is a shepherd or keeper unto every other, and accountable for the welfare of the entire fold (Bukhari). Further, mankind are the creatures of God, and most beloved of them before Him is he who is the best to His creatures (Baihaqi). These and other sayings of the Prophet stress the point that one has to identify his interests with the interests of others. The duties to one's self and the duties to others are here placed side by side as the component parts of one's responsibility in life. Only when the individual has a developed sense of such responsibility that he is a moral being and of greater service to society.

Duties are generally expressed in terms of duties to God and duties to society, but the spirit underlying duties to God is the spiritual development of one's self so as to be mindful of duties to others – a harmonious interaction between the sense of God and the sense of fellow-men resulting in righteousness. Such is the concept of morality in Islam and, therefore, Islamic law is the law of duties rather than of rights. Generally, rights have corresponding duties but in Islamic law duties are more than rights. This has its own advantages.

Right is a claim on someone and duty is a responsibility to someone. The emphasis merely on rights gives rise to the sense of one's own power and authority over others which may be injurious to peace, while emphasis on duties creates harmony in social life and is conducive to peace. A generalized sense of duty is a sense of being bound by that which is right because of its rightfulness. Conformity to the letter of the law ' then takes the place of faithfulness to its spirit, *i.e.*, its usefulness in calling attention to the welfare of not only one's self but also of others. The sense of duty, thus, reminds us of our responsibility towards our fellow-beings. This sensitive is specially needed whenever our desire tends to blind us to everything but itself. There are occasions in life on which, under the influence of strong desire, we are apt to lose control upon ourselves and it is the sense of duty to God and to our fellow-men which keeps us away from evil-doing and directs us to the right path—the path of eternal peace and prosperity. Here we realize the importance of duty and comprehend why Islamic law is the law of duties.

Peace for Everyone : The Model World according to Islam, is a world of peace. Islam in itself means a religion of peace. The Quran says: And God calls to the home of peace. This is the message of Islam to mankind. It means that a world of peace on earth so that you may be granted a world of peace in your eternal life in the Hereafter.

Now what are the basic elements of building of a culture of peace, according to Islam to be brief, these are three—compassion, forgiveness and respect for all.

Let's take compassion first. If you go through the Quran and Hadith, you will find many verses in the Quran and Hadith which lay great stress on compassion. For instance, the Prophet of Islam said: O people, be compassionate to others so that you may be granted compassion by God.

Thus, Islam makes compassion a matter of self interest for

every man. As one's own future depends on one's compassionate behaviour to other fellowmen. In this way Islam motivates us to be compassionate in our dealings with each other. One who wants to receive God's grace will have to show compassion to others.

Let's take forgiveness. The Quran has to say this in this regard "when they are angered, they forgive." There are a number of verses in the Quran which promote forgiveness.

Then there is a hadith. Once a person came to the Prophet and asked him, "O Prophet, give me a mature advice by which I may be able to manage all the affairs of my life." The Prophet replied: "Don't be angry." It means that 'forgive people even at provocation.' That is, adopt forgiveness as your behaviour at all times.

Respect Others to be Respected : Now let's take the third principle—Respect for all. There is a very interesting story, recorded by al-Bukhari in this regard.

The Prophet of Islam once saw a funeral procession passing by a street in Medina. The Prophet was seated at that time. On seeing the funeral the Prophet stood up in respect. At this one of his companions said: 'O Prophet, it was the funeral of a Jew (not a Muslim), The Prophet replied: 'Was he not a human being?' What it meant was that every human being is worthy of respect. There may be differences among people regarding religion and culture, but everyone has to respect the other. For, according to Islam, all men and women are blood brothers and blood sisters. And all are creatures of one and the same God.

These three principles are the basic pillars to form a peaceful society. Wherever these three values are to be found the result no doubt will be a society of peace and harmony

The above references are enough to show that Islam is a culture of peace. It is true that some Muslims are engaged in violence in the name of Islam. But you will have to differentiate between Islam and Muslims. You have to see Muslims in the light of Islam and not vice 'versa.

Concept of Peace : A believer is necessarily a lover of peace. In his mind faith and a desire for peace are so closely interlinked that, regardless of the circumstances, he will strive to the utmost for the maintenance of peace. He will bear the loss of anything else, but the loss of peace he will not endure.

The life that the true believer desires in this world can be lived only in the propitious atmosphere which flowers in conditions of peace. Conditions of unrest breed a negative atmosphere which to him is abhorrent.

But if peace is to be maintained, it calls for a certain kind of sacrifice. That is, when conditions become disturbed, the believer must overlook both the misdeeds leading up to this situation and the identity of the wrongdoers. He must suffer all the harm and injustice done to him without making any attempt either to retaliate, or to bring the miscreants to book, so that a state of peace should continue to prevail. The believer has to be willing to pay this price, so that his pursuance of constructive ends should proceed unhampered.

The believer is like a flower in the garden of nature. Just as a hot wind will shrivel up a bloom and cause it to die, so will constant friction distract the believer from achieving positive goals. And just as a cool breeze will enable the flower to retain its beauty for its natural life-span, so will a peaceful atmosphere enable the believer to fulfil the obligations of divine worship in a spirit of great serenity. Peace is thus central to the life of the believer. Islam is a religion of peace. And peace is a universal law of nature. That is because God loves the condition of peace, and disapproves of any state of unrest. God's predilection for peace is quite enough reason for the believer also to love peace. In no circumstances will the true believer ever tolerate the disruption of peace.

Human Rights in Islam

A believer has important responsibilities towards both God and man. His duty towards God means believing in Him with all His attributes, worshipping Him, regarding himself accountable to Him; and making himself ready to carry out wholeheartedly any such demands that God may make upon him.

Another responsibility of the believer is one which concerns the rights of human beings. This responsibility devolves upon him in his relations with others. Every man or woman, a relative or neighbour, a fellow townsman or compatriot or one with whom he has dealings in business - everyone has some rights over him. It is incumbent upon a believer to fulfil those rights, failing which he will not be deserving of God's succor.

What is meant by recognising the rights of human beings (Huquq ul-Ibad)? This means that whenever and wherever a believer meets another person, he should give him such treatment as is in accordance with Islamic teachings. He should refrain from such behaviour as does not come up to the standard of Islam.

Examples of proper Islamic behaviour are giving respect to other, never humiliating others while giving them help, acting for the good of others, and if unable to benefit them in any way, at least doing no one any harm, fulfilling trusts, never breaking them; never usurping the wealth and property of others; dealing justly with others regardless of the circumstances; giving the benefit of the doubt to others, not believing in allegations made against others without proper proofs; advising others in earnest.

Everyone has a duty to fulfil these responsibilities towards other human beings according to the Islamic Shariah. This is called Huququl Ibad, or human rights.

Expression and Freedom

Islam grants human beings total intellectual freedom. Rather it would be truer to say that it was Islam which for the first time in human history brought about a revolution in freedom of thought. In all the ages of history prior to Islam, the system of despotism prevailed, and man was consequently denied freedom of thought. This was a matter of the utmost gravity for it is a fact that the secret of all human progress lies hidden in such freedom.

The first benefit of intellectual freedom is to enable man to achieve that high virtue which in the Quran is called "fearing the unseen." That is, without any apparent compulsion or pressure from God, man, of his own free will, acknowledges God and leads his life in this world, going in fear of Him. In the absence of an atmosphere of total freedom, no one can undergo this spiritual experience-an indescribable spiritual pleasure-which is called in the Quran, going in fear of the Lord. Without such freedom it is not possible to give credit to anyone for this highest of human virtues.

Man is a thinking creature. Of necessity he forms opinions. If curbs are placed on the independent expression of his views, the content of his thought may remain unchanged, but his ideas will never find expression in his speech and writings. Curbs of this nature, imposed by a community or a state, will ultimately produce a society of hypocrites. No sincere person can ever flourish in such a repressive atmosphere. It is only freedom of thought and expression which can save man from hypocrisy.

Moreover, intellectual freedom is directly related to creativity. A society with freedom of thought will produce creative human beings; a society which places curbs on freedom of expression will necessarily witness intellectual stagnation; it will stop producing creative minds, and its development will come to a standstill.

In matters of criticism or expression of differences, the right approach is for people to end unnecessary, sensitivity to it instead of attempting to put an end to criticism and differences. This is the demand of Islam as well as of nature.

According to the hadith it is a virtue on the part of believers: to accept the truth without any reservation when it is presented to them. That is to say, a believer is one who has the ability in the perfect sense of the word to accept the truth. Whenever truth is brought before him, whenever his faults are pointed out to him, no complex comes in the way of his accepting of the truth. This quality is present to the maximum degree in one who is ready and waiting to accept the truth when it is brought before him. Eager for his own improvement, he accepts the truth with pleasure. This keenness for self-reform through acceptance of the truth is perfectly expressed in the words of 'Umar ibn al-Khattab: "May God bless the man who sends me gifts of my own shortcomings."

It is a fact that acknowledgment of truth is worship, nay, it is the greatest form of worship. It is an act for which man has to make the greatest sacrifice. What makes it such a great sacrifice is that it involves the setting aside of one's prestige.

It amounts to the sacrifice of one's ego. But that is the occasion when man assures his entry into heaven.

When does one find the opportunity for this great form of worship and this great good fortune? This opportunity comes one's way only when there is full freedom of expression. When one can criticise another with impunity. When such an atmosphere prevails in a society which permits the speaker to air his views freely and the listener may freely appreciate what is being said. Just as a mosque is the right place for the performance of prayer in congregation, similarly freedom of expression is the right atmosphere in which to foster the great virtues of expressing the truth and acceptance of the truth.

Human Equality **:** According to Islamic tenets, all human beings are equal. In prayer, all members of the congregation stand in the same rows together, and on the Hajj pilgrimage, all the believers belonging to different countries don identical white seamless robes for the performance of the obligatory rites. On the occasion of the Final Pilgrimage, it is noteworthy that the Prophet of Islam declared that no Arab was superior to a non-Arab and that no white was superior to a black. All were equally servants of God. In Islamic society, everyone is accorded the same status, there being, ideally, no higher or lower social strata.

How then can we rationalise what are apparently very great differences in human beings in terms of colour and race, etc., considering that the concept of human equality ranks so high in the value system of Islam? We find the answer in the Quran, which makes it clear that such outward differences are meant to serve as means of identification and were never intended as indicators of superiority (or inferiority). People in different parts of the world may have a diversity of skin colourings and other distinctive racial characteristics, but that is only so that they may be easily distinguished from each other. By Islamic standards, this is designed to facilitate social and national interaction.

The sole basis of superiority in Islam is *taqwa* - the earnestness with which one leads a God-fearing life; as such, it bears no relation to colour or race. Physical attributes certainly have their effect on the social interaction of this world, but in the Hereafter, no value is attached to them. There, the only things which count are inner qualities, for upon them depends the essential excellence of man's distinctive character. That is why, according to a hadith, God sees the heart and not the body. He reserves a place in Paradise only for those found deserving in terms of their inner worth.

According to Islam, all greatness belongs to God. God as

the Supreme Being is ineffably superior to all men. While there is this infinitely great difference between God and man, there is no difference whatsoever between man and man.

Human Brotherhood and Islam

According to Islam, all human beings have been created by one and the same God, and for this reason belong to one great brotherhood. So far as their earthly origin is concerned, they are all descendants of the first pair of human beings ever created by God -Adam and Eve. In their subsequent spread over different parts of the world, variations in geographical conditions produced a diversity of skin colourings, languages and other racial characteristics.

The teaching of Islam in this regard is that despite differences of colour, language, etc., people should harbour no ill-will towards those who are apparently unlike themselves, for differentiating between one man and another is not approved by God. They should rather promote fellow feeling towards others, even if at first glance they appear like total strangers to them. Bearing in mind that they are all traceable back to Adam and Eve, they should be each other's well-wishers and willingly come to one another's assistance, like members of the same large family.

Ideally, the relation between one man and another ought not to be one of strangeness but one of familiarity; not of distance but of nearness; not of hatred but of love.

When all human beings are descendants of the same progenitors, that means that all are equal: no one is superior or inferior. The distinction between great and small is not between one human being and another, but between God and man. And before God, certainly, all human beings are equal; all are equally His creatures and His servants. For God does not discriminate between one or the other of His creations.

Non-violence in Islam

Islam is a religion which teaches non-violence. According to the Quran, God does not love *fasad*, (violence). What is meant here by *fasad* is clearly expressed in verse 205 of the second surah. Basically fasad is that action which results in disruption of the social system, causing huge losses in terms of lives and property.

Conversely, we can say with certainty that God loves non-violence. He abhors violent activity being indulged in human society, as a result of which people have to pay the price with their possessions and lives. This is supported by other statements in the Quran. For instance, we are told in the Quran that peace is one of God's names (59:23). Those who seek to please God are assured by verse 5 of the sixteenth surah chat they will be guided by Him to "the paths of peace." Paradise, which is the final destination of the society of God's choice, is referred to in the Quran as "the home of peace"' (89:30), etc.

> The entire spirit of the Quran is in consonance with this concept. For instance, the Quran attaches great importance to patience. In fact, patience is set above all other Islamic virtues with the exceptional promise of reward beyond measure. (39:10)
>
> Patience implies a peaceful response or reaction, whereas impatience implies a violent response. The word *sabr* exactly expresses the notion of non-violence as it is understood in modern times. That patient action is non-violent action has been clearly expressed in the Quran. According to one tradition, the Prophet of Islam observed: God grants to *rifq* (gentleness) what he does not grant to *unf (violence)*.
>
> (Sunan, Abu Daud, 4 /255)

The word *rifq* has been used in this hadith as an antithesis to *unf*. These terms convey exactly what is meant by violence and non-violence in present times. This hadith clearly indicates the superiority of the non-violent method.

God grants on non-violence what He does not grant to violence is no simple matter. It has very wide and deep implications. It embodies an eternal law of nature. By the very law of nature all bad things are associated with violence, while all good things are associated with non-violence.

Violent activities breed hatred in society, while non-violent activities elicit love. Violence is the way of destruction while non-violence is the way of construction. In an atmosphere of violence, it is enmity which flourishes, while in an atmosphere of non-violence, it is friendship which flourishes. The method of violence gives way to negative values while the method of non-violence is marked by positive values. The method of violence embroils people in problems, while the method of non-violence leads people to the exploiting of opportunities. In short, violence is death, non-violence is life.

Both the Quran and the hadith have attached great importance to jihad. What is jihad? Jihad means struggle, to struggle one's utmost. It must be appreciated at the outset that this word is used for non-violent struggle as opposed to violent struggle. One clear proof of this is the verse of the Quran (25:52) which says: Perform jihad with this (i.e. the word of the Quran) most strenuously.

The Quran is not a sword or a gun. It is a book of ideology. In such a case performing jihad with the Quran would mean an ideological struggle to conquer peoples' hearts and minds through Islam's superior philosophy.

In the light of this verse of the Quran, jihad in actual fact is another name for peaceful activism or non-violent activism. Where qital is violent activism, jihad is non-violent activism.

Non-violence therefore should never be confused with inaction or passivity. Non-violence is action in the full sense of the word. Rather it is more forceful an action than that of violence. It is a fad that non-violent activism is more powerful and effective than violent activism.

Non-violent activism is not limited in its sphere. It is a course of action which may be followed in all matters.

Whenever individuals, groups or communities are faced with a problem, one way to solve it is by resorting to violence. The better way is to attempt to solve the problem by peaceful means, avoiding violence and confrontation. Peaceful means may take various forms. In fact, it is the nature of the problem which will determine which of these peaceful methods is applicable to the given situation.

Peaceful Beginning : When the Quran began to be revealed, the first verse of the revelation conveyed the injunction: "Read!" (Iqra) (96:1). By perusing this verse we learn about the initiation of Islamic action. It begins from the point where there is hope of continuing the movement along peaceful lines, and not from that point where there are chances of its being marred by violence.

When the command of 'Iqra' was revealed, there were many options available in Mecca as starting points for a movement. For instance, one possible starting point was to launch a movement to purify the Kaaba of the 360 idols installed in it. But, by pursuing such a course, in such a case the Islamic movement would certainly have had to face a violent reaction from the Quraish. An alternative starting point could have been an attempt to secure a seat in the Dar-ul-Nadwa (Mecca's parliament). At that time almost the whole of Arabia was under the direct or indirect influence of the Roman and Sasanid empires. If the freeing of Arabia from this influence had been made the starting point, this would also have been met with an immediate violent reaction on the part of the Quraish.

Leaving aside these options, the path followed was that of

reading the Quran, an activity that could be with certainty continued along peaceful lines: no violent reaction would ensue from engaging in such an activity.

> The Prophet of Islam followed this principle throughout his life. His policy was that of adopting non-violent methods in preference to violent methods. It is this policy which was referred to by Aishah, the Prophet's wife, in these words: Whenever the Prophet had to opt for one of two ways, he almost always opted for the easier one. (Fath ul Bari 6/654)

What are the advantages of non-violent activism over violent activism? They are briefly stated as under:

1. According to the Quran there are two faculties in every human being which are mutually antipathetic. One is the ego, and the other is the conscience called respectively *nafs ammara* and *nafs lawwama*. (The Quran, 12:53; 75:26) What the violent method invariably does is to awaken the ego which necessarily results in a breakdown of social equilibrium. On the other hand, non-violent activism awakens the conscience. From this results an awakening in people of intro-spection and self-appraisal. And according to the Quran, the miraculous outcome of this is that "he who is your enemy will become your dearest friend." (41:34)

2. A great advantage of the non-violent method is that, by following it, no part of one's time is wasted. The opportunities available in any given situation may then be exploited to the fullest extent-as happened after the no-war pact of Hudaibiya. This peace treaty enabled the energies of the believers to be utilised in peaceful constructive activities instead of being dissipated in a futile armed encounter. One great harm done by violent activism is the breaking of social traditions in the

launching of militant movements. Conversely, the great benefit that accrues from non-violent activism is that it can be initiated and prolonged with no damage to tradition.

Generally speaking, attempts to improve or replace existing systems by violent activism are counter-productive. One *coup detat* is often the signal for a series of coups and counter-coups, none of which benefit the common man. The truly desirable revolution is that which permits gradual and beneficial changes. And this can be achieved only on the basis of non-violence.

Good Life : Since the objective good is known to God alone, the good life is that which is lived in accordance with the law of God and men ought to behave in the manner which pleases God and what pleases God most are the righteous deeds. We are given a beautiful description of righteousness:

"It is not righteousness that ye turn your faces towards East or West ; but it is righteousness — to believe in God and the last Day, and the Angels and the Book, and the Messengers; to spend of your substance, out of love for Him, for your kin, for orphans, for the needy, for the wayfarer, for those who ask, and for the ransom of slaves; to be steadfast in prayer, and practise regular charity; to fulfil contracts which ye have made; and to be firm and patient, in pain (or suffering) and adversity, and throughout all periods of panic, such are the people of truth, the righteous'. (2 : 177).

The emphasis laid upon this verse is so great that most of the Quran seems to be nothing else than the exposition of its implications. Among the duties; enumerated in this verse, the first and foremost is to believe in the Unity of God. This is the basic concept into which the Quran desires to initiate human mind. The late Rev. C. F. Andrews has said :

"One of the greatest blessings which Islam has brought to East and West alike has been the emphasis which at a critical period in human history it placed upon the Divine Unity. For during those Dark Ages both in East and West, from 600 to 1000 A.D. this doctrine was in danger of being overlaid and obscured in Hinduism and Christianity itself, owing to the immense accretions of subsidiary worships of countless demi-gods and heroes. Islam has been, both to Europe and India, in their dark hour of aberration from the sovereign truth of God's Unity, an invaluable corrective and deterrent. Indeed, without the final emphasis on this truth, which Islam gave from its central position, – facing India and facing Europe – it is doubtful whether this idea of God as one could have obtained that established place in human thought which is uncontested in the intellectual world today" (*The Genuine Islam*, Singapore, Vol. 1, No. 8, 1936).

Unity of God is to express itself in the Unity of man. The enforcement of the sense of Unity and brotherhood has been the chief aim of Islam. Every one who embraces Islam, enters into its fold and is treated as a brother, since believers are but one brotherhood (49 : 10). Suffice it to quote from the Prophet who says :

"A Muslim is a brother of another Muslim, he neither wrongs him, nor leaves him helpless, nor humiliates him" (Muslim).

"It is forbidden for a Muslim to take the life, honour and property of another Muslim" (Muslim and Bukhari).

"In mutual compassion, love" and kindness, you will find the faithful like a body, if one of its parts feels pain, the whole body responds with wakefulness and fever" (Muslim and Bukhari).

Believe and work righteously are the injunctions to be strictly observed. These are the words that reverberate and echo in the Quran. The Quran expects man who believes in God to express that belief in an earnest endeavour to promote the unity of man, it is by action that he has to prove his belief in God, even as the Prophet said:

> "God doth not accept faith if it is not expressed in action, and doth not accept action if it does not conform to faith" (Bukhari).

Next to belief in God is the importance attached to the deeds of charity. So mindful is the Quran of the economically depressed classes of society that it calls upon every earning member to assign, in his earnings a share to the needy and the poor: "And in their wealth is a share of the needy and deprived" (51: 19). The supreme note in regard to social security is struck in the verse (3 : 92). It runs:

> "Ye shall never attain righteouness unless ye give (the needy and poor) of that which ye love (particularly your wealth); and whatever ye give of a truth God knoweth it well."

Charity is not to give something worthless but it is to give what we love and value greatly. Faith is not merely a matter of words, we must be prepared to show it in deeds of charity to our fellow-men. Practical deeds of charity are of value when they proceed from love, and from no other motive. In this respect our duties take various forms in the gradation as arranged in the above cited verse (2 : 177). The importance attached to these duties is manifest from the fact that their mention precedes that of the duties to God such as Salat (Prayers) which is one of the five pillars of Islam. These are the pillars devised to purify the soul of man and build his character in such a manner that he takes pleasure in self-sacrifice—the essence of righteousness.

The above verse is remarkable in that it renders the individual conscious of his duties on which depends the welfare of society and also teaches him to be firm and patient in pain (or sufferings) and adversity and throughout all periods of panic. The virtues of firmness and patience help man preserve his dignity and enable him to bear with fortitude all that falls to his lot of the vicissitudes of life.

The Arabic word 'Sabar', which occurs in this verse, is translated as patience but it implies many shades of meaning which is impossible to comprehend in one English word. In addition to its meaning of not being hasty, the word 'Sabar' connotes perseverance, constancy, steadfastness, firmness of purpose, self-restraint, endurance of sorrow, pain, and other evils. But it is never used in the sense of despair and disappointment for Islam is not passivity but active striving with the hope for the better. 'Sabar', thus, means patient perseverance and firmness of purpose which bear good fruits. In proof of the importance of this word it is enough to say that it has appeared in the Quran on more than ninety occasions and the Caliph Umar is reported to have stated that he had found the best way of life in patience, for patience is the key to success.

Here, it may be said that there is no peculiarity about Islam, for all the revealed religions profess the same truth. But their teachings are not in the original form. Further, they cannot claim to be the religions of universal character. Islam is the only religion, universal and for all time, for the Prophet Muhammad was sent as a Universal Messenger to mankind (34 : 28), and the Quran is the Book preserved in the original purity. Being universal in character Islam is neither Judaism which has the concept of a particular covenant or a specially chosen people, nor is it Christianity whose mission, as Jesus made it clear, was confined to recovering the 'lost sheep of Israel'. Further, the Christian view of the 'Kingdom of God in heaven and Kingdom of Caesar on earth' has no place in Islam.

Says Kerr : 'In professing to provide man with a political and legal system as well as a spiritual faith, Islam denies, at the outset, the conception familiar to Christendom of a separation between temporal and spiritual matters' (*Islamic Reform*, p. 3).

Observes Hitti : 'Moses was a prophet, so were Ibrahim, Nuh, Christ and others, each with a dispensation appropriate for a certain time or place. But Muhammad's dispensation, sums up as well as supersedes all earlier ones. It is final. After it there is none' (*The Near East in History*, p. 197).

Being the last of the Prophets, the message delivered by Muhammad is final and for all time and the law contained in the Quran is perfect and comprehensive. Good life is, therefore, to live in conformity with such a law.

Laws of Islam

Islamic law is the Command of God revealed to the Prophet Muhammad. It precedes the state and is not preceded by it; it controls the society and is not controlled by it; state and society both have ideally to conform to its dictates. Observes Jackson:

> "Islamic law finds its chief source in the will of Allah revealed to the Prophet Muhammad. It contemplates one community of the faithful, though they may be of various tribes and in widely separated locations. Religion, not nationalism or geography, is the proper cohesive force. The state itself is subordinate to the Quran, which leaves little room for additional legislation, none for criticism or dissent. This world is viewed as but the vestibule to another and a better one for the faithful, and the Quran lays down rules of behaviour toward others and towards society to assure a safe transition. It is not possible to separate political or juristic theories from the teachings of the

> Prophet, which establish rules of conduct concerning religious, domestic, social and political life.
>
> This results in a law of duties rather than of rights, of moral obligations bindings on the individual, from which no earthly authority can relieve him, and which, he disobeys at peril of his future life"
>
> (Jackson, Foreword to *Law in the Middle East*, pp. vi, vii).

The doctrine of the Umma or one Community of the Faithful lies at the root of Islamic political concept. The Umma consists of the totality (jamaa) of individuals bound to one another by ties, not of kinship or race, but of religion, in that all its members profess their belief in the One God, and in all their relations to Him, all are equal, without distinction of rank, class or race. Differences of function are recognised, but 'the noblest among you is the most god-fearing' (49:13). See Gibb, 'Constitutional Organisation' in *Law in the Middle East*, p. 3.

According to Plato, law belongs to the class of convention; it rises through use and wont, while Islamic law is based upon Divine Revelations. Being Divine in origin, Islamic law is distinct from human law which is the product of reason and outcome of customary rules which can never, with perfectness, produce uniformity of conduct within the field of action to which they apply as do the Divine laws with their specified norms of good and bad, virtue and vice.

Divine laws are the standards of right conduct and provide guidance not only in establishing a well ordered society, but also in distinguishing between 'good' and 'evil'. As a well-knit system of obligations, they safeguard the rights of all and as a product of Divine Wisdom which alone knows what the objective good is, they ensure the welfare of the entire humanity.

The peculiarity of divine law is that it is eternal and immutable. The basis of life, as conceived by Islam, is spiritual.

A society based on such a conception must have eternal and immutable laws, but since it does not lose sight of the material world which is subject to change, the laws contain broad principles that admit of interpretation so as to accommodate the change in life and to provide for the growing needs of society. Over and above is the Rule of Necessity and Need to provide facilities to those who are confronted with hardships.

> Divine laws, thus, take in their sweep not only this world, but the world to come : 'Ye prefer the life of this world although the Hereafter is better and more lasting' (87 : 17). Islamic life, as such, is the harmonious blend of the material with the spiritual. Bare spirituality is never preached in Islam as it says 'yes' to life and to the worldly things. God has made all things in nature available for man so that he may harness them to suit his purpose: 'Whatever is in the heavens and whatever is in the earth are made of service unto him' (45 : 13).

Divine law is unique in that it has its own permanent standards of justice. Hence justice according to Divine law is much higher than all other systems of justice, be they Greek, Roman or any other human law, for it searches the innermost motives. Justice, as conceived by Islam, is not only to give each his due, but also to return good for ill. What Islam suggests is the objective approach to the problem of justice, to put ourselves in the place of another, to see things from the standpoint of an impartial observer. Here are some of the Quranic verses to give an idea of impartiality :

> 'And when ye judge between people, judge with fairness' (4:58). 'O ye who believe! stand fast to justice, and for the sake of God always be truthful in giving evidence, though it be against your own selves or (your) parents or kinsfolk, whether the party be rich or poor: God safeguards the interests of both (parties).

> Therefore follow not your own inclinations lest you should swerve from justice. If you prevaricate or decline (to speak the truth), then verily God is aware of what you do' (4:135). 'O ye who believe! For the sake of God, stand up to uphold justice and let not ill-will towards any people impel you to deviate from justice. Act justly. This indeed is akin to piety. Be mindful of God ; for assuredly, He knoweth all that ye do' (5 :9).

Justice in Islam is conceived as a sacred trust, a duty imposed upon man to be discharged in all sincerity. 'To render justice', says Sarakhsi, 'constitutes one of the most noble acts of devotion' (*Mabsut*, vol. 16, p. 67). According to Kasani, 'it is one of the best acts of devotion and one of the most important duties after belief in God' (*Badai al-Sanai*, vol. 7, p. 4). Says the Caliph Abu Baker :

> 'By God, to me the powerful among you will be weak, and the weak among you powerful until I have taken for them their right'
>
> (Abu Ubayd, *Kitab al-Amwal*, p. 8).

The Caliph Umar is reported to have said :

> 'No one will be allowed by me to treat others unjustly or to encroach upon their rights. Should anyone do so I will punish him severely so that he returns to others their rights'
>
> (Abu Yusuf, *Kitab-al-Kharaj* p. 167).

The above sayings are in obedience to the Command of God which lays a preponderant stress on moral values :

> 'Verily, God enjoineth fairness of dealings and kindly behaviour (with others), and the giving to kindred (out of what you have) ; and forbiddeth lewdness and wrong-doing and oppression' (16 : 90). 'And do not touch the property of the orphan except to replace it

with something better until he comes of age; give measured weight with, (full) justice;—no burden do We place on any soul but that which it can bear;—whenever ye speak, speak justly, even if a nearer relative is concerned; and fulfil the covenant of God: Thus doth He command you, that ye may remember' (6 : 152). Such is the morality and law of Islam. For details we refer the reader to our work Philosophy of Islamic Law I and the *Orientalists,* Islamic Publications, Lahore (Pakistan).

Conept of Predestination : This has been the most disputed problem in the past and continues to be so in the present. For, if everything is determined or predestined by God, why should man be held responsible for his acts? This issue has given birth to two parties of opposite-views—Jabriyya or Fatalists and Qadriyya who are opposed to Fatalists.

To Fatalists, God must be tyrant and unjust if He punishes man for acts which, are not under his^ power and control. As opposed to this view, the Qadriyya hold that God is Just and is bound to be so. He would not punish man for such acts as are not in his power. Man, they say, has complete power over his actions: he has free-will and also choice and, as such, responsible for his acts.

Before we enter into further details, let us try to know, in the light of Quranic verses, the scheme of God and how it is carried out. It cannot be denied that God has power over all things (67 : 1), He created all things and ordered them in due proportions (2 : 52). He also created Death and Life, that He may try which of His creatures (men) is best in deed (67 : 2). Creation, therefore, is not without a purpose. God has created things with a measure (54 : 49) and also created their opposites, for things are known through their opposites. Night has been created to "know the importance of Day and vice versa. Thus, world has been made a glittering show with all sorts of things to test the quality of man: 'That which is on earth, We have made but a glittering show for the earth, in order that We test them—as to which of them is of best conduct' (18 : 7). Evil and Good are both created by God as a trial, and test for us: 'And We test you by evil and by good by way of trial, to Us must ye return' (21 : 35).

As to the Will of God, 'He doeth what He will' (2 : 253). This is further supported by the Quranic verses: 'Thy Lord is doer of what He will' (11 : 107). 'His verily is all Creation and Commandment (7 : 54).

It may be noted that there are two aspects of His Commandment—Commandment relating to Creation (*amr takwini*) and Commandment relating to Right Conduct (*amr tashrii*). Creation includes both what He likes and what He dislikes, for example, He created the Devil and wickedness, while Righteousness is His love and approval. Man has to choose for himself, what is liked by God, with the help of the Rules of Right Conduct. Wickedness and sin do not fall under His liking and approval: 'He loveth not mischief (2 : 205). Ha liketh not ingratitude from His servants' (39 : 7). And when ingratitude and wickedness transgress their limits punishment becomes inevitable. Even then God's Mercy gives every chance to the wicked to mend themselves and to repent. They are given a definite warning and if they still persist in their wickedness, the charge is proved against them and it is at this stage-that God's Commandment takes effect: 'When We decide to destroy a township, We send Commandment to its folk who live at ease, and afterwards they commit abomination therein, and so the Word (or doom) hath, effect for it, and We destroy it utterly' (17: 16); and it was never God's (part) that He should send a folk astray after He had guided them until He had made clear unto them what they should avoid' (9 : 115).

God's will is expressive of His unlimited power which renders everything possible for Him. 'He cannot be questioned for His acts but men will be questioned for theirs (21: 23). He may forgive whom He pleaseth and punish whom He pleaseth but, at the same time, He is Oft-Forgiving, Most Merciful (3 :129). This shows the tremendous Power which He commands and can use it at His Will and Pleasure but His Mercy gives chances to men so that they may correct themselves. If they fail to do so, it becomes just and fair for God to set seal on their hearts and on their hearing (2 : 7), and give rope to such as do not receive guidance and try them in their contumacy and then mete out a severe punishment for them. All this shows that God is not tyrant.

The Quranic verses which deal with God's severe penalty indicate His Power and Possibility to do any thing but the use of such power is not without justice-Although God can deal with His creatures in whatever manner He Hikes and is not bound by any law) to be just, yet 'not one will He treat with injustice' (18 : 46); 'nor shall He suffer to perish the reward of any who do a (single) righteous deed' (18 : 30). 'He never harms those who serve Him' (3 : 182); 'nor is He unjust' (41: 46).

From the foregoing it is proved that God is just and deals justly and as such, His determining of good and evil cannot be without justice. Further what is predetermined is not known to us, so why dispute it and call its fairness in question and why not believe in His Justice and Mercifulness. The best course is, therefore, to have implicit trust in the justness of God and ascribe every good to Him and evil to ourselves: 'Whatever good (O man!) happens to thee, is from God; but whatever evil happens to thee is from thyself (4 : 97). We have no reason to doubt God's fairness Who takes into consideration even an atom's weight of good and evil and passes His judgement in accordance therewith: 'And who so doeth good an atom's weight will see it then, and who so doeth the atom's weight of evil will see it then' (99: 7,8).

We cannot evaluate our acts. May be, we pride ourselves on our works and take them to be the righteous ones but in the judgement of God they are quite reverse. We may be under the impression that our efforts will be rewarded, while we are among 'those whose efforts have been wasted in this life, but they thought they were acquiring good by their works' (18 : 104). We cannot judge our acts, God alone is the best judge.

Coming to the question of the Fatalists we feel that they are unnecessarily obsessed with the idea of determination. They must always expect good from God, for He does not intend anything evil for His creatures. Even' in the severe punishment which He has meted out there is our welfare. To meet the strict claims of justice equality is prescribed in cases of murder (2: 179). Life is taken for a life and in this law of equality, says the Quran, is the saving of life. And, indeed, it saves lives, being a lesson for all. Though the life of the murderer is lost but it brings peace to the society. Likewise hands of the thief are cut off (5 : 41) and in this lies the safety of property and protection of innocent people from crime. All the acts of God are, therefore, a Mercy to mankind and in their own interest.

We do not know what is really good for us and what is evil, 'Perchance ye dislike a thing which is good for you and that ye like a thing which is bad for you but God knoweth and ye know not' (2 : 216). So instead of questioning the predestination, of which we know nothing it is profitable to beseech God for His guidance and entreat Him to give what is good for us. The Prophet has rightly prescribed *istikhara* (asking good of God) in place of discussion on this topic. God in all His bountiful Mercy may grant us, what we ask for. 'Call Me', says He, 'I will answer your prayer.' (40: 60). Further, He has the power to efface the evil: God doth efface what He will and establishes what He will and with Him is the source of ordinance' (13 : 39).

Here the question may arise that God's knowledge of things would be defective if such changes take place. To this we answer that He is All-Powerful and can withhold Decree of Command which brings destiny into existence.

And it is for this reason that the Prophet laid stress on prayers. Pray often and in real earnest,' said he, 'for prayers can avert that which is inevitable (destiny).' We have to act upon it, for it is possible that God might have intended for us a better destiny on account of our entreaty and earnest prayer. Thus, His knowledge of things cannot be defective.

The followers of the Prophet asked him once as to what actually predestination meant and whether they should cease to work, for what is predestined is bound to happen. The Prophet in answer, exhorted them to work and to do righteous deeds and cited the Quranic verse:

> 'As for him who giveth (in charity) and is dutiful (toward God) and believeth in goodness: surely We will make smooth for him the Path of Bliss. But he who is greedy miser and deemeth himself self-sufficient and disbelieveth in goodness; surely We will make smooth for him the Path of Misery.
>
> (92 : 5-10).

This is the best solution offered by the Prophet. Obsessed with the idea of determinism we should not cease to work, nor be indifferent to the world. The Path of Bliss will be made smooth for us if we have faith in God and do righteous deeds. For details, we refer the reader to our work Islam, its Theology and the Greek Philosophy, Islamic Publications, Ltd. Lahore (Pakistan).

Assessment and Examination

On analysis we find that ethics is not a finished and complete subject. Socrates has rightly remarked: 'No system of ethics could be constructed until full attention had been devoted to the special features of moral experience and to the vagueness and contradictions of ordinary moral opinions. This required the philosophical intellect of the first rank concentrated on the problems of conduct' (*Ency. Britannica,* vol. 10, p. 762).

He went about showing that those who claimed to teach men how to live, poets, orators, and sophists were unable to define their views by argument or even to give adequate definitions of what they were claiming to explain. They were both inconsistent and ignorant. The problem is, therefore, to find what is absolute or objective good.

Nietzsche adopts an attitude of moral relativism. To him, that only is good which leads to enhancement of the will to power, and because in different times and climes it is possible to achieve this result with the help of different moral devices, he did not see any point in prescribing a universal code of morals. He insisted on the inversion of values because he saw in the prevailing Christian values nothing but nihilism and decadence.. Morality, he says, has been only a weapon in the hands of those who had the will to gain power, hence various systems to suit the various ends. He who is strong and powerful is on the right side, and who is weak is destined to be reckoned as false.

The classical ethical theories are characterised by their efforts to answer two questions: 'What is the good life ?' and 'How ought men to behave ?' Moral theories like Hedonism, Cynicism, Stoicism, Utilitarianism and so on seem to be of highest complex nature. We find ourselves constrained to support G. E. Moore who claimed, in his *Principia Ethica,* that the classical theories were attempts to deduce moral precepts from theological, metaphysical or scientific premises and that such arguments are fallacious, since one cannot argue from premises of one logical type {i.e., descriptions) to conclusions of a different logical type (i.e., prescriptions).

Moral theories which appear plausible at a first glance, such as Hedonism, are found upon careful examination to suffer from serious defects. How can the good life be identical with a life of pleasure, since there are pleasures which are bad? For example, pleasures such as drinking alcohol, give us momentary pleasure but may result in a life of subsequent pain and travail.

The various answers which classical theories give are in the form of advice rather than an effort to define moral words like 'good', 'bad' and so on. Hedonism, for instance, may be regarded as advising men that good life consists of pleasure, and further that they ought to act so as to acquire pleasure. But the word 'good' is not defined and, indeed, 'good' like all moral words, is indefinable and that 'goodness' is an unanalysable property. Any attempted definitions of moral words will be in terms only of their descriptive meaning and no more.

> Good and evil are thus, described in terms of pleasure and pain. So far as 'Utilitarian Ethics' is concerned it assumes that man is motivated by the desire to secure pleasurable and avoid painful experiences. The Utilitarians have their own suspicions of reason and look to human observation and experience in order to find what men actually value. Instead of judging the conduct by the feelings and motives, they would judge it by its consequences. Each individual, they held, is really seeking his happiness above everything else. If then we are to find a moral standard in what men actually value, we must find it not in the heavens alone but in human happiness.
>
> (Dewey, *Ethic*, p. 167).

> The essence of Bentham's philosophy is that nature has placed man under the empire of pleasure and pain. We owe to them all our ideas; we refer to them all our judgements, and all the determinations of our life. He who pretends to withdraw himself from this subjection knows not what he says. His only object is to seek pleasure and shun pain... .These eternal and

> irresistible sentiments ought to be the great study of the moralist and the legislator. The principle of utility subjects everything to these two motives' (Bentham, *The Theory of Legislation*, p. 2).

Bentham's theory is criticized as contradictory in itself. According to its conception of desire and motive, the whole object of all actions is the obtaining of personal pleasure, while the proper standard for judging the morality of act is its contribution to the welfare of others. In Bentham's theory 'desire for private pleasure as the sole motive of action and universal benevolence as the principle of approval are at war with each other'.

'It would be only a poor sort of happiness' remarked George Eliot in her *Romola*, 'that could ever come by caring very much for our narrow pleasures'. Personal pleasure is indeed a low sort of pleasure and it is better to be a human being dissatisfied than a pig satisfied.

Further, pleasure has no sound basis, for it depends mostly upon the existing state of a person:

> 'What is agreeable at one time, disagrees at another; what pleases in health is distasteful in illness; what annoys or disgusts in a state of repletion is gratifying when one is hungry and eager. And on a higher scale, that which is pleasant to men of generous disposition arouses aversion in a mean and stingy person; what is pleasant to a child may bore an adult; the objects that gratify a scholar are repulsive to a boor'
>
> (Dewey, Ethics, p. 213).

In fact, there can be no standard of judgement as to know what exactly constitutes pleasure and, morally speaking, pleasure as an end cannot be considered 'good', for a villain takes pleasure in his wickedness. The Utilitarian theory, that pleasure is the good and the end, is baseless and immoral.

It may have been clear by now that Morality cannot be adequately defined and Ethics fails to be a science. But the subjectivists, for instance, Hedonists contend that their moral judgements are not false but true. Moral theories, in this respect, are classified into subjectivistic and objectivistic. This raises the question of defining subjectivism and objectivism.

Subjectivism**:** Subjectivism is the doctrine that all knowledge is subjective only and incapable of objective proof. It is commonly held that there is no reality other than the reality of things which we see, touch, hear, smell or taste. This leads to deny the existence of an order of reality which is not open to the investigation and subject to the laws of science and equally denies, with regard to human conduct, that there is anything real in the psychological realm other than the series of emotions, desires, impulses, hopes and thoughts which make up the stream of our consciousness. Hence a thing is good not because it is characterized by goodness or is really good but because we desire it and it gives us happiness.

Suppose if someone denies this sort of conclusion as ascetics are said to have done, maintaining that we should mortify the flesh here for the happiness to be attained in the Hereafter, what will be the reply? Further, if we ask a subjectivist, 'How do you know that pleasure is a good ?' He has no reasoned answer, he just sees to be so. Finally, as we have already-explained pleasure has no definite meaning.

The argument which is advanced in support of subjectivism may be called the argument from Sentience. The subjectivists argue that no question of good or bad can arise in a world which has no sentient being – beings that are capable of feeling, for it would not make sense to say that anything good or bad could happen to inanimate objects such as a rock or stone. It is only if some sentient being is affected by these events, or could be affected by them, that it makes sense to say that they are good or bad. Goodness and badness thus seem to depend upon the feelings, attitudes and desires of sentient beings. From considerations such as these it is argued that some form of subjectivism must be true.

But if we probe deep into such argument it becomes evident that what it proves is not the good or bad as it actually is but as it is thought or felt. Moral judgements of this type cannot be called sound ethical judgements since they depend not only upon emotions,, desires, and feelings of persons making such judgements but also on their ethical, traditional, social, economic and other sentiments. It is on this account that these judgements not only differ from one another but are also conflicting so much so that even vices and crimes-are considered virtues. Says Canon Rashdall, a well-known authority on ethical philosophy:

> 'There is hardly a vice or crime (according to our own moral standard) which has not at some time or other in some circumstances been looked- upon as a moral and religious duty. Stealing was accounted virtuous for the young Spartan and among the Indian caste of Thugs. In the ancient world Piracy, i.e. robbery and murder, was a respectable profession. To the Mediaeval Christian religious persecution was the highest of duties, and so on'
>
> (C. E. M. Jood, *Philosophy*, P- 31).

Under the circumstances it may be said that just as science is content with a world of matter in motion, the subjectivist ethics is content with a world of human consciousness which consists of nothing except the stream of emotions, desires, impulses, hopes and thoughts. The peculiarity of the subjectivist theories of ethics is that they do not accept the view that there is an 'object' which possesses ethical qualities of its own, with the corollary that there can be correct ethical judgement.

For a better understanding of subjectivist theories let us call a person making an ethical judgement 'the subject' and the character to which the judgement refers 'the object'. The ethical judgements are called subjectivistic as they do not refer to the object which they support but to the subject, being judgements to the effect that the subject is experiencing certain feelings. The good according to such theories is not the good in its own right but according as is experienced by the subject, i.e., the maker of ethical judgement. It, therefore, follows that if such theories are considered to be correct then 'good' has no ethical quality of its own, for, the good, in such a case, is only what is thought 'good'. Let us turn to objectivism and see whether its ethical judgements are correct.

Objectivism : Objective means actually existing, not Subjective only. Hence objectivism is the tendency to lay stress upon what is objective or external to the mind.

> The main argument in favour of objectivism is that; it provides a theory which corresponds more closely to the views of men of common sense about moral matters than subjectivism. To mark the difference between subjectivism and objectivism we cite an example of 'two persons who have just entered a room and asked to guess its temperature; the one is supposed to have recently emerged from a refrigerator, the other from a hot-house; the former guesses 75°F., the latter 70°F. It is clear that two subjective conditions prevailing in the bodies of the two judges have determined the guesses that they make as to the temperature of the room; what they do not determine is the temperature of the room. What both judges are purporting to assess is a certain condition which prevails in the world independently of their judgements, and most of us would agree that, since the temperature of the room can be measured by a thermometer, there is a perfectly definite sense in holding that judgement according to thermometer is

> Objective and correct, while another judgement to the effect that it is something else is wrong and incorrect'
> (C. E. M. Jood, *Philosophy*, pp. 133,134).

The difference between the case in which we judge about the temperature and the case in which we judge about ethical qualities is that in the former we can refer to an instrument, the thermometer, by reference to which we can determine what the objective temperature is and pronounce our judgement to be nearer to the truth than the other, whereas there is no equivalent instrument wherewith to measure ethical judgements. Here is the difficulty and it is perhaps for this reason that the subjectivists contend that all knowledge is subjective and incapable of objective proof. Let us turn to Kant and see if his moral theory can solve this problem.

In his analysis of human impulses and desires Kant goes all the way with subjectivists that man is merely a creature of likes and dislikes, of wants and needs, of impulses and tastes, of preferences and prejudices, but, he says, there is one characteristic unique in nature, and man being possessed of it, cannot be adequately regarded as wholly a child of nature. In addition to the impulses and desires which tell him -what he would like to do, he is, on occasion, conscious of something else, namely, what he ought to do which may be very opposite to what he would like to do. Thus, for man there is a distinction between 'want' and 'ought', between 'desire' and 'duty'; moral sense is innate in him and not derived from experience. Moral sense, says Kant, is our unescapable feeling in the face of our temptation that this or that is wrong. An act is good not because it has good results or because it is aright, but because it is done in obedience to the inner sense of duty. Morality is not properly the doctrine how we make ourselves happy but how we make ourselves worthy of happiness.

To comprehend the unique significance of 'ought' Kant insists that man must be a member of some other order of reality. Thus, he can win free from the influences of heredity, circumstances and environment which otherwise determine his psychology. To see Kant's moral philosophy in its proper setting we have to study it in its association with his metaphysical theory.

Kant says that when we will to do our duty in pursuance of ought' and in the face of disinclination, we are making direct contact not with the familiar world which appears to our senses, but with the world as it is independently of ourselves—a moral world and an order of reality which contains the value of morality such as right and good. It is not with our minds and our intellects that we recognize what is right and realize what ought to be done, but by the 'practical' as opposed to the 'theoretical' reason—a faculty similar, in modern concept, to intuition. The central feet of morals appeared to him to be the voice of duty from within the soul itself.

Thus the familiar world of common sense is not the only world, there is another world and order of reality which is spiritual and which contains values of morality. This implies the existence of a mind, other than our own, which not only knows but also creates values—a Law-giver who lays down the moral law or order of the universe. The argument, in this way, passes over from ethics to religion.

With God as the Law-giver the problem is solved. He alone knows the objective good and we cannot know it as we often dislike a thing which is good for us and like a thing which is bad for us: 'Perchance you dislike a thing which may be good for you ; and perchance you like a thing which may be bad for you'. To know the objective good is beyond our power and it is in His law alone that we find the required instrument and standard for correct ethical judgements. 'Good', here is not what is thought 'good' but the 'objective and absolute good'. The question, is now, 'What is the good life, in its real sense, and' how ought men to behave?'

Classical Theories

Plato: Evil is Due to Lack of Knowledge : In most of the classical theories it is assumed that if we know what the good life is we will naturally behave in such a way as to try to achieve it.

Platonism, for instance, holds that evil is due to lack of knowledge; if a man discovers what is right he will never act wickedly. But the problem is how to discover 'the right' or 'the good' and how can this be done when men hold different and conflicting opinions about the good life?

In answer to this Plato says that the discovery of the nature of things is an intellectual task, hence to discover what the good life is one must be trained in various disciplines such as mathematics, philosophy and so on. It is only through such intellectual training that men would have the capacity to know the nature of the good life. Even without this sort of training it is possible for some men to lead good life but they will do so haphazardly or blindly. There may be some men who do not have intellectual power to apprehend what the 'good life' is, but they will act virtuously if they follow those who have knowledge of the good. This finds expression in Plato's famous work 'The Republic', which speaks of Philosopher King as the most efficient ruler, for he is possessed of knowledge of 'the good' and can lead men to the good life.

According to Plato, there is fundamentally one and only one good life for all men to lead because goodness is something which is not dependent upon man's inclinations desires or wishes but is absolute as it exists independently of men and remains to be discovered if men can be properly trained. Such is the absolutism in Plato's philosophy.

From the above it is evident that Plato regards morality as being a matter of knowledge but only a few are intellectually gifted to have such ability. It is not sufficient to say that those of us who have not the ability- can live good lives by being led by those who have, since to behave morally presupposes that one has responsibility for one's actions and an action is not truly moral or immoral unless it is the result of free choice of the individual performing it. Aristotle seems aware of these defects in Plato's theory, since he adopts his own doctrine of morality.

Aristotle: Doctrine of the Golden Mean : Aristotle, though a great metaphysician, but, curiously enough, in his ethical writings he adopts a scientific or empirical approach to ethical problems. Instead of trying to discover the nature of the good life for all men by reflection alone, he examined the behaviour of various people in every day life. He noticed that the various lives that men of common sense consider to be good all contain, one common characteristic, i.e. happiness. Hence he frankly admits that the aim of life is not goodness for its own sake, but happiness.

His doctrine of Golden Mean is explained as follows:

> Being happy, according to Aristotle, is like being well-fed. How much food should a man eat in order to be well-fed? To Aristotle, there is no general answer to this question in the sense of specific amount. It depends on the size of the man, what sort of work he does, whether he is ill or well, and so on. The proper amount for anyone to eat can be ascertained by trial and error: if we eat a certain amount of food and still feel hungry, we should eat more ; if we eat the same amount and feel uncomfortable, then we should eat less. The correct amount is a 'mean between eating too much and too little.

But the 'mean' cannot be interpreted as being synonymous with 'average'. Suppose that one pound of food per day is too little, and that two pounds is too much. Does this suggest that the average amount (i.e., one pound and a half) is the correct amount ? Aristotle's answer is that it may or may not be—but in general, one cannot say that the correct amount is exactly one pound and a half ; all one can say is that it is an amount somewhere between one pound and two pounds; and this is what Aristotle intends by the word 'mean'. Further, it will be seen from the above that Aristotle's mean varies from man to man.

The golden mean, however, is not, like the mathematical mean, an exact average of two precisely calculable extremes; it fluctuates with the collateral , circumstances of each situation and is subject to flexible reason.

The theory of Aristotle is subject to some criticism as in certain situations it is difficult to follow the mean. For example, there is no 'mean' between keeping a promise and not keeping one. The same applies to telling the truth: either one does or does not tell the truth. But we have to bear in mind that the question of mean arises only when there is the possibility of going to extremes.

Hedonism : To Plato, the good life is in no way connected with pleasure, but Aristotle moderated this doctrine in holding that 'pleasure must be in some way an ingredient of happiness'. Epicurus disagreed with both of them and held a view which is called 'Hedonism', the doctrine that pleasure is the sole good. To him, morality is identical with expedience.

The ethical philosophy of Epicurus consists mainly of advice for living moderately but pleasantly. While discovering pleasure to be good he also realized that if a person pursues pleasure too arduously, pain will follow. For example, if a man drinks too much, it will result in headache. Since some pleasures are obviously followed by pain, Epicurus distinguished between those pleasures which are followed by pain and those which are not and regarded only the latter as good. He called the former 'dynamic' pleasures and the latter as 'passive' pleasures. Sexual love, for example, is bad because it is accompanied by fatigue, remorse and depression. He advocated avoidance of such pleasures as are bad, for he believed that it is better to avoid pain than to seek pleasure if it will produce pain.

Hedonism, though theoretically attractive, may be seen to violate our ordinary feelings about what constitutes behaviour. The objection is not that it seeks superficial and narrow pleasures but, more fundamentally, that pleasure is not the sole object which men should strive for.

Cynicism : It is the philosophy of the Cynics, founded by Antisthenes, a pupil of Socrates, who condemned ease, -wealth, and enjoyment of life. The most famous was Diogenes who carried principles to an extreme. This is the philosophy which holds that if salvation is to be found it is to be found in a rejection of society and in a return to simple life—to a life of asceticism.

The word 'Cynic' comes from the Greek word 'Kunos', which means 'dog-like'. Diogenes, for example, is supposed to have lived in a large tub, and rejected all refinements—of dress, food, personal cleanliness. The Cynics believed that the world was fundamentally evil; in order to live properly a man must withdraw from participation in it. Cynicism is not only anti-social, but also contributed largely to undermine the social standards, contending that only individual virtue was of essential importance. As a philosophy Cynicism has had a great influence upon plain man and is considered to have been a major factor in the development of early Christian philosophy. The monk is no better than a Cynic for he casts aside the world and lives the life of a cave or monastery, while monasticism is not permissible in Islam.

Stoicism : Stoicism has been the most influential ethical doctrine of the ancient Western World before Christianity. Zeno was the founder of Stoicism and is supposed to have lectured in the third century B.C. from a porch, and stoicism gets its name from this fact, since 'stoa' is the Greek word for 'porch'. The basic tenet of stoicism for achieving personal salvation is just like that of the Cynics and can be summed up in one-sentence. Learn to be indifferent to external influences! It is a philosophy of indifference. By practising indifference one becomes independent of the world.

The Stoics believed in predestination, i.e. that all happenings in the world are fixed by God according to some preconceived plan, and that virtue consists in a will which is in agreement with the happenings of nature. Further, they considered it important to free oneself from desires and passions.

Stoicism differs from Cynicism in that the Cynics felt that they were powerless to prevent the collapse of the world in which they lived and hence they renounced it, while the Stoics argued that this sort of renunciation was unnecessary, for man need not renounce the material things of the world provided that he does not become involved in them. If he remains indifferent to them and uneffected by them there is no reason why he should not continue to enjoy them.

The Stoics hold that man is not free but instead is chained to his destinies in accordance with the divine-plan. But this view is inconsistent with their view that, a man can alter his character and can change his frame of mind in such a manner that he will become-indifferent to things that he formerly prized. If man is free and has power to alter his character and to-change his frame of mind, then the thesis that all events are predetermined by some master plan must be false.

The problem of Freedom of the Will is the most baffling one. It has not only appeared in Stoic-philosophy but also occurs in religious philosophy as-well as in modern psychology. Islam is the religion, which has found a clue to its solution as will be explained later.

Spinoza: The Ethics : Spinoza is reckoned as one of the towering figures in the history of Ethics. He was a rigid determinist as he says, 'All things come to pass, come to pass according to the eternal order and fixed laws of Nature'. Thus he was in the metaphysical tradition of the Stoics-In holding that nothing is good or bad in itself, but is only so in relation to someone, Spinoza is a relativist. From this point of view of Spinoza riches, fame and sensual pleasure are all not inherently worthwhile. They are not worth acquiring for their own sake but only as means to making human life more happy. When these things affect men in desirable ways, they are good, but when they affect them in undesirable ways, they are bad.

According to him good life consists in the recognition of the truth that all events are determined and a man will be happy when he comes to understand that there are limits to human power and that everything which happens must happen necessarily. This sort of attitude, says he, if developed, will liberate men from fear, anxiety and unhappiness. These arise only when a man becomes slave tc his emotions.

Spinoza's masterpiece is The Ethics which is considered to be his great work by many philosophers but he did not effectively resolve the conflict that exists between determinism and freedom. He believed that all events in nature are determined which means that man is essentially powerless. The question is: 'how can he change his attitude and frame of mind towards life and be free from anxieties when he is powerless ?'

Bentham and Stuart Mill: Utilitarianism : One of the earliest exponents of this moral theory was Francis Hutcheson but the most famous exponents of it are Jermy Bentham and John Stuart Mill who attempted to lay down a principle for determining the rightness or wrongness of an act and called this maxim the Principle of Utility. According to this principle an action is right in so far it tends to produce the greatest happiness for the greatest number and happiness is taken to mean pleasure. The fundamental point is that it is consequences of a given action which determine its rightness or wrongness, not the motive from which it is done. The object is to separate the rightness or wrongness of an action from the goodness or badness of the person who performs the action.

There are certain objections raised against Utilitarianism and Nietzsche describes Mill as a 'block head' for his assumption that in computing the amount of happiness or unhappiness, which an action creates, each man will count equally for one unit of happiness. Nietzsche believed that some people were inherently more important than others and their happiness or unhappiness counted for more than the happiness or unhappiness of the average man. Carlyle, on the other hand, condemned Utilitarianism as 'a universal syllabus of sentimental twaddle'.

Further, there are some philosophers who rejected Utilitarianism on the ground that consideration in assessing the moral worth of our action must be given to the motive from which it is done.

Kantian Moral Philosophy : According to Kant ethics is the most important subject in philosophy. He believes in the moral basis of religion. He even used ethical arguments to establish the existence of God. Since men who are not virtuous are happier in this world there must be another world for virtuous men to be rewarded and this leads him to the conclusion that there is God and an eternal life.

'What is the nature of morality' is the main question which Kant's moral theory was formulated to answer. Kant believed that the key to answer this question lay in distinguishing between acts done from 'inclination' and acts done from a 'sense duty-or obligation'. An obligations that which a map ought to do despite his inclination to do otherwise.

Some philosophers have held that in matters of morality

one should act upon his inclinations but Kant rejects such an account of morality. For him, a man is acting morally only when he suppresses his inclinations and obeys the command of duty. Further, he makes a distinction between actions which are 'in accord with duty' and those done 'from duty'. The former are not moral acts but the latter are. Most parents, for instance, are inclined to take care of their children because they are fond of them but this does not amount to moral act as it is in accordance with duty and not from duty. A man who understands the nature of his duty and acts upon it is moral and not otherwise. According to him the concept of goad and evil must not be determined before the law. But only after it and by means of it'. Thus he subordinates good to moral law. Briefly, a moral action is that which is done from 'a respect for duty and a moral person is he who acts 'from duty', not from inclination or even in accord with duty.

Kant differs sharply from the Utilitarians in that he stresses the point that the essence of morality is to be found in the motive from which an act is done. A man who keeps promises by accident is not a moral man. Every action, says he, must be judged in the light of how it would appear if it were to be a universal code of behaviour. All that is required is to know our duty in a particular case and ask ourselves if the motive of that act can be made universal without falling into self-contradiction. For example, says he, 'May I when in distress, make a promise with intention not to keep it?'

Evidently, this principle, if made universal, simply contradicts itself, for with such a promise there would be no such thing as a promise. No one would like to be content with a false or deceitful promise. The principle of right action, in this light, may be summed up as: 'Act in a way that you would like to be paid back in your own coin' or 'Act as if the maxim of thy action were to become by thy will a universal law of nature'. This is according to Kant, the unconditional command of our conscience – a categorical imperative. Another categorical imperative formulated by Kant is: 'So act as to treat humanity, whether in thine own person or in that of -another, in every case as an end, never as a means only.' Another way of putting such maxim is 'Do unto others as you would have them do unto you.' We should treat others as ends in themselves because that is how we regard ourselves. To treat another man only as a means to achieve our end is to disregard his humanity, hence immoral.

It is said that Kant's theory is inconsistent in that he has not held to his original claim that he is concerned solely with motive and not consequences. The objection is on the basis that Kant introduces consequences of the act in tacitly showing that the effect of not behaving in accordance with the categorical imperative would be to make human life impossible.

8

Islamic Ethics

Good Life : Good character is the sum of personal virtues which guarantees correct and agreeable behaviour in daily social interaction. A person of good character will invariably conform in his behaviour to a strict code of ethics.

What should be the underlying principle of this code of ethics? According to a hadith it is simply this: you should like for others what you like for yourself, that is, you should treat others just as you want to be treated by others.

Everyone likes to be addressed with good manners and pleasing words. So everyone should speak gently to others. Everyone wants his existence to be problem-free, so he should avoid creating problems for others.

Everyone wants others to deal with him in a sympathetic and cooperative manner. So what everyone ought to do while dealing with others is to give them his full sympathy and cooperation.

This standard of ethics is very simple and natural. It is so simple that anyone may easily learn it, be he literate or illiterate, able bodied or disabled, and regardless of his likes and dislikes. This hadith has given such a criterion for human ethics that no one can find difficult to understand. In this way Islam has set forth, in the light of everyone's personal experience, what behaviour may be indulged in and what behaviour has to be refrained from.

According to another hadith, the best of us is one who is best in moral character. Accordingly, becoming a good human being has nothing ambiguous about it. Its simple formula is that of avoidance of double standards. One who lives his life by this formula is indubitably a person of the highest moral character.

The Intention of Man : Islam attaches the utmost importance to intentions (*Niyyat*). No action is acceptable to God purely on the basis of its outer appearance. He accepts only such actions as are performed with proper intention, and rejects those performed with ill intention. Right intention is the moral purposiveness which underlies all actions performed solely for God's pleasure. One who acts on such feelings will be rewarded by God in the Hereafter.

An ill-intention, on the other hand, is a negative spur to worldly attainment. Ostensibly religious acts, if performed for worldly gain or public commendation, are in this sense ill-intentioned. Any fame, honour or popularity which ensues from an ill-intentioned act is a hollow triumph and is looked upon by the Almighty with extreme disfavour.

Intention is rooted in man's inner thinking and feelings. A common man is unable to penetrate the inner recesses of a person's mind but God knows full well what a man's thought processes and feelings are. People can be deluded by appearances, but God has complete knowledge of everything. He will deal with people according to His knowledge and will reward everyone exactly as he or she deserves.

Intention has to do with the inner reality. A thing which

loses its reality or its meaningfulness is valueless. Similarly, an act which is performed with ill intention or with no good intention, has no value-neither in the eyes of man, nor of God.

Things are of value only when they are pure, without any adulteration. An act done with right intention is a pure act, and an act performed without right intention is an impure act.

Speaking the Truth : A believer in God is also necessarily a truth-loving person. He always speaks the truth. In all matters he says just what is in accordance with reality. A true believer cannot afford to tell lies, or hide facts. What does it mean to speak the truth? It is to have no contradiction between man's knowledge and the words that he utters and for that matter, whatever he says should be what has come to his knowledge. Falsehood, by contrast, is the utterance of statements which do not tally with knowledge.

Truth is the highest virtue of a believer's character. A believer is a man of principle. And for such a person telling the truth is paramount. For him no other behaviour is possible, for he finds it impossible to deny the truth.

The world of God is based wholly on truth. Here everything expresses itself in its real form. The sun, the moon, rivers, mountains, stars and planets are all based on truth. They appear just as they really are. In this unfathomably vast universe of God nothing is based on untruth. There is nothing which shows itself in any form other than its real form.

This is the character of nature, which is spread out on a universal scale. A believer too has exactly the same character. He is totally free from falsehood or double standards. A believer is all truth. His whole existence is moulded to truth. From the very first he appears to be a true person both inside and out.

Speaking the truth is not only a matter of policy for the believer it is his very religion. Compromising in the matter of truth is not possible for him. He speaks the truth as he cannot live without doing so. He speaks the truth because he knows that not speaking the truth is the negation of his own personality and commitment to something which is the negation of the self is not possible for any worthy person.

Patience in Islam

Patience (Sabr) is the exercise of restraint in trying situations. It is a virtue which enables the individual to proceed towards worthy goals, undeflected by adverse circumstances or repeated provocations. If he allows himself to become upset by opposition, taunts or other kinds of unpleasantness, he will never reach his goals. He will simply become enmeshed in irrelevancies.

The only way to deal with the irksome side of daily living is to exercise patience. Patience will ensure that whenever one has some bitter experience, he will opt for the way of tolerance rather than that of reaction to provocation. It will enable one to absorb shocks and to continue, undeterred, on one's onward journey

Patience, as well as being a practical solution to the problems faced in the outside world, is also a means of positive character building. Failure to exercise patience, gives free rein to negative thoughts and feelings, resulting in the development of a negative personality. While one who remains patient is so morally bolstered by his own positive thoughts and feelings that he develops a positive personality.

Sabr is no retreat. Sabr only amounts to taking the initiative along the path of wisdom and reason as opposed to the path of the emotions. Sabr gives one the strength to restrain one's emotions in delicate situations and rather to use one's brains to find a course of action along result-oriented lines.

The present world is fashioned in such a way that everyone is necessarily confronted with unpleasant matters at one time or another. Things which are unbearable have somehow to be borne; harrowing events have to be witnessed and all kinds of pain have to be suffered. In such situations, succumbing to impatience leads to the kind of unnecessary emotional involvement which is counter-productive, while a demonstration of patience has a healing, beneficial effect, allowing one to tread the path of discreet avoidance. Success in the present world is destined only for those who adopt the path of patience in adverse circumstances.

No Prejudice : During the lifetime of the Prophet of Islam many of his fellow men opposed Islam and engaged in plotting against Islam and Muslims. The Quran has mentioned this at several places. But the counter strategy advocated by the Quran was not to unearth their plots and launch movements to defeat them or even finally to wage war against them, On the contrary, the Prophet and his companions were enjoined to place their trust in God alone.

That is to say, ignoring the plots and antagonism, trusting only in God and rising above circumstances, they were to continue all activities which were of a positive nature.

This was an extremely important injunction. By giving this guidance, God set them on a course of positive thinking, which left no room for negative thinking. In short, this Quranic teaching encouraged the early Muslims to live in a self-sufficient way, free of baneful influence of their opponents.

If you have this obsession that others are plotting against you, and that everyone has turned your enemy, it will result in your starting to suspect everyone, to the extent that even if a member of your own community underscores the importance of tolerance and avoidance, you will take it in a negative light and dub him an agent of the enemy. In this way, you will weaken yourselves by turning your own people away from you.

One harmful aspect of such negative obsession is that one loses all objectivity in thinking. One's entire outlook becomes partisan and prejudiced. One is unable to see reality as it is. One becomes like the man who can see only the thorns in a garden of roses or the colour blind person to whom a garden blossoming with flowers will appear in melancholy shades of grey.

The Tolerance in Islam

Tolerance is a noble humanitarian and Islamic virtue. Its practice means making concessions to others, Intolerance on the other hand, means showing a self- centered unconcern for the needs of others. Tolerance is a worthy, humane virtue, which has been described in different terms in the Shariah: for instance, gentle behaviour, showing concern for others, being soft-hearted, being compassionate.

When true God-worship and religiosity is born within a person, he reaches above all those evils which emanate from selfishness. Instead of living within the confines of the self, he begins to live in the world of reality. The truly pious person begins to look upon people with love and compassion. He does not expect anything from anyone, that is why even when others differ from him or do not behave well towards him, he continues nevertheless to make concessions to them, and continues to be tolerant towards them.

Tolerance implies an unswerving respect for others, whether in agreement or disagreement with them. The tolerant man will always consider the case of others sympathetically, be they relatives or friends, and irrespective of the treatment he is given by them, be it of a positive or a negative nature.

Tolerance means, in essence, to give consideration to others.

In social life, friction between people does occur in every society, differences arising from religion, culture, tradition and personal tastes persist. In such a situation the superior cause of action is to adopt the ways of concession and large-heartedness without any compromise of principle.

That is to say that the pious man should be a man of principle as far as he himself is concerned, but should be tolerant towards others. He should judge himself in the light of the ideal but in the matter of his fellow men he should show tolerance and broad-mindedness. This being inseparable from human gentility and nobility. Islam aims to produce this fine human quality of gentlemanliness by preaching tolerance.

The Simplicity

A beliver is one who finds God. God's discoverer starts living by nature on the plane of higher realities. He rises above outward, superficial things and finds sources of interest in the world of piety.

Such a person by his very nature becomes a simplicity loving person. His motto is: Simple living and high thinking.

One who has acquired the taste for the meaning of the divine reality can have no taste for outward and material things. Such a person relishes simplicity. In his eyes pretensions lose their attraction. His soul finds peace in natural things. Unnatural and artificial things appear to him as if they are causing his inner world disintegrate and creating obstacles to the progress of his spiritual journey.

Simplicity is a support to the believer. It contributes to his strength. By opting for simplicity he is able to put his time to the best use by not wasting it on irrelevant matters. He does not let his attention be diverted to things which are inessential so far as his goal is concerned. And in this way he is able to devote himself whole-heartedly to the achievement of higher goals.

Simplicity is the food of the believer, and, having its own internal beauty, it serves as an apparel for his modesty. It is in an atmosphere of simplicity that his personality finds the scope for its growth. On the contrary, if the believer builds up an artificial glamour around himself, he will eventually feel as if he is imprisoned in a cell.

A believer considers himself God's servant in the ultimate sense of the word. His thoughts and feelings are all perfectly attuned to this servitude, to this condition of being God's servant. One who consistently thinks in this way inevitably finds his whole disposition veering towards simplicity. Since ostentation, artificiality and social pretensions are at variance with his disposition, he resolutely avoids them throughout his life, in his manner of living and in his daily dealings.

The Piety : Taqwa means piety, that is, leading a life of caution and restraint in this world.

Umar Farooq, the second Caliph once asked a companion of the Prophet what *taqwa* was. He replied, "O leader of the believers, have you ever crossed a path which has thorny shrubs on both sides?" But the companion instead of replying asked another question, "What did you do on such an occasion?" Umar Farooq replied, "I gathered my clothes close to me and moved ahead cautiously."

The companion said, "Now I know what is meant by taqwa." The present world is a testing ground. Here, various kinds of thorns have been scattered for the purpose of testing man, such as negativity, false issues raised by non-serious people, the lure of-worldly things. Besides these, there are many unpleasant occurrences which disturb people's minds and lead them away from the path of virtue.

All these things are like thorny shrubs lining both sides of the path of life. At any moment it is feared that man may embroil himself in these thorns and then instead of going forward, remain entrapped in these snares of life.

In such a state of affairs the wise man is one who travels the paths of life by gathering up his clothes to avoid becoming entangled in these unpleasant snares. In this way, he is able to continue his journey unhampered. Yet at all times he must remain conscious of the fact that he must protect himself . He has to adopt the path of avoidance, not of entanglement.

Man has been created with an upright nature. If no hindrance comes in the way, then every man will, on his own, take the right course. That is why, the utmost precaution must be taken against allowing unnatural obstacles to come in the way.

Then, guided by this upright nature, man will continue to walk along the right path until he meets his Lord.

Thanksgiving and Islam

Thanks giving for man is to acknowledge the blessings of God acknowledgment first arises in the heart then, taking the form of words, it comes to the lips of the grateful person.

From birth, man has been superbly, adorned in body and mind by his Creator. All his requirements have been amply catered for, every object in the heavens and on earth having been pressed into his service. All the things necessary for his leading a good life on earth and the building of a civilization have been provided in abundance.

Man experiences these blessings at every moment. It is, therefore, incumbent on man to thank God for His blessings at all times. His heart should be eternally brimming with gratitude for these divine blessings.

Thanksgiving is the most comprehensive term of worship: gratefulness is the essence of the godly life. The best expression of that gratefulness is the expenditure of time and money in the way of God. It is God, after all who has given man the reason to worship Him and the means to do so.

The Trial in Islam

Man is free in this world. God has not placed any curbs on him. But this freedom is for the purpose of putting man to the test, and is not meant to encourage him to lead a life of permissiveness like the animals and then just pass away one day. Rather its purpose is that man should lead a morally upright life of his own free will, thus demonstrating that he is of the highest moral character.

One who conducts himself in this matter should be reckoned as God's special servant who, without any apparent compulsion chose to be a man of principle; who, without being subjected to any external force, did of his own free will, what his Lord would have desired. This liberty accorded to man gives him the opportunity to gain credit for being the most superior of all God's creatures.

All the things in this world are God's subjects. The stars and satellites rotate in space entirely at their Lord's bidding. Trees, rivers, mountains, and all other such natural phenomena are functioning according to the unchangeable ways of God laid down by Him in advance.

Similarly, the animals follow exactly those instincts instilled in their species as a matter of Divine Will. Man is the only creature who has been given, exceptionally, the gift of power and freedom.

This freedom has opened doors of two kinds for man, one leading to success and the other to failure. If, on receiving freedom an individual becomes arrogant and insolent, it will mean that he has failed to pass the test.

But if on the other hand, he remains modest and humble,

bowing to his Lord's will on all occasions, he will have made the right use of his God-given freedom: he will, without any compulsion, have bound himself by divine principles. One who chooses this course will succeed in the test of freedom. He will be handsomely rewarded by God as no other creature. Held to be the chosen servant of God, he will remain in an everlasting state of blissfulness and blessedness.

Concept of Salvation : What is the greatest issue facing man in this world? It is how to secure salvation in the life after death so that he may find his true abode and have a share in God's eternal blessings.

Every man who is born in this present world has to enter another world after death. In this world man was granted life's opportunities as a matter of being tested by them. Whatever man receives in the next world will be purely on the basis of his deeds in this world. This means that in the world before death, man has been given a great number of things and opportunities, whether or not he deserved them. But after death, the criterion of receiving will only be a matter of his just deserts; nothing will be given to him to try him.

This means that those who are held to be deserving will be granted not out of God's blessings but more that they actually merited. But those who have done nothing to deserve God's blessings will have nothing whatsoever in store for them. They will be compelled to live in a state of utter deprivation.

This is man's greatest problem. To what should he give the greatest attention so that he may not be held undeserving in the life to come? Everyone has to exert himself to the utmost in the consciousness that in the next stage of his life he may by default be considered without merit. Then there would be no further scope for him to earn God's blessings, salvation would elude him completely.

The next world is the most perfect and eternal world. There, all kinds of pleasures and happiness which have been stored up for mankind. It is that world which man should cherish most, and it should be the place to which he most earnestly aspires But the time for action to secure a place in that blessing-filled world is not the world after death, but the world before death. The present world is the place for action, while the next world is the place for reaping the reward for one's deeds.

Salvation in the life Hereafter is only for those who prove themselves deserving of it.

9

The Fraternity

The Islamic community is governed by a sense of both individual and collective responsibility to Allah Who has defined the limits of human behaviour. In discussing the collective aspects of human interaction in any community, it is only logical to start at the beginning, that is, with the family. The Islamic teachings are designed to strengthen and protect this important nurturing ground of future generations with the utmost care and concern. Marriage, which is the cornerstone of the family is strongly encouraged in Islam. The purpose of marriage, according to Islam, is that a man and woman build a home, live together in love, kindness, support and com panionship, meet each other's sexual needs and bring up children together. By their marriage, they form a family unit which also supports and strengthens the existing families of the pair.

Since men and women have different natures, Islam assigns different but complementary roles to each, dividing the work between them in a way that best suits their capacities and natures. It assigns the leadership role, the financial responsibility and the support and maintenance of the women and children, to men. Women are responsible for looking after their family and husband's comfort and well being, guarding their honour and properties, providing for the physical and emotional well being of their children and bringing them up as true Muslims. That a woman must do the household work is not required by Islam, as she is free to hire domestic help if she can afford it. She can pursue her own work and interests, provided the family is not neglected. They are not required to provide for the family's maintenance because Islam has made this the responsibility of men.

Islam lays great stress on raising children properly. Young people, on their part, are required to develop a sense of responsibility for their own conduct from an early age. A young Muslim is considered by Islam as accountable for his actions from the age of puberty by which time he is considered to be capable of possessing a sufficient understanding of the Islamic teachings and of what is allowed and what is prohibited.

Thus, there is a continuity of values from one generation to the other and rebellion against them is not only a rebellion against parental guidance but against Allah. Islam also requires that Muslims take responsibility for their elderly parents or relatives who may need their care and support.

Islam considers the honour of women sacred and insists that they be treated with dignity and respect. Women are required to guard their modesty and purity. The Islamic community should be free from the exploitation and degradation of women and of any influences which weaken marriage, the family life or people's morals. Islam lays down certain limits to govern the relations between men and women so that their interaction may be characterized by integrity, purity and honesty.

The material development of the community is considered a religious obligation in Islam. However, the aim of all such efforts must be the welfare of the people and the community, keeping in mind the needs of future generations as well.

Charity and feeling of brotherhood which is unique amongst Muslims is intended to distribute wealth equally so that wealth is not concentrated among a few people while the rest live in poverty. Every Muslim is expected to help and to accept responsibility for those living in his community as far as his means allow.

The social life of a Muslim is based upon principles that are designed to secure happiness and prosperity for the individual as well as for the community. There can be no superiority due to class or origin or wealth according to the Quran and the sayings of the Holy Prophet (PBUH). On the contrary, there are many Quranic verses and sayings of the Holy Prophet (PBUH) which remind mankind of the fact that all humanity represents one family springing from the same parents. The relation between the individual and the community is based on this unity of origin. The role of the individual is complementary to that of the community. Between the two, there is solidarity and cooperation. The individual is responsible for the welfare and prosperity of his community. The community life of Islam is marked by cooperation in goodness and piety. The individual is enjoined to play an active part in the establishment of sound social morals by inviting the members of the community to good and forbidding evil. In doing so, not only does he himself avoid evil and does good, but he also helps others to do the same. The individual who feels indifferent to his community is a selfish and irresponsible person.

Thus, the structure of community life in Islam is very lofty, sound and comprehensive. Among the main elements of this structure are sincere love for one's fellow human beings, mercy for the young, respect for elders, comfort and consolation for the distressed, visiting the sick, genuine feelings of brotherhood and solidarity, respect for the rights of other people with regard to life, property and honour, and mutual responsibility between the individual and the community.

Community Life and Principles

The believers are brothers.

Quran: Sura 49: 10 *The Apartments*

None of you can be a believer unless he loves for his brother what he loves for himself.

Tradition of the Prophet Muhammad

Muhammad was both a prophet and a ruler. The first few years of his mission were spent in his native Mecca. It was a flourishing centre of trade, and persecution grew as one person after another joined him in a way of life that threatened the prevailing materialism.

To escape assassination, he and his followers moved to Medina. There for ten years he ruled a community which has always been regarded as the embryo of the Islamic state. He was succeeded by four of his close companions, the "just" caliphs: Abu Bakr, 'Umar, 'Uthman and 'Ali.

The role of the Prophet as a social reformer, and of the first Muslim community in Medina as a social order, are still a stimulus to political thought in the Muslim world.

This section gives one man's answer to the question, "What does the life of the Prophet of Islam mean to us today?": and another man's insight into the relation between an individual and the community to which he belongs.

What Does the Life of the Prophet Mean to Us? Each year the Birthday of the Prophet gives an opportunity for general rejoicing and family parties, and also for fresh assessment of the role of Muhammad and of the relevance of his life and message to contemporary needs. One such assessment was made in the mosque at Zurich, on the occasion of the Prophet's Birthday, 1972, by Dr Ismail Izzet Hassan, Doctor of Music and formerly of Cairo.

Fourteen centuries ago, in a land which was at that time

backward and out-of-the-way, a successful and happily married young businessman retired to Mount Hira near Mecca to pursue quiet meditation. At the age of forty he was shaken to his depths by a vision of the Archangel Jibbrail, and after that he understood that God had chosen him as a prophet.

When he died at the age of sixty-three, his life's work had completely transformed his native land. Not only did a new, pure faith prevail. The whole of existence had become different. The status of the poor and of the slaves, the rights of women, the protection of minors, had been put on a totally new basis; politics and economy were reorganised, democracy brought into public life, all in a manner incredibly audacious for those days.

A hundred years after the quiet meditation of Mount Hira, Islam had spread a new civilisation from Central Asia to the Atlantic. It challenged other civilisations to rid themselves of decadence and barbarism. One single man had initiated a revolution and a renaissance that had spread across the known world. How was this possible?

The Prophet of Islam always maintained that he was only a man like all others, but that he had been called by God to be His messenger and God had revealed His Word, the Holy Quran, to him. The secret of Muhammad's effectiveness lies in his complete obedience to his Lord, in his total self-dedication to the execution of the instructions he received from Him. He did not fulfil his task out of his own strength, but as an instrument of a Higher Power. A *Hadith* (tradition of the Prophet) says: "My Lord has formed my character and formed it well."

No personal ambition drove him on. Again and again it cost him great inner struggles and conquest of self to hold to his mission. Temptations, crushing difficulties, bitter enemies opposed him. Dedicated friends helped him. He experienced successes, some of which could hardly have been expected by human foresight. First he arose to proclaim a faith. Later he acted as law-giver, as head of state, as military commander. He was a husband and a father, as well as a friend and counsellor to many people. He was active in the world - a human, like us - yet always completely for God.

In this manner the Prophet Muhammad fulfilled the true task of Man, the purpose of humanity, and so he is also called "the perfect human" *(al-insanu-l-kamil).* According to Islamic teaching, God has appointed Man as His agent on earth, has made him responsible for executing His Will and commanded him to stand up for Good against Evil. The Prophet taught the Muslims in the new community which grew around him how to live and be effective in this manner.

The Founder of Islam has not only shown a way to salvation in a future life, but has also brought practical answers to the problems of this life. He leaves us not only a theory that is preached, but concrete experience and historical facts.

And we do need concrete facts. In today's situation of crisis the call for renewal, change and progress is heard everywhere. The Prophet Muhammad is a prime example of a personality who understood how to bring about revolutionary progress and build a community of true brotherhood. The deep trouble and distress in today's world may have a simple root cause: that we humans - and, unfortunately, we must also add, we Muslims too - have not properly obeyed God's essential instructions and thereby have missed our main goal. Whoever studies the life of the Holy Prophet of Islam in earnest finds himself confronted with the question: "Are you also ready to follow the highest that God shows you?"

Individual versus Society : There are two sources of social legislation in Islam. One is the Quran, which contains the laws on which life in Muhammad's Medina was built. The second is the *Sunna,* the "custom" of the Prophet: what he said and what he did. His personal life was recorded in detail by his family and friends. Each of his sayings is known as a "tradition", *hadith.*

Dr Hassan Hathout, writer, poet and surgeon, illustrates his theme, "Individual versus Society", by examples drawn from the experience of the Prophet and his immediate successors. These stories are part of the furniture of the mind of every Muslim – told to children as well as studied by lawyers. They are, he says, "formative elements in the Muslim mentality."

In our present-day world, both the capitalist and the communist camps suffer from a conflict between the right of the individual and the right of the community. Whereas capitalist societies protect the individual and his rights, often pushing this so far as to trespass on communal welfare, communist countries almost disregard the individuality of the individual for the sake of society as a whole. The results of both are far from satisfactory. The so-called "free world" boasts of political freedom, and freedom of thought and expression. Yet under the banner of private enterprise such perversions as greed and selfishness have become acceptable. Freedom to become rich has often added to the miseries of the poor. Freedom of thought has often been converted into freedom to pollute thought. As people become more and more material-minded, they become less and less God-guided. The result is an unhappy society.

When we turn to communist societies, the scene is even worse. Individuals are but the bricks used for a building. Society looks like a beehive or an ant colony - very active, very disciplined. In this atmosphere, a sign of individuality is looked upon as political opposition. Since the conception of God is non-existent, it is difficult to imagine any source from which values such as conscience, love, self-restraint and charity can derive. The inevitable result is also an unhappy society.

It seems that both sides have been willing to reconsider their systems. The communist camp has had to permit some kinds of private ownership. In capitalist countries it has been found inevitable to impose certain limitations on the absolute rights of the individual: rising taxation, state ownership, the welfare state, for example. The ideal ratio of individual to communal interest has not yet been found. Against this background, it may be asked how Islam views this question. It is interesting to note that the views here given are not derived from the theories of communism and capitalism. The religion of Islam as conveyed by the Prophet Muhammad is nearly fourteen hundred years old.

The communal and individual viewpoints have been so blended in Islam that it is difficult to separate them. Fraternity and love are the cement which binds various individuals to form a society. In the Prophet's words: "The faithful are to one another like (parts of) a building - each part strengthening the others." And: "The faithful in their mutual compassion, sympathy and love are exemplified by the whole body. If one of its organs falls ill, the remainder will suffer."

These ideas are not merely of moral value. They are legally implemented, for Islam brought with it a legal system. A legal principle introduced by the second caliph 'Umar decrees that if a person dies of starvation, the penalty for wrongful death should be imposed on all the citizens of the town, as though they had killed him.

Duties and Rights : Many of the teachings of Islam bear a dual nature. An individual's right may also be his duty, and as such cannot be surrendered. Islam thus protects vital communal rights by asking the individual to be clear about his own rights.

The right to be educated - recognised by law - is also the duty to leant. The Prophet said: "Seeking knowledge is a duty for every Muslim, man or woman."

The right to express an opinion involves the duty to speak out. If you believe that something is right, you have not the right to remain silent about it. The Prophet teaches: "He who remains silent about truth is a dumb devil." Related to this is the duty to give testimony in court, and this may also be applied to the duty to vote. The Quran says: "Do not withhold testimony, and whoever does so must have a wrongful heart."

The right of political opposition and of honest criticism of authorities is also a duty. The first caliph, Abu Bakr, in his inaugural speech, said: "If I do right, support me. If I do wrong, correct me." The second caliph, 'Umar, asked: "What will you do if I go wrong?" One of those present stood up and shouted: "By God, we will put you right with the edge of our swords." 'Umar replied: "If you do not do so, you will lose God's blessing. And if I do not accept your correction, I shall lose God's blessing."

This attitude is not confined to political issues, but concerns every aspect of life, in accordance with the saying of the Prophet: "Whoever sees wrong being done must change it - with his hand, if he can, or else with his tongue or his heart." Even obedience to government, commendable as it is in Islam, may become a crime if the government disobeys God. The Prophet said: "There is no obedience if it entails disobedience to God." The first caliph declared: "Obey me as long as I obey God. If I disobey Him, then you owe me no obedience."

The right to work is coupled with the prohibition of unemployment, for it is also a duty to work. Beggary is forbidden in Islam. If a person is completely unable to earn a living the community has to provide for him. The Prophet said: "It is better to collect wood and sell it, than to seek charity." 'Umar said: "No one should be lazy, for the sky does not rain gold and silver."

Liberty, Fraternity and Equality : It puzzles the Muslim to find that historians in the West date "Liberty, Fraternity and Equality" from the French Revolution. And never a word about Islam!

Freedom is sacred in Islam. The basic freedom is to free oneself from passions and desires. For instance, the main aim of fasting all through the month of Ramadan (no food or drink from sunrise to sunset) is to train the individual to be able to say "No" to himself whenever it should be said. This type of freedom is so important that the Prophet likened it to winning a major battle. Returning from a battle, he commented, "We are back from the minor *Jihad* (holy war) to the major *Jihad,*" referring to conquering one's moods and passions. And again. "Might is not to be assessed in terms of physical strength. The strong man is he who can control himself when angered."

Freedom from greed is stressed, and freedom from the fear of other mortal men. The Quran is very rich in verses emphasising full regard for God alone. "Fear them not, and fear Me." "Worship God, and let nothing share (worship) with Him." "They fight in the cause of God and they never fear blame from any blamer."

Freedom from the fear of men is much encouraged by the fact that in Islam man's relation with God is a direct one, without intermediary. There are no clergy in Islam and all are equal in the eyes of God. The Quran stresses this direct relationship: "When those who worship Me ask you concerning Me, I am indeed close to them. I listen to the prayer of every suppliant when he calls on Me. Let them also with a will listen to My call, and believe in Me, that they may walk in the right way." Other aspects of freedom were stressed by Islam fourteen centuries ago. Freedom of religious belief is expressed in the Quran. "Let there be no compulsion in religion. Truth stands out clear from error." Personal security and freedom from unlawful arrest are established Islamic rules. The second caliph 'Umar, for example, was unable to prosecute people caught drinking (illegally) in their own houses because he had no right of entry. As to equality before the law, and equality of opportunity, there is only one respect in which one person can be considered better than another, and that is in good deeds and the fear of God. "Dearest to God are those that fear Him most," says the Quran.

Community and the Minorities: An Islamic society is not formed of Muslims only, but of Muslims, Christians and Jews living together under the legal system of Islam.

The legal principle applying to Christians and Jews is: "They have the same rights, and owe the same duties (as we do)."

As a religion, Islam does not put itself in an attitude of conflict towards other God-sent religions. The word *Islam* literally means surrender (to God). God's guidance has been sent through a succession of messengers and prophets who are all revered by a Muslim. Islam is thus the last link of a chain. The Quran reads, "Say (O believers) we believe in God and in that which has been transmitted to us, and in that which has been transmitted to Ibrahim, Ismail, Ishaq, Jacob and the Tribes; and that which was given to Moses and Jesus; and that which was given to the Prophets from their Lord. We do not discriminate between them and to Him do we surrender."

Muslims and the People of the Book (Christians and Jews, who have their own sacred writings) can eat each others' food, unless it is specifically prohibited, like pig and alcohol.

A Muslim can take a Christian or a Jewess for a wife, and she has the right to stick to her faith. The People of the Book have freedom to worship in churches and synagogues, which are to be protected by the Muslim ruler. They are equal under Islamic law. Yet on legal points specified in their own religions concerning their private affairs (marriage, divorce, inheritance, etcetera) the Islamic law does not apply and they are left to settle these matters according to their own religion. This is an example of preserving the rights of minorities.

Equality is not only in the court room. Minorities also share the benefits of the principles of social security and "welfare state" laid down since the earliest days of Islam. One day the caliph 'Umar saw a blind old man - a Jew - begging. The man told him, "I beg so as to be able to pay the tribute." (The tribute was a tax imposed on non-Muslims, who were exempted from military service.) 'Umar took him by the hand to his own house and gave him what he needed. He sent orders to his treasurer: "Look after people like him. It would not be fair to take from him when he is young and neglect him when he is old." He decreed that old age should be a reason for exemption from the tribute, as well as illness and disablement. On his way to Damascus, 'Umar once encountered a group of Christian lepers, and ordered food and money to be given them.

The Right of Ownership – Private Property : Private ownership in Islam is a concept radically different from that of either communism or capitalism.

In Islam total ownership is God's.

The right of ownership that has been bestowed on us is secondary to this.

"To God belongeth whatever is in the heavens and the earth." "Give them something yourselves out of the means which God has given you."

The owner of property should realise that he is God's agent. In his capacity as owner, he must behave in accordance with the ways of God.

Indeed, God's ownership extends to the owner himself. Islam pervades all aspects of life, all the time. In the eyes of a Muslim, whatever he does or thinks, while at work or at leisure, be it private or public, personal or social, concealed or revealed, popular or unpopular, is a matter of the relationship between God and himself.

Private ownership in Islam entails a God-owned owner, given the right to own a God-owned property and to exploit it fully in the ways of God. This right of ownership, once assumed, is very strongly protected in Islam. But in its respect for private ownership. Islam does not foster greed or materialism. These are tempered by conscience, and by legal safeguards. For instance, it was conscience, and that ever-vivid mutual relation with God, that induced the third caliph 'Uthman to give away a caravan full of foodstuffs free, rejecting an offer to sell it at tenfold price, when Medina was struck by famine.

The right of ownership is the rule. Limitations on it are the exception (contrary to communist theory). Ownership in Islam is a social function, and is interpreted in Islamic law as aiming at the welfare of the community. Where the actions of the owner conflict with this welfare he can be restrained: for instance, in cases of mental incapacity, hoarding, abuse of others' rights, injury to the community (such as monopoly), or neglect of the needs of the poor.

A prerequisite of enjoying the right of ownership is recognition of the rights of the needy. The Prophet was heard to say: "He cannot be a believer. He cannot be a believer. He cannot be a believer." When asked "Who?", the Prophet answered: "He who sleeps the night with a full stomach, while his neighbour is hungry." Private ownership is so sacred that in ordinary circumstances a thief might have his hand amputated: but if he proves needy the punishment is suspended. It is the duty of the governor to fulfil this need for food. If the alms tax *(zakat)* together with money given for charity do not suffice, the governor must impose heavier taxes on those better off, in favour of the needy.

In times of war or famine resources are to be shared. In a year of famine, 'Umar suggested that each household should double the number of people they were feeding, "for people will not perish of half-empty stomachs."

No individual right or freedom can be regarded in isolation. The Prophet told this story. A group of men shared a ship - some on the upper deck, some on the lower. Whenever they wanted water, those below had to come up.

So they thought it might be a good idea to cut a hole in their part of the vessel so as not to bother the ones above. If those on deck allowed them to do this, the ship would sink and all would be drowned. If they prevented them, all would survive. Whole nations today are faced with similar dilemmas.

The State: Authority and Responsibility : Islam couples authority with responsibility, as in our day the welfare state sets out to do.

The fourth caliph 'Ali wrote instructions to his viceroy in Egypt: "Fear God in regard to the lowest class in society, who are helpless, poor and miserable. You are responsible to God, for He entrusted them to you. The distant should receive as much as those who are near. Give each his due, and if you think this is beneath your dignity, do not make excuses. You will not be forgiven if you ignore minor matters to concentrate on those which seem important. Look into the affairs of those who are so weak that they cannot reach you. Appoint Godfearing and humble persons to bring their affairs before you. Give attention to the helpless orphans and the young who would never beg. The burden of responsibility on a viceroy is indeed a heavy one."

The caliph Umar ibn Abd el-Aziz said: "If a mule stumbles in Iraq (far away in the empire) I shall find myself responsible to God for it on the day of judgment: why had I not paved the road properly?" There are innumerable examples of this coupling of authority with responsibility. As the Prophet said: "Every one of you is a shepherd and is responsible for his flock. The governor is a shepherd - so is the man with a family, the woman in her household, the servant with his master's money. All these are shepherds, responsible for the flock entrusted to them."

This is a passing glimpse of Islam, And it has much to offer to our restless world. But it seems to be an abandoned treasure, abandoned by those who bear its name. No wonder they are so different from the glory I describe, And unless they go back to it again, they will remain Lost in bewilderment, at the rear of Humanity's procession. For it is the remedy, the light and the guidance from God For them - and for the world.

Modesty in Community

Modesty plays a vital role in character building. It restrains a man from behaving in an undesirable manner. It also acts as a shield against immoralities. It holds the key to piety. It is related by Zaid bin Talha that the Holy Prophet (PBUH) said:

> "Every religion has a distinctive quality and the distinctive quality of Islam is modesty."

This Hadith shows that in every faith, some particular aspect of moral behaviour receives importance and an extraordinary emphasis is laid on it; in Islam modesty is of fundamental significance as the Holy Prophet (PBUH) said:

> "Modesty is a part of faith."

The word, modesty, in common use, signifies that a man should abstain from indecent acts. However, in the terminology of the Quran and the *Hadith,* it is used in a wider sense. In Islam, it stands for a feeling which is intolerant of everything that is not desirable or produces disgust in a person. Faith and modesty are so closely related to each other that either both will be present in an individual or community or none of the two would be present. It is related by Abdullah bin Umar that the Prophet of Allah said:

> "Modesty and faith exist together and when one of them goes out, the other too goes out,"

The rule of modesty is prescribed for both men and women that is, to lower their gaze and not stare at each other as the Quran says:

> "Say to the believing men that they should lower their gaze and guard their modesty." (24: 30)
>
> "And say to the believing women that they should lower their gaze and guard their modesty. " (24: 31)

Modesty is not to be observed only in relation to human beings. The Almighty Creator comes first. No one can be more unfortunate than the person who, knowing that Allah sees and hears all that he does and speaks, feels no shame in saying dirty and deplorable things in His presence. If the sense of modesty is alive and active in a person, his life will not only be clean in the sight of his fellow beings but also in the eyes of Allah. The primary requirement of modesty is that a person should feel disgusted at everything that is displeasing to Allah. Therefore, he should abstain from it.

It is related in *Tirmidhi* that once the Holy Prophet (PBUH) observed while speaking to his Companions:

> "Practice modesty towards Allah as it ought to be practiced towards Him. "

The proper way of observing modesty towards Allah is that you take care of the head and all the ideas and notions that are contained in it, and you take care of the belly and all that is contained in it (i.e., protect the mind against evil thoughts and the stomach against unlawful food).

Teachings on Economy

Islam provides guidance to its followers in all phases and activities of life. Its teachings with regard to economics are mentioned in several passages of the Holy Quran. Islam encourages sharing and a just distribution of wealth.

> "To those weak of understanding make not over your property, which Allah hath made a means of support for you, but feed and clothe them therewith, and speak to them word of kindness and justice." (4:5)

In another place Quran says:

> "Seek with the (wealth) which Allah has bestowed on thee, the home of the hereafter, nor forget thy portion in this world: but do thou good." (28:77)

The Quran reminds us in Surah Baqara:

> " There are men who say: "Our Lord give us (thy bounties) in this world!" But they will have no portion in the Hereafter. And there are men who say "Our Lord give us good in this world and good in the Hereafter and defend us from the torment of fire" To these will be allotted what they have earned;"
>
> (2:200-202)

In an Islamic society adequate fulfilment of basic material needs is as necessary for human welfare as spiritual uplift. Therefore, while arranging for the spiritual guidance of men through prophets, Allah has also provided all necessary resources for his material well-being. The individual is required to fulfil his material needs through his own efforts. Islam condemns begging and laziness and places great stress on hard work. The Prophet (PBUH) is reported to have said:

> "Beg not anything from people,"

and also:

> "A man has not earned a better income than that which is from his own labour."

Hadrat Umar once said: "Seek of the bounty of Allah and be not a burden on others."

The economic life in Islam therefore is based upon Divine instructions. Earning one's livelihood through labour is not only a duty but a great virtue as well. Dependence of any able person on someone else for a livelihood is a sin and disgraceful humility. All kinds of work and hard labour is respected in an Islamic society. The Holy Prophet (PBUH) is reported to have said that it was far better for a person to take his rope, cut wood, pile it up and sell it in order to eat and give charity than to beg for sustenance from others. According to Islam, the status of honest hard working men cannot be lowered because of the kind of work they do for a living. The economic system of Islam is based upon a comprehensive system of morals and principles. A person employed by another or by a company has the moral responsibility to do his work efficiently and honesty. The Holy Prophet (PBUH) said that if any of you undertakes to do any work, Allah loves to see him do it well and with efficiency. Upon the completion of work, the worker is entitled to a fair wage. Failure by the employer to pay just wages or to cut it down is a punishable act, according to the Law of Allah.

Honest trade is permitted and blessed by Allah. This may be carried out through individuals, companies or agencies. But all business deals should be conducted with honesty. Cheating, hiding defects of goods and exploiting the needs of customers are all sinful acts and punishable by the Islamic law. All methods of earning a living have to be honest, anybody brought up on unlawful provisions, according to the Holy Prophet (PBUH) will be a fuel for the fire of Hell. Islam forbids usury or charging interest in return for lending money to the needy. This is to show man that he rightfully owns only what he works for and that any exploitation of other people's needs is immoral and inhuman and against the teachings of Islam. There are several traditions of the Holy Prophet (PBUH) excluding the cheaters, exploiters and dishonest businessmen from the band of true Muslims.

It is essentially the responsibility of the individual to support his family by earning an honest income. However it may not always be possible. In all societies there are some people who cannot achieve that goal and so become dependent upon the state or on others. It then becomes the responsibility of the Islamic State to play a positive role in guiding and regulating the economy to ensure a respectable standard of living for all the people who are unable to take care of their own needs and require assistance. The Holy Prophet (PBUH) clearly declared:

> "He whom Allah has made an administrator over the affairs of Muslims but remains indifferent to their

> needs and poverty, Allah will also be indifferent to his needs and poverty."

In order to fulfil this obligation, the Islamic state needs financial resources. The means of income for the Islamic state are:

Zakat: Islam has instituted a social security system with religious sanctity. It is a part of the religious obligations of a Muslim to pay Zakat at a prescribed rate. The significance of the institution of Zakat in Islam is so great that whenever the Quran speaks of the obligation, to establish prayers, it also simultaneously stresses the obligation of Muslims to pay Zakat. The Holy Prophet (PBUH) went so far as to say that whoever offers prayers but does not pay Zakat, his prayer are in vain.

The purpose of the establishment of the institution of Zakat is to setup up a society which is like a single family, where wealth is justly distributed where the essential needs of all deserving individuals are met through mutual help with planning and organization by the state. There is a general consensus among jurists that collection and distribution of Zakat is essentially the duty of the Islamic state. This was the practice during the day of the Holy Prophet (PBUH) and the first two khalifas. However Hadrat Uthman, the third khalifa, allowed the payment of Zakat directly to the needy.

Income from Natural Resources: Natural resources have been provided by Allah for the welfare of all people, therefore, the monetary benefit derived from these resources should be distributed to all people, and not to any particular group or individual.

Taxation: The right of the Islamic State to raise funds through taxes is defended on the basis of the Holy Prophet's (PBUH) saying:

> "In your wealth there are also obligations beyond Zakat."

Most jurists have upheld the right of the state to levy taxes, because if these funds benefit the people themselves, it is their obligation to bear the cost. However, only a just tax system has to be appiied in harmony with the spirit of Islam. The khalifas are reported to have stressed that taxes should be collected with justice and kindness, that they should not be beyond the ability of the people to bear, and should not deprive the people of the basic necessities of life.

Borrowing: If total revenue from all the above mentioned sources is not sufficient, the Islamic state would stand in need of borrowing. In this case because of the Islamic injunction against interest, the borrowing would need to be free from interest. Although man is encouraged to work, is free to engage in business and trade, is entitled to earn and possess wealth and has the authority to invest and spend, he is guided by principles which save him from going astray. There are certain rules of expenditure to be followed. God enjoins upon man to fulfil his financial obligations towards his fellowmen and to be moderate in his spending.

The Quran says:

> "And render to the kindred their due rights, as (also) to those in want, and to the wayfarer: But squander not your wealth in the manner of a spendthrift. Make not thy hand tied (like a niggard's) to thy neck, nor stretch it forth to its utmost reach, so that thou become blameworthy and destitute. (17:26, 29)

The main purpose of the Islamic laws that deal with economic and commercial matters is to secure the rights of the individual, to maintain the solidarity of the society, to encourage morality in the world of trade and to enforce the law of Allah in business as well. It is logical that Islam should be concerned with such aspects as these, because it is not merely a spiritual formula but a complete system of life.

10

Family in Islam

Offsprings and Parents

Show kindness to parents ...
Lower to them the wing of humility
out of tenderness.

Quran Sura 17: 23-14 *The Israelites*

***Parents and Children in the Quran*:** Profound issues of love and obedience often arise between parents and children. An Indian mother and daughter discussed their mutual duties, and a subsequent study of what the Quran has to say on the subject revealed an emphasis somewhat different from what they expected. To parents, the utmost kindness is due: and to God, obedience.

Four well-known passages from the Quran are quoted here, followed by some notes from the commentary of Yusuf Ali:

> Thy Lord commanded, "Worship none but Him, and show kindness to parents. If one or both of them attain old age with thee, never say unto them any word expressive of disgust nor reproach them, but address them with excellent speech. And lower to them the wing of humility out of tenderness. And say,

'My Lord have mercy on them even as they nourished me in my childhood.'"

Quran: Sura 17: 23—24 *The Israelites*

We enjoined on man kindness to his parents. But if they strive to make thee associate with Me that of which thou hast no knowledge, then obey them not. Unto Me is your return, and I shall inform you of what you did. Quran: Sura 29: 8 *The Spider*

We have enjoined on man concerning his parents - his mother bears him in weakness and his weaning takes two years — "Give thanks to Me and to thy parents. Unto Me is the final return." ... And if they contend with thee to make thee set up equals with Me concerning which thou hast no knowledge, obey them not. Be a kind companion to them in all worldly affairs: and in spiritual matters follow the way of him who turns to Me. Then unto Me will be your return and I will inform you of what you used to do.

Quran: Sura 31: 14-15 *Luqman*

We have enjoined on man to be good to his parents. His mother bears him in pain and brings him forth in pain ... When he comes to maturity he says, "My Lord, make me grateful for Thy favour which Thou hast bestowed upon me and my parents, that I may do such good works as please Thee. And make my seed righteous for me. I do turn to Thee, and truly I am of those who submit to Thee." ... But the one who says to his parents, "Fie on you both! God's promise ... is nothing but tales of the ancients," ... will be utterly lost. Quran: Sura 46: 15-18 *The Sandhills*

In his notes on the passages in the Quran dealing with parents and children, Abdullah Yusuf Ali makes the following comments:

> In matters of faith and worship even parents have no right to force their children ... Children and parents must all remember that they have to go before God's tribunal, and answer each for his own deeds. In cases where one set of people have lawful authority over another set of people (as in the case of parents and children), and the two differ on important matters like mat of Faith, the latter are justified in rejecting authority: the apparent conflict will be solved when the whole truth is revealed to all eyes in the final judgment.

Where the duty to man conflicts with the duty to God, it means that there is something wrong with the human will, and we should obey God rather than man. But even here, it does not mean that we should be arrogant or insolent. To parents and those in authority, we must be kind, considerate and courteous, even when they command things which we should not do and therefore disobedience becomes our highest duty...

In any apparent conflict of duties our standards should be God's Will, as declared to us by His command. That is the way of those who love God: and their motives in disobedience to parents or human authority, where disobedience is necessary by God's law, is not self-willed rebellion or defiance, but love of God, which means the true love of man in the highest sense of the word. And the reason we should give is: "Bom you and I have to return to God; therefore not only must I follow God's Will, but you must command nothing against God's Will."

These conflicts may appear to us strange and puzzling in this life. But in God's presence we shall see their real meaning and significance. It may be that was one way in which our true mettle could be tested: for it is not easy to disobey and love man at the same time.

Told to the Children: Teaching children religion is reckoned as one of the most important aspects of family life. This is primarily the responsibility of the parents. Children are taught to pray by the time they are seven, often by older brothers and sisters. Much of the teaching comes in story form: tales of brave and generous men and women who did great things for their fellow men, or about rich and poor people who are unequal in possessions and yet are equal before God.

"Muslim women have a great responsibility for passing on tradition and culture. So it is important to give the children the right examples. Prophet Muhammad's life is rich in this way," said one mother. It may be one of the older members of the household - grandmother or even great-grandmother - whose story-telling is unforgettable.

The Prophet's life - his boyhood as an orphan, his honesty in business, his calling, his escapes, his struggles as well as his victories is told and retold, as are the lives of other prophets. "After the Prophet," said another mother, "my favourite characters are Virgin Mary and Caliph 'Umar. Girls can learn much from Virgin Mary. They can be pure and virgin till they are married - dedicated in a way as she was."

'Umar, the second successor to Muhammad, is especially popular. He was not only a warrior, but a father to his people. He used to move about Medina at night, to find out how his poorer subjects were living. One of many tales is of his hearing the cry of a hungry child, and himself fetching and cooking food for the family. His conversion—from violent opposition to Muhammad — was a dramatic turning point in the early growth of Islam. The story is told here from the Children's Page of *The Islamic Review and Arab Affairs* (Working, September 1967). It is part of a series on the life of Muhammad, written by Mrs Olive Toto.

Conversion of Umar : Please remember, all you little girls who will grow up to be women, that Muhammad's first believer was a woman, Khadijah his wife ...

His next believers were 'Ali and a little slave boy Zayd, who were about twelve or fourteen years old. Maybe they were young, but they were very serious boys and knew what they believed to be right! Abu Bakr, an old and trusted friend, joined Muhammad. Other friends also came forward. A small band of fifty people joined Muhammad in his belief.

Now a change came about. The citizens of Mecca turned against Muhammad and his followers were persecuted. After three years an open opposition was organised and acts of violence started. A youth leading prayer was attacked and he fought back. Islam does not say turn the other cheek. It is common sense that one has to defend oneself.

In the fourth year of his mission, Muhammad was given a friend's house to hold meetings for people who wanted to know about God. The name of this friend was Arqam ...

There was a man called 'Umar. He thought about things and decided to have his peace of mind by killing Muhammad, and then his followers would forget him. So he took his sword in his hand and went to Muhammad's house to kill him. 'Umar was a man of great influence in Mecca. He did not know that his sister Fatima and her husband had become Muslims. On his way to the Prophet's house with his sword in his hand he met a man who had recently embraced Islam. Seeing the sword the man said, "Where are you going?" 'Umar said, "To kill Muhammad." "Oh," said the man, "don't you know that even your sister and your brother-in-law have embraced Muhammad's religion?"

'Umar was furious: he decided his relations must die first and then Muhammad. On reaching the house he heard his relatives reading verses that had been revealed to Muhammad from God. 'Umar was so furious that he beat his brother-in-law very badly. 'Umar's sister was hurt whilst trying to stop the fight. 'Umar snatched away these verses and started to read them. One could have heard a pin drop, so engrossed was

'Umar. His rage had calmed down, and his breathing was once more like a human being's. Gradually, as he was reading the words, peace came into his heart. He was reading something that calmed his soul with its truth and beauty. It had set him thinking.

On seeing this altered man, the followers talked to him, and soon the harsh and proud 'Umar joined Islam.

'Umar then went to the house of Arqam, where Muhammad met him at the door. 'Umar said, "O Prophet of God! I declare my faith in God and believe in His Prophet." Things became much easier with 'Umar on Muhammad's side.

Mary and Jesus : Of all the women honoured in the Quran, Mary mother of Jesus stands highest. Her own family upbringing is recounted in the third sura of the Quran, which is named after her father 'Imran. The visit of the angel, and the birth of Jesus, are told more than once. Here is the story as it is given in the chapter named after Mary:

> In the name of God, the Merciful, the Compassionate.
> And make mention of Mary in the Scripture, when she had withdrawn from her people to a chamber looking East,
> And had chosen seclusion from them. Then We sent unto her Our spirit and it assumed for her the likeness of a perfect man.
> She said: Lo! I seek refuge in the Beneficent One from thee, if thou art God-fearing.
> He said: I am only a messenger of thy Lord, that I may bestow on thee a faultless son.
> She said: How can I have a son when no mortal hath touched me, neither have I been unchaste?
> He said: So (it will be). Thy Lord saith: It is easy for Me and (it will be) that We may make of him a revelation for mankind and a mercy from Us, and it is a thing ordained.

And she conceived him, and she withdrew with him
to a far place.
And the pangs of childbirth drove her unto the trunk
of the palm tree.
She said: Oh, would that I had died ere this, and had
become a thing of naught, forgotten!
Then (one) cried unto her from below her, saying:
Grieve not!
Thy Lord hath placed a rivulet beneath thee,
And shake the trunk of the palm tree toward thee,
thou wilt cause ripe dates to fall upon thee.

So eat and drink and be consoled. And if thou meetest any mortal, say:

Lo! I have vowed a fast unto the Beneficent, and may
not speak this day to any mortal.
Then she brought him to her own folk, carrying him.
They said: O Mary! Thou hast come with an amazing
thing.
Oh sister of Aaron! Thy father was not a wicked man
nor was thy mother a harlot.
Then she pointed to him. They said: How can we talk
to one who is in the cradle, a young boy?
He spake: Lo! I am the slave of Allah. He hath given
me the Scripture and hath appointed me a Prophet,
And hath made me blessed wheresoever I may be,
and hath enjoined upon me prayer and almsgiving so
long as I remain alive,
And (hath made me) dutiful toward her who bore
me, and hath not made me arrogant, unblest.
Peace be upon me the day I was born, and the day
I die, and the day I shall be raised alive!
Such was Jesus, son of Mary.

Quran: Sura 19: 16-34 *Mary*

Life with Family Members

> The family is a divinely-inspired institution that came into existence with the creation of man. The human race is a product of this institution and not the other way round. Khurshid Ahmad

Woman must be regarded as equal to man and must shed the remaining shackles that impede her from taking a constructive part in life.

> The family is the primary cell in society, and as such it must be afforded every protection in the national interest. Abdul Moghny Said

Of all the questions that exercise the minds of Muslims, those connected with family life are the most sensitive. Muslims are proud of their traditions, and wish to maintain them. Western culture with its permissive standards has an impact on their sons and daughters which they see as a threat to their whole way of life. Advance in technology is regarded as essential: but there is widespread fear of the retrogression in character that often seems to accompany it.

Certain practices are an essential part of religion.. Others are a matter of custom, and can be set aside. Every Muslim community is in process of some degree of adjustment in regard to the position of women, to marriage customs and to relations between the generations.

These dilemmas are reflected in what Muslims say about their family life. But in comparison with the ever-increasing rate of marital breakdown in the Western world they understandably feel that they have something of value not only to preserve, but to offer. Mr Khurshid Ahmad, Chairman of the Islamic Foundation, Leicester, writing on "Family Life in Islam", says, "It is the family that provides the most congenial climate for the development and fulfilment of human personality." Marriage and the family in Islam should be studied in the context of the scheme of life Islam wants to establish. "We refuse to accept the value-neutral approach that willy-nilly fashions the life and perspectives of man in the secular culture of the West today. We think the disintegration of the family in the West is, in part, a result of confusion about the place and the role of the family in society and about the purpose of life itself."

About a third of the legal injunctions in the Quran deal with family matters, and with the network of rights and obligations that provide the basis for family life. These aim to produce the attitudes and behaviour patterns that Islam wants to foster in society. The Muslim family is an extended family, normally with three or four generations within its circle. Marriage in Islam is not a temporary union and is meant to last for life. Dissolution of marriage is, however, permitted if it has irretrievably broken down: but before divorce the law demands an attempt at reconciliation by the families concerned. "The natural prevalence of monogamy as the normal type of sexual relationship" is more and more the practice in Muslim countries. Nevertheless, a limited polygamy is seen as a realistic need in certain circumstances: and indeed as preferable to the "concealed polygamy" without responsibility, in some ways tolerated in Western society. "Islam is a practical religion and is meant for the guidance of human beings made of flesh and bones." The ideal is a loving, stable family in which the best of human nature can flower.

An Arab Family : A Muslim lawyer, Mr Jamil Nasir, head of an Arab family in Jerusalem, made the following observations on the social traditions of Arab family life. In 1966, his daughter invited me to spend an evening in her home. She was then Vice-Principal of a Teacher Training College, and had just returned from a course in "counselling" in the United States. She is one of ten children, who include two medical doctors and a Ph.D. Three of her sisters were living at home: two of them principals of schools, and the youngest a teacher. Present also was an Irish sister-in-law, whose doctor husband had refused better paid posts so as to continue to work in Jerusalem.

Awkward questions arise as one sits in such homes. "What is happening to your life in America, in Britain?" "What about these attacks on old people for their money?" "Why do you let young people treat your lovely parks as bedrooms?" On this particular evening, the conversation turned on a tragic event. In London, the sons of a mutual friend had been attacked in the street. One had lost an eye and was in a serious condition.

My friend's father, the lawyer, said: "How can these things happen in a civilised country? Here, the police find and punish thieves within a few days. In your cities, I hear, they cannot find them. Our young men feel responsible to their families. They are more afraid of what the family would do or say than they would be of the police."

I asked him to tell me more about the ties which bind Arab families, and which, he said, still implant a sense of privilege and responsibility in each member, young and old. He said:

> Arab social life is based on ancient traditions, and on the teaching of the Quran. The individual is responsible to the family, and the family to the tribe or community. If an individual commits wrong, the family and community will be held responsible: and if wrong is done to an individual his family and community automatically support him.

Thus an individual is very cautious in his dealings and behaviour, because he will be subject to reprimand by his relatives and his community, all of whom he will have involved by his wrongdoing. The reputation of the individual man or woman reflects on his family and community, and they have to pay any fine he incurs.

From an early age, children are taught not to cause any

inconvenience to parents and relatives by bad behaviour. They grow up in this spirit, and there is therefore hardly any juvenile crime, theft or injury committed. They learn to respect older people, to help their neighbours and to be generous to guests. Thus we find a high level of security in Arab countries.

When a man marries, he remains closely connected with his father and mother, sisters and grandparents. Together they share happiness and sorrow, and meet the events and accidents of life, and take the lawful and customary procedures if their rights are infringed. If necessary, all the relatives will act together. Marriage and funeral expenses are corporate responsibilities.

Girls are treated equally with boys, and every man is obliged to protect his women relatives as far back as the connections of the "fourth grandfather". A woman after marriage retains her father's family name, rather than taking that of her husband, as an indication that her father is responsible for her all her life. Her parents must visit her during every big holiday season, and take her a present. Thus she feels the strength and protection of her male relatives. This encourages her, and if she gets into difficulties it helps to deter her from wrongdoing.

There are customary procedures to be followed, as well as legal ones, if something goes wrong between families. For example, news came that my son had been involved in a car accident in Amman. While he was driving, a boy was knocked down. The police completely exonerated the driver, but this was not the point as far as the family was concerned. We went straight to Amman, found three respected men of standing, and sent them to the boy's family to arrange a week's truce between the families. (Among the Bedouin, if someone is killed and such a truce is not quickly settled, a life will be taken to restore the family honour.) The boy was lying in hospital with concussion. After a week, the truce was renewed for two months. The boy was unconscious for fifteen days. If he had died, we would have had to pay the sum enjoined by the Prophet Muhammad to be paid for an accidental death, now reckoned as £350. Every one of our family — "until the fourth grandfather" and the cousins connected in this degree - would have been liable to contribute. But, thank God, the boy recovered. When the two months were over, there was a ceremony. A sheep was killed and many members of both families were present at the feast. "Thank God, the boy is well," we said. "We forgive you and realise it was an accident," they said. Peace was restored, and documents signed to say so.

The father is responsible for his sons and his daughters. If a girl does something wrong with a man, the family honour is at stake. There are cases when the brother kills her, or kills the man who wronged her. The law takes into consideration "defence of life, property and honour," and a lenient sentence may be given: three years' or seven years' imprisonment, rather than hanging.

Hospitality is another side of Arab tradition. There still exists the custom among Arab chiefs of generously welcoming a guest for three days before asking him his name and the purpose of his visit. Then he is offered any help he needs.

> Mutual assistance and cooperation; help for the poor and needy; respect for others' faith and rights as well as safeguarding one's own; obedience to law and custom; the inclination to treat others as one wishes others to treat oneself: all these are part of the Arab attitude and way of life. Jamil Nasir, Jerusalem'

Position of Women : The traditional place of women in Islam is a high one. Modern writers all stress the improvements the Prophet Muhammad brought about in their position and rights. Undue restrictions prevalent at certain periods of history have been, it is said, a matter of social custom, not of religion itself.

Equal and Different **:** According to the Quran, women are equal to men as human beings - different in their role. In the presence of their Creator, their basic duties are the same. Daily prayer, fasting and pilgrimage are incumbent on them. They are alike in their hopes of paradise and certainty of judgment.

> Men who surrender unto Allah,
> And women who surrender,
> and men who believe,
> And women who believe,
> And men who speak the truth,
> And women who speak the truth,
> And men who persevere in righteousness,
> And women who persevere,
> And men who are humble,
> And women who are humble,
> And men who give alms,
> And women who give alms,
> And men who fast,
> And women who fast,
> And men who guard their modesty,
> And women who guard their modesty,
> And men who make mention of Allah much,
> And women who make mention of Him,
> Allah hath prepared for them forgiveness and a vast reward. Quran: Sura 33:35 The Clans
>
> If any do deeds of righteousness - be they male or female - and have faith, they will enter paradise.
> Quran: Sura 4:124 Women

Women have the right to own property, and to inherit it, and to run their own businesses. It is often pointed out that these measures of equality were only won in western society in the Nineteenth Century, whereas they have existed in Muslim law since the time of the Prophet. At the same time, men have duties towards the women of the family. A wife must be maintained by her husband, even if she has means of her own. This is used to explain the inequality of inheritance — a man receives a larger share of a family legacy than does a woman.

Women in History : Women played an important part in the early days of the Prophet's mission and the coming of Islam. His wife Khadijah - a business woman in her own right- was the first to support him in his calling. In their home in Mecca their daughter Fatima and her sisters grew up. After Khadija's death, and his move to Medina, much of our knowledge of what he said and what he did is owed to the loving insight and acute perception of his young wife Aishah. These three names are very often given to Muslim girls.

In seeking their role in society, today's Fatimas, Khadijahs and Aishah's have the example of these early pioneers of Islam, and also of many others who played their part later in the flowerings of Islamic life and civilisation. In every age some outstanding women make their mark.

Many saintly women are recorded, among them Rabia al-Adawiyya, whose life of poverty in Basra challenged the rich and powerful in the early days of the Abbasid empire. The great philosopher and mystic Al-Ghazzali quoted what he learned from her about the love of God, and her prayers still sift the motives of those who use them.

Oh my Lord ! the stars are shining and the eyes of men are closed and every lover is alone with his beloved, and here I am alone with Thee.

Oh God ! if I worship Thee for fear of hell, burn me in hell, If I worship Thee in hope of Paradise, exclude me from paradise, But if I worship Thee for Thine own sake grudge me not Thine everlasting beauty.

In contrast with Arabia's life of dedication in poverty, many women have been honoured for the use they made of their wealth. One of the most famous of these a generation after Rabia was Zubaida, wife and cousin of the caliph Harun al-Rashid. She is still remembered with gratitude by pilgrims to Mecca for the beneficence of her provision of water in the city and along the road from Iraq.

Most women who have wielded influence in Muslim society have done so through their sons. The position of the mother in the family is central, and an often-quoted saying of the Prophet is, "Heaven lies at the feet of a mother."

Education for Women : The present resurgence of Islam was already gathering momentum at the beginning of this century. Leading thinkers - the Egyptian Muhammad Abdo and the Indian Amir Ali among them - called for the restoration to women of rights given to them in the Quran but often ignored in practice. During the Ottoman period women's education had been almost totally neglected, and in the early 1900's experiments in the education of girls began simultaneously in different parts of the Muslim world. Today, such education is given high priority by the governments of Muslim countries, including Saudi Arabia. Women are graduating from scores of universities, and there is a growing body of skilled professional women: doctors, nurses, teachers, lawyers, also architects and engineers. There are also widespread literacy programmes, reaching the country women.

Freedom for Service : Many tensions arise in the effort to give maximum service to the community without disrupting the pattern of family life and without losing prized traditions and identity. To understand these tensions it is necessary to take into account the revulsion against elements of decadence in western society. The idea that "progress" lies in imitation of the West is rightly rejected. The excesses of some upholders of "liberation" for women have made it more difficult for women in Muslim countries to pursue their own path towards fuller responsibility. To find the way to this, without eroding the importance of motherhood, or of loyalty to Islam, is the challenge this generation is facing.

Two quotations show these concerns from very different points of view. The first comes from a woman who has held cabinet office in Jordan, the second from a Shite scholar in Iran.

Mrs Inam Mufti was appointed Minister for Social Affairs in Jordan in January 1980. She was formerly Principal of the UNRWA Women's Vocational College, Ramallah, in the West Bank. She has been a pioneer of education in many forms, and in the 1940's was herself one of the first girls to go to college from her home town in Safad, in Northern Palestine. She is concerned with what women will bring with them into public life, with questions of values as well as of skills. Women, she thinks, can bring into every branch of a nation's work a sense of service and a care for individuals. As they do so, they will become pace-setters for standards of excellence and integrity.

We want to find a balanced formula for partnership which takes into consideration all the responsibilities of women. The role of the mother in the community must never be underestimated. But apart from women with young children, there are many who do not find full employment and expression in their homes. Here is a potential that the nation cannot afford to neglect.

Certain old attitudes and prejudices must change, and they are changing. In the past, these have limited the activities of women, and their freedom of expression. But there is nothing in the true tradition of Islam to hold women back. The Quran says that every man and woman must search for knowledge, and also tells them to engage in honest work.

We need to move with caution so as not to lose the family life we prize. We do not want to find ourselves neglecting either our children or our old people. There is a give and take between the generations, a mutual interplay of service and responsibility, which we must maintain. The preparation of women citizens must be personal, as well as vocational. They bring up the men, and character building for the future is their most vital role.

Sayid Mujtaba Musawi Lari is the son and grandson of respected Shite scholars in Iran. His grandfather was one of those instrumental in bringing into being the Iranian constitution of 1906. He himself studied theology for ten years in the city of Qum, an ancient centre of religious training not far from Tehran. He then spent some time in Germany for health reasons. His shrewd observations and wide reading during this period of ill health formed the basis of a book *Western Civilisation through Muslim Eyes.*

He portrays the inconsistencies, the absurdities, alongside the arrogance, which he finds in western society. The workless, the hungry, the lonely old and the delinquent young, the pampered dogs and battered wives, for him mirror the callousness of a society which appears to have lost its heart and soul. If the picture is overdrawn, it is nevertheless a genuine expression of views widely held. It makes it understandable that western strictures on other societies are not better received.

To his picture of the West he adds his own reflections on Islam's contribution to the solution of social problems. In a chapter on the family he speaks of marriage, and the importance of "steering the life-force into its God-given legitimate channels where peace of mind and calm of conscience accompany the happiness of a shared life."

Modern disrespect for the bond of marriage is due to the neglect of this high conception of wedlock. It has been degraded by a mass of petty dreams and twisted imaginations. Men's thinking about marriage was in ruins before their families began to fall apart.

On the position of women Sayid Musawi Lari writes:

> The West's vociferous partisans of Women's Lib have no idea of the revolutionary leap forward in women's position which Islam brought about. Islam regards both man and woman as created by God to rise to the full stature of the perfect human. Each is a precious soul. They are complementary to each other. Many women possess such personal excellence and intelligence that they attain great heights of true humanity and happiness. Many men, alas, fall to the lowest depths because they flout reason and abandon themselves to their passions.

A woman, he says, tackled the formidable caliph 'Umar on a legal point in public. 'Umar could not deny the accusation and said, "It was a man who erred and a woman who uttered the truth." He contrasts the property rights of the Muslim woman with the legal position of women in Europe until recent years, quoting the Sura of Women (4: 33) "Whatsoever a man earns is his own. Whatsoever a woman earns is her own." He continues:

> It is true that today far too many women are condemned in the East to an unsatisfactory way of life. But this is not due to Islam's regulations. It is due to the neglect of religious precept in political, social and financial institutions.

Poverty is one important reason for the bad conditions under which Eastern women have to live. A few are too rich; but the majority far too poor, victims of hunger and wretchedness. The resultant weakness has deprived people of the strength to rise up and insist on a change in their environment, for the sake of their families and their children. Nor have the women the power in such a situation to make use of their legal rights and to take men to court for the violence and tyranny of their behaviour. Women fear the difficulties of having to live without a male companion in a man's world.

Economic needs cause a diminution in morals and in human affections. Violence and injustice replace moral values.

Although Islamic lands are amongst the worst sufferers from these modern disasters, it is not Islam itself, but the deliberate neglect and abandonment of Islamic principles by Muslims and their leaders which has brought these tragedies upon us. For Islam is the very acme of the counterforces to poverty and injustice, and insists that wealth must be fairly divided amongst people of all classes, declaring that it is wrong for people to have to live under the torture of indigence and its pressure on hearts and souls, not least those of women and children.

Have we not men wise and just enough to eradicate these wrongs? To cure the bitterness which they produce? To reenact sound Islamic measures? To restore respect for the dictates of piety and reverence for God and men? Should not the same Islam which once rescued woman from degrading depression, now raise her again by instituting a new society?

The Veil : "The true veil is in the eyes of the men," runs a saying of the Prophet. Women on pilgrimage are not allowed to veil their faces. What is clearly commanded in the Quran is a modesty of dress and behaviour - for both men and women.

The relevant passages are as follows:

> Tell the believing men to lower their gaze and be modest. That is purer for them. Lo! Allah is Aware of what they do. And tell the believing women to lower their gaze and be modest, and to display of their adornment only that which is apparent, and to draw their veils over their bosoms, and not to reveal their adornment save to their own husbands or fathers or husband's fathers, or their sons or their husband's

> sons or their brothers or their brother's sons ... and turn unto Allah together, Oh believers, in order that ye may succeed. Quran 14:30-31 Light
>
> Oh Prophet! Tell thy wives and thy daughters and the women of the believers to draw their cloaks close round them when they go abroad. That will be better, that so they may be recognised and not annoyed.
> Quran 33: 59 The Clans

The commentator Abdullah Yusuf Ali says in notes on these two passages, "The rule of modesty applies to men as well as to women." "The times were those of insecurity, and the women were asked to cover themselves when walking abroad. It was never contemplated that they should be confined to their houses like prisoners." "The object was not to restrict the liberty of women, but to protect them from harm and molestation under the conditions then existing in Medina."

The covering of the face by a veil has never been universal in the Muslim world. Country women go to the fields without a veil, women in some parts of the Muslim world have not adopted it, others during the last decades have discarded it. But the Quranic injunction to modesty, however it is applied, cannot be set aside. Its interpretation has varied, and does vary, but its importance is basic. One interpretation of what constitutes modesty is the long skirt and head scarf worn by many young women – a stricter interpretation than that of some of their mothers.

Some Muslim women note an obsession among western observers with the question of the veil, an emphasis that tends to trivialise an important debate. The point at issue in the many discussions on the subject of women's role and women's dress is not the veil itself, but the values which Muslim society treasures and seeks to maintain. High among these are honour and good faith, premarital chastity and fidelity in marriage. "If the veil still exists, it is because those who are wearing it feel it is part of their tradition and part of their lives," says one woman lawyer.

Asked about the question of the veil, a western-educated Iranian woman student said:

> I think the profound reason for the veil in Islam is that a woman should not draw the attention of others. But if deeply inside her aim *is* to draw attention to herself she will do so even by being covered. Therefore it is a question of motive. If our motive is to gain the respect of others we will do this through the way we are: our behaviour, our acts, our thoughts, what we say and what we wear.

A woman can be a centre of attention or she can decide to give attention to others. She can be a cause of crime or a cause of creation. It depends on her deep motives.

Today we talk a lot about "la femme objet", the woman as a material object and not a real human being. And we often blame men for this attitude. They may deserve part of the blame, I do not know. But we are the real cause. We must be able to attract through our naturalness, our freedom from jealousy, hate and selfishness, and through what we think. Dressing in an extravagant fashion must not be the test of being charming and attractive. We can change such values by rethinking our role and our place in society and the world.

The Prophet's Marriages : On the Prophet's own family life, the following comment comes from Professor Seyyed Hussain Nasr, author of *Ideals and Realities of Islam, Man and Nature,* and other works:

> During the period of youth when the passions are most strong the Prophet lived with only one wife, who was much older than he, and he also underwent long periods of abstinence. And as a prophet many of his marriages were political ones, which, in the

> prevalent social structure of Arabia, guaranteed the consolidation of the newly founded community ... The multiple marriages of the Prophet, far from pointing to his weakness towards "the flesh", symbolise his patriarchal nature and his function, not as a saint who withdraws from the world, but as one who sanctifies the very life of the world by living in it and accepting it with the aim of integrating it into a higher order of reality. Seyyid Hussain Nasr

Origins of Muslim Marriage : The fourth chapter of the Quran is called *Women,* because it deals largely with women's rights. It begins:

> O Mankind! Be careful of your duty to your Lord Who created you from a single soul and from it created its mate and from them twain hath spread abroad a multitude of men and women.

It goes on to urge respect for mothers and for the rights of orphans, then continues:

> Marry of the women who seem good to you two or three or four; and if ye fear that ye cannot do justice (to them) then one (only) ... Thus it is more likely that ye will not do injustice.

The trend today is to interpret this as a clear discouragement of polygamy. One man commented, "The Quran tells us, 'Marry more than one if you can be fair to them – but you never will be fair.' The Prophet for certain special reasons married more than one wife and treated them justly. But how can we disregard the word of God in the Quran telling us that we shall not act justly?"

The origins of Muslim marriage, and the special circumstances in which arose its permission of a limited polygamy are explained in *A Muslim Commentary on the Declaration of Human Rights.* The author is Sultan Hussain

Tabandeh, leader of the Nematullahi Sultanalishahi Sufi Order, Iran.

A glance at the situation in the Arab communities of the Pre-Islamic Times of Ignorance reveals how much Islam in fact advanced women's status and improved the conditions of their life.

The enemies of the Muslims attacked them with military force and in the ensuing battles so many men perished that great numbers of women were left without a protector, an almost impossible situation in the desert society of the Arabia of those days. It was to ensure the safety of women bereaved ... that the Prophet was told to grant permission to the Companions each to take one of the bereaved women with her children under his aegis as part of his own family ... and so to extend to the solitary women the assurance of protection and family life.

The new religion at once set to work to purge society of abuses. The imposition of a strict limit of four on the numbers of marriages allowable was one of the first beneficent new regulations.

The legalising of the number of four wives was not a command to take four wives. It was not an order but a limit. This permission is hedged about with many conditions. For instance, the man's finances must be sufficient, his circumstances favour a multiple establishment. His intention must be to be absolutely fair to each wife, his companionship and provision for each be equally shared.

> If polygamy is not allowed, circumstances may arise which cause difficulty, sin, confusion or unnecessary strain ... Many reasons make polygamy sensible, reasonable and right. But if a man's motive is merely to satisfy his carnal lusts, polygamy is frowned on, since men are commanded to allow their reason to

> control their passions. The acceptance of this inner discipline increases the intellectual powers and diminishes the force of fleshly desire.
>
> Sultanhussein Tabandeh

Marriage : An eminent Indian lawyer, A. A. A. Fyzee, discusses the legal aspect of marriage in his authoritative text book, *Outlines of Muhammadan Law.*

Marriage, in its legal aspect, is a contract and not a sacrament. There can be no marriage without consent. In its social aspect, three important factors must be remembered.

(i) Islamic law gives to the woman a definitely high status after marriage.

(ii) Restrictions are placed upon the unlimited polygamy of pre-Islamic times.

(iii) The Prophet, both by example and precept, encouraged the status of marriage. He positively enjoined marriage for all those who could afford it. And the well-known saying attributed to the Prophet, "There is no monkery in Islam", expresses his attitude to celibacy briefly and adequately.

In its religious aspect... marriage is recognised in Islam as the basis of society. It is a contract, but it is also a sacred covenant. Marriage as an institution leads to the uplift of man and is a means for the continuance of the human race. Spouses are strictly enjoined to love and honour each other.

> Muslim law permits polygamy but does not encourage it, and the Quranic injunction (Sura 4: 3) shows that in practice perfect equality of treatment on the part of the husband is, for all practical purposes, impossible of achievement. Hence Muslim law as enforced in India has considered polygamy as an institution to be tolerated but not encouraged. Asaf A. A. Fyzee

Divorce **:** There are strict rules and safeguards in the Quran in regard to divorce. Abdul Moghny Said discusses these in his book, *Islam - A Progressive Faith for a Dynamic World:*

> Marriage is a noble communion between man and woman, a communion which is blessed by Allah and based on freedom of choice. It is to be made or dissolved by the free consent of both parties.
>
> Islam leaves room for divorce as an undesirability, but not as a right to be excessively used. If it is deemed impossible for a couple to live together, after exhausting all means of conciliation and arbitration, they have but to separate. "If you fear a breach between the two of them, appoint an arbiter from his folk and an arbiter from her folk. If they desire amendment Allah will make them of one mind." (Quran Sura 4: 35 *Women)* It is clear that divorce is permitted only as a last resort. As Prophet Muhammad said, "Divorce is the most hateful to Allah among that which is permitted." When divorce is deemed inevitable it must be carried out in a decent and kind way. "Divorce must be pronounced twice and then (a woman) must be retained in honour or released in kindness."
>
> (Quran: Sura 2: 229 *The Cow)*
>
> We would like to emphasise that humanity has learned through its long experience that divorce is an unavoidable necessity in certain cases. This is why divorce is permitted even in countries whose religion does not allow it. As regards this issue, Islam has proved to be realistic. Abdul Moghny Said

Family Planning **:** Statements by Muslim religious authorities have been sought on the question of the use of contraceptive methods, in view of Family Planning programmes. These statements agree that contraception - but not sterilisation- is permissible under Muslim law:

> The use of medicine to prevent pregnancy temporarily is not forbidden by religion, especially if repeated pregnancies weaken the woman due to insufficient intervals for her to rest and regain her health. The Quran says: "... Allah desireth for you ease; He desireth not ... hardship for you ..." (Sura 2: 185) "... And hath not laid upon you in religion any hardship ..." (Sura 22: 78) But the use of medicine to prevent pregnancy absolutely and permanently is forbidden by religion.
>
> The Fatwa Committee, Al Azhar University, March 10 1953"
>
> There are genuine traditions which allow methods for restricting procreation, such as coitus interruptus ... A corollary of this is the dispensation for the use of medicine for contraception.
>
> The Grand Mufti of Jordan, December 1964

In his book, *The Lawful and the Prohibited in Islam,* Dr Yusuf Al-Qaradawi, Dean of the Department of Shariah, University of Qatar, says:

> The preservation of the human species is unquestionably the primary objective of marriage, and such preservation of the species requires continued reproduction. Accordingly, Islam encourages having many children and has blessed both male and female progeny. However, it allows the Muslim to plan his family due to valid reasons and recognised necessities.

Valid reasons given for the use of contraceptives are: fear that the pregnancy or delivery might endanger the life or health of the mother; fear that the burden of children may straiten the family's circumstances so much that one might do something *haram* (forbidden) to satisfy their needs; fear that the children's health or upbringing might suffer, especially that a new pregnancy might harm a previous suckling child. Dr Qaradawi adds:

Imam Ahmad bin Hanbal [founder of one of the four traditional schools of Islamic Law], is of the opinion that contraception requires the consent of the wife, because she has the right both to sexual enjoyment and to decide whether or not she wants a child. It is reported that 'Umar forbade the practice of coitus interruptus without the consent of the wife. This was, on the part of Islam, a noteworthy step toward establishing the rights of women in an age in which they had no rights.

Abortion : While Islam permits preventing pregnancy for valid reasons, it does not allow doing violence to the pregnancy once it occurs, says Dr Yusuf Al-Qaradawi. However, there is one exceptional situation, he says. If it is reliably established that the continuation of the pregnancy would necessarily result in the death of the mother, then, in accordance with the general principle of the Muslim legal code, that of choosing the lesser of two evils, abortion may be performed.

The Islamic position on abortion is examined by Dr Hassan Hath out, FRCSE, Chief Medical Officer, Maternity Hospital, Kuwait.

In February 1971, a seminar was held in Beirut by the International Planned Parenthood Association, on "Induced Abortion - a Hazard to Public Health". Among divergent views, says Dr Hathout, there was a strong current in favour of abortion, but a new impetus was given to the discussion when Islam's attitude was broached. The need was expressed for a study of Islam's stand on planned parenthood from all angles, and especially in relation to abortion, so as to clarify what Muslim law sanctions and proscribes in regard to it.

Dr Hathout's paper, "Induced Abortion", was presented at a further gathering of the association in Rabat, December 1971. A summary of his argument follows:

> I am no stranger to the subject (of abortion) as I encounter it almost daily as obstetrician and gynaecologist. Quite a sizeable part of my life has been spent in study of the human foetus. And I am a believer in Islam who holds that Islam is and should remain the foundation upon which the life of the Muslim should rest.

History shows that man's civilisation has rested on one unique concept, namely man's control over his passions. Without this, he would not have scaled the heights of moral glory nor would his intelligence have proceeded along the path of scientific research. If man were to give his passions free rein, mankind would become a community bent on self-destruction - a disintegrating civilisation.

Lust today is portrayed as an irresponsible beast. Chastity is held to be unreasonable and unacceptable. In Muslim societies, however (and among Christians living among them), virginity before marriage is practically one hundred per cent. This means it is not beyond the reach of possibility. It might be argued that fear and social pressures contribute largely to this figure. But fear is not - and should not be -the sole reason for chastity. Indeed I have known men who practise self-restraint not out of fear but out of self-respect and respect to those they love. If you love somebody you should not subject them to possible harm.

When doctor and patient discuss this question, there is always a third party present: the foetus, the newcomer waiting at the door. Perhaps the foetus has the added privilege of having his whole life ahead of him. I have come to know the foetus in its various phases, arriving at the conclusion that the foetus is an individual. I have been unable to draw a line between the foetus as a human and a non-human. I have moreover been unable to draw a line telling me where I would have to feel concern for the foetus and where I would have to disregard it. It is confusing and contradictory to hear those voices loudest in the defence of the illegitimate baby, which were most willing to have sacrificed him a few months before, when he was a foetus *in utero.*

Muslim legal views on abortion were unanimous on some points, varied on others. Some were based on the early medical belief that "quickening of life" took place when movement of the foetus could be felt, about four months after conception. This is not now scientific.

Abortion differs from contraception, being an assault on life and therefore a criminal act. All agree that abortion is a crime after" quickening" has taken place, and blood money is due. Opinions differ as to before "quickening". Ghazzali and others hold it a crime against existing life. But if the mother's life is endangered, the lesser evil is to be allowed and the mother saved. The foetus has the right to inherit – and the right to live. To deprive it of this right is prohibited by religion, unless there are strong grounds. These may be the certainty of danger in the present or immediate future to the mother's life, or the strong probability of the baby being born deformed.

To say that a foetus is "unwanted" is a delusion. We have conducted a survey on a group of women - married - who had demanded abortion. When they were delivered of their babies, we asked each one if she still felt the baby was unwanted. The reply of one and all was in the negative.

11

Society in Islam

Main Characteristics : Islam has given laws based on the Book of Allah, preached and practiced by the last Messenger of Allah which guarantee the rights of human beings, their life and property, their honour and prestige, security and peace. They guarantee social, religious and political rights to all its citizens, irrespective of race, caste, creed or colour. All enjoy equal rights and equal freedom in an Islamic society.

In the way ward society of Arabia, women were treated as animals, life and honour of none were safe. Men buried their daughters alive. No law existed and men bowed before idols. In that society robbery was not considered a crime, trust had no sanctity and a man could lose all his possessions including his wives and children through games of chance. It was Hadrat Muhammad (PBUH) who brought about a marvellous change in the life of such people.

He cast kindness into their hearts and converted robbers into custodians. People constantly fighting among themselves became brothers. They learnt to stand side by side, shoulder to shoulder in a row while praying. It was Hadrat Muhammad (PBUH) who taught that all human beings belong to one brotherhood and that they are all equal. He made life easier by his teachings of tolerance of other people's views and opinions, especially in matters of faith. The Quran says:

> "Let there be no compulsion in religion." (2:256)

Everyone in the Islamic society is free to practice his religion. This philosophy of religious freedom is further explained in the Holy Quran:

> "If it had been the Lord's will
> They would all have believed
> All who are on earth!
> Will you then compel mankind,
> against their will to believe!" (10:99)

The protection of life and property is fully guaranteed to every citizen in an Islamic society.

> "take not life, which Allah hath made sacred, except by way of justice and law:" (6:151)

And with regard to property:

> "And do not eat up your property among yourselves for vanities, nor use it as bait for the judges, with intent that ye may eat up wrongfully and knowingly a little of (other) people's property." (2:188)

In an Islamic society, wealth should remain in circulation. For this purpose, Islam has established the institution of *Zakat* which is collected from the rich and distributed amongst the poor of the society. *Zakat* is compulsory and, therefore, if one does not pay it, he goes against the commandment of Allah and for him, is prescribed a painful punishment.

As regards the acquisition of wealth, Islam encourages all lawful means and condemns the unlawful ones. Muslims are required to earn livelihood by honest means; it regards begging and unemployment as undesirable. Its emphasis is on lawful and legal trade and it considers hoarding, games of chance and gambling as illegal.

Yet another feature of an Islamic society is justice which is to give every deserving person his right. It is the duty of every individual member of the society to cooperate with the society towards this end, to the best of his ability.

In order to eradicate evil, the Holy Prophet (PBUH) first attacked the basis of corruption. He prohibited all alcoholic drinks and gambling in the Islamic society. He encouraged people to adopt piety, goodness and justice in their individual as well as social dealings. He also discouraged slavery and used all possible methods to get rid of this evil from society.

The social system based on these principles has been working successfully till the present times. In these comprehensive principles, the most balanced Divine Guidance is given to mankind to purify their life and to lay the foundation of a healthy, pious and chaste society in which people can live in peace and happiness. These are the distinctive features of the society set up by Prophet Hadrat Muhammad (PBUH) which provides honour, peace and security to every human being.

***Promiscuous Society* :** There seem to be four main types of sexual relations, of which we either have a society of pure homosexuals, an entirely promiscuous society, a society in which no sexual relation exists except between husband and wife, or a *laissez-faire* society in which all these forms are tolerated. Are there any rational and objective bases on which we can choose among these types of society ?

Let us start with the easiest one to rule out. If men continue to be moral then a society of pure homosexuals is a self-defeating one, since it severs the enjoyment of sex from its reproductive function. An entirely promiscuous society seems to many to be the best, and in the long run the inevitable form of sexual relations. In such a society, sex, it is thought, ceases to be a problem, since here we shall for the first time combine complete freedom with the deepest enjoyment as well as the procreation of children. This, however, is a mere dream in which one does not see the facts as they are but as one wants them to be. Here are some of the difficulties that beset such a society.

Far from being the natural or ultimately the inevitable, and even if man is viewed as a mere animal, this is a dream which shall never be realised. This is because the human being is basically and biologically a pair-forming species. As the emotional relationship develops between a pair of potential mates it is aided and abetted by the sexual intimacies they share. The pair-formation function of sexual behaviour is so important for our species that nowhere outside the paining phase do sexual activities reach such a high intensity.

The facts are therefore against those who argue that man is basically promiscuous. "It is true that in many cultures economic considerations have led to gross distortion of the pair-forming pattern, but even where this pattern's interference with officially planned 'pseudobonds' has been most vigorously suppressed, with savage penalties and punishments, it has always shown signs of reasserting itself. From ancient times, young lovers who have known that the law may demand no less than their lives if they are caught, have nevertheless found themselves driven to take the risk. Such is the power of this fundamental biological mechanism."

As a dream, a promiscuous society is one where everybody chooses whoever he likes at whatever time he prefers. As a reality it is a society in which sexual deprivation becomes the main problem.

The young and the beautiful are universally more attractive than the plain or the ugly, and the old. And then there are personal tastes as to voice, form, culture, gesture, dress, etc. And if a person fails to find the mate of his or her liking, then even if he or she is physically satisfied, he or she is most likely emotionally deprived.

In such a society people are sure to be obsessed with sex, the search for the younger, the more attractive, the what not, becomes a full-time job. If time is a valuable asset, then much of it is unnecessarily wasted in such a society.

And this leads inevitably and naturally to the commercialization of this human need, a commercialization which through advertisement, pictures, specialised magazines, the employment of sexually attractive girls and, only very occasionally boys and men, and a hundred other cunning devices, yet increase the obsession with sex.

And the natural outcome of this is a distortion of human values. We do not mean by this anything metaphysically or mysterious. We only mean that in such a society a person's worth will depend on the accident of her or his being of a certain age or having good looks and/or a beautiful body. Girls are rewarded socially, and materially, and even 'crowned', not for anything they achieved but for a thing they had at their hour of birth. By implication the less beautiful girls are punished for no fault of theirs. How manifestly unjust an arrangement, one might say, even cruel !

And the fact of the matter is that a promiscuous society is definitely a cruel one. Even in a normal society, the feeling that one is getting older — and hence less attractive and less wanted therefore — is somewhat annoying, but how much worse it must be in a society where the worth of a person is determined, above all, by the degree of physical attraction, almost to the exclusion of other considerations.

If many criminal tendencies among both the young and the old are discovered to have their origins in broken homes and unstable families, what is going to be the fate of the army of parentless children which a promiscuous society produces? We cannot go here into details of the problems of the mass bringing up of children, but we have pointed to some of the consequences. Contemplating them, some might say : "Well, no-one ever seriously advocated this kind of society.

All we stand for is a society where every individual or group of individuals shall have the freedom to lead the kind of sexual life which they prefer. In such a society, married people will live side by side with promiscuous individuals and homosexuals, each appreciating and respecting the ideas and choices of the others and tolerating their behaviour." But, on even a little reflection one will realise that this will not do either.

First, because the bad consequence of homosexuality (with the details of which we are not presently concerned) and promiscuity, will not be eradicated by having those who practise them living among married people. All the complications will be there, though on a narrow scale.

Secondly, if the consequences are admitted to be harmful, then why encourage, and not lessen, the factors responsible for them ? And, the unfortunate fact is that tolerating homosexuality and promiscuity means encouraging them and pushing more and more people to practising them inasmuch as tolerance leads to others to experiment, and in due course, to come to practise them – as is invariably the case with any other aberrance that is 'tolerated.' The inevitable result will be that the society will become more and more homosexual and promiscuous and it is the married people who will come to be looked upon as 'eccentric', as happened in the case of the people of Prophet Lut (peace be upon him):

> "And Lut : (Remember) when he said unto his folk:
> Will you commit abomination such as no other people
> ever did before ? Lo ! you come with lust unto men
> instead of women. Nay, but you are a wanton folk !
> And the answer of hie people was only that they said

(one to another) : Turn them out of your township.
They are folk, forsooth, who keep pure !" (7 : 80-82)

Although wicked people have always been committing this most heinous sin that has given the people of sodom an everlasting notoriety yet it has always been considered a filthy and detestable act. But the only people who have tried to raise it to a moral excellence, were the Greek Philosophers in the ancient world, and the Europeans in the modern world. The latter are doing their utmost to make up the deficiency by making an open propaganda for it, and have succeeded in giving this filthy act a legal sanction. So much so that the legislatures of some countries have legalized it. It does not require elaborate argument to show that homosexuality is a horrible social crime and a heinous sin. For the Creator has made the male and the female of each and every living species different from and complementary to each other for their reproduction. Then this difference in the human species has been created to serve another purpose.

This is to urge the two to live together in order to form a family along with their offspring. For this is the foundation of a civilized life for which man has been created. That is why their bodies have been made complementary to attract each other for the satisfaction of sex urges and for the service of the natural function of reproduction of the species. Therefore the one who satisfies this sex urge in an unnatural way becomes guilty of many crimes at one and the same time :

1. Such a one, so to speak, wages a war against the natural and physical functionings of his own organs and those of the victims of his lust. This inevitably produces very harmful effects on their physiques, their minds and their morality.
2. He becomes guilty of treachery and dishonesty against Nature for he enjoys sexual pleasure, without performing the necessary service of his species and

civilization and without fulfilling the rights and obligations attached to it.

3. He commits a breach of trust against the society in general for he enjoys all the benefits of the civilized society, but in his turn does not take on himself the responsibilities of the married life and wastes all his powers in the unnatural satisfaction of his sexual desires. This selfish and unworthy attitude is not only useless but also positively harmful to the collective morality. Thus he makes himself unfit for the service of the family and of the human race and produces unnatural feminine characteristics in, at least, one other male, and opens the way to adultery and moral degradation for at least two women.

By elimination then, and also by implication, the society with the least evil and most good is a society of married people who do not tolerate, but do their best to eradicate, all the causes of homosexuality and promiscuity.

Muslim World and Society

Islam teaches that God is concerned not only with moral and ethical reform, but also with social emancipation and economic conditions.

Abdul Moghny Said

Islam strikes a balance between the two extremes of capitalism and socialism. Muhammad Qutb

The simultaneous stress on both the material and the spiritual aspects of life is a unique characteristic of the Islamic economic system. This synthesis of the material and the spiritual is what is missing in the other two systems, capitalism and socialism. Both the capitalist and the socialist systems have neglected the spiritual needs of the human personality.

Muhammad Umar Chapra

Contemporary attempts to base the life of nations on Islamic principles cover a wide range. All are profoundly influenced by the example of the Prophet and of the early Muslim community in Medina. They are also strongly influenced by reactions to events and trends in the Western world, both capitalist and communist.

The great adjustments that are taking place in Muslim society are happening at a time when it feels itself under threat from a dominant civilisation which, while no longer politically imperialist, is imposing its norms of behaviour and its materialism on others. Reactions towards the "West" face Muslims with difficult dilemmas.

The search goes on for answers to social and world problems that are consonant with Islamic tradition, neither merely reactions to nor adaptations of alien thought.

"The dominant, permanent factor in Muslim countries," says Dr Fathi Uthman, former editor of the *Islamic World Review*, "is Islam as a comprehensive way of life." It is important to realise, he adds, that those who hold this view can be progressive - recognising that not everything "modern" is tied to secularism. The Islamic revival is many-sided, forward-looking as well as traditional.

The tide of renewal in the Muslim world began to flow more than a century ago, with movements such as that of the Wahhabis in Arabia, the Arab awakening in the Near East, and the expansion of Islam south of the Sahara.

The Twentieth Century has seen a war of ideologies — of powerful ideas regarding man and society. Every tide of ideology that has swept through the world during the course of the past decades has had its observers, its critics and sometimes its supporters in the Muslim world. Liberalism and socialism in turn were interpreted in Muslim terms. The atheistic creed of communism has never been acceptable to Muslims, but the Marxist diagnosis of society and history has had its influence in various quarters. Nationalism, though contrary to the Islamic concept of the universal community, the *Ummah,* helped to raise many local and regional loyalties, as well as to inspire the larger vision of Pan-Arabism. Young men – and women also of each succeeding generation pinned their hopes of radical change to one banner or another: often to suffer disillusionment when the promises of their leaders were not fulfilled.

More and more, hopes of profound change on a national and global scale came to focus on a return to the teachings of Islam. Islam itself could be viewed as an ideology, in the sense of a comprehensive system of ideas that embraces the whole of life.

Some of many trains of thought and action are indicated here: a view on Arab Socialism; the principles of Islamic banking by one of its pioneers; an insight into the universal nature of science; and how the West is seen. Is it irretrievably decadent, or are its people possible partners in fashioning a new age? The key to all progress is in the renewal of faith.

***Origins of Arab Socialism*:** The Islamic principles on which Arab socialism was based differ fundamentally from dialectical materialism.

One of those who contributed to the development of independent Arab socialist thinking is Abdul Moghny Said, until 1975 Under-Secretary in the Ministry of Manpower, Cairo. He is known for his pioneering work in the field of workers' education. In his book, *Arab Socialism,* he traces its origins in the thought and practice of the Quran and the Prophet.

The concept of Arab socialism actually existed for many centuries before modern Arab nationalism came upon the scene. Its roots were planted long before Marx. They lie deep in the soil of Islam and in the cultural heritage of the Arabs.

All the great monotheistic religions were cradled in these Eastern Mediterranean lands which have always been the home of the Arab people. The impulse towards social emancipation is found in all these religions, but it is perhaps most developed in the precepts of Islam. The Quran makes it clear that, as well as setting up moral standards as a basis of decent behaviour and better human relations, religions must bring help to the poor and improve the living standards of the masses. In previous revelations the message was simple: "Do not exploit; be charitable; practise unselfishness." In Islam, for the first time, an economic theory of equal opportunities and fair distribution was outlined.

Without being too theological, it is possible to explore the social and economic implications of Islam and the principles which have influenced contemporary Arab socialist thought... Islam teaches that God is concerned not only with moral and ethical reform, but also with social emancipation and economic conditions.

The Quran provides a basis for a moral interpretation of history; an interpretation which is deeper and broader than that of Karl Marx because it covers both the moral and material aspects, while that of Marx concentrates entirely on the material aspects, being greatly influenced by the materialistic evolutionary philosophies of his time. Religion is not the opium of the people. The great religions aimed at a classless society, where equality, justice and prosperity would prevail. In their principles, and particularly in Islam, which Marx completely ignored, we can trace much that pointed towards socialism.

A New Economic Order: Muslims responsible for the policy of nations - Asian and African as well as Arab — see the teachings of the Quran as having relevance to major questions of economics, and also to the stewardship of money and the distribution of world resources.

Banking is one field where practices based on these teachings have been increasingly explored and expanded. In the 1970's and 1980's numbers of Islamic banks were set up, based on the principles of partnership and the sharing of profit and loss. It is essential that the system should be interest-free; since the Quran specifically forbids usury, and this is generally taken to include any form of interest. But the emphasis is on working out a positive system, not merely on excluding an incentive regarded as wrong. By 1987 there were more than 100 Islamic banks and financial institutions throughout the world, including multinational banking companies. The Islamic Development Bank (IDB) was established in 1975 by the Organisation of the Islamic Conference (OIC) to undertake long-term financing of development projects.

One of the pioneers of these developments is Prince Muhammad Al-Faisal Al-Saoud, Chairman of the International Association of Islamic Banks. In 1981 he founded the Geneva-based Dar-ul-Mal al-Islami (DMI). The aim is that Islamic banks and interest-based banks should view each other not as competitors but as partners. One of many steps towards this goal was a symposium of bankers held in Baden-Baden, West Germany, in May 1981, organised by the Syma Institute and chaired by Prince Muhammad.

In his inaugural address he outlines some value premises of Islam. (1) The unity *(tawhid)* of thought under God: His power and direction are relevant to every aspect of life. (2) The vice-gerency of man who is God's deputy and who has to act as a trustee: with no extravagance, no waste, but positive utilisation of the available resources. (3) The search for justice, political and social as well as individual. From such a value-framework, he says, the economist will derive a new set of policy conclusions. The thrust of economic analysis will move from what people demand, to what the world needs, and this will be a revolutionary change in economic thinking.

The basic principles of Islamic banking and finance are not new. What is new is only in the application. Our philosophy is based on the Quran in which there are certain things that are given, things which do not bear discussion, because we cannot in any way adjust them. However, there is a wide area in which innovation, new approaches and methods can be applied. We feel we can contribute to the solution of some of the problems in the economies of the world today. We are trying to help in relieving the pressures on the Third World by mobilizing the resources of the Islamic countries through Islamic banking.

Man has been created as God's surrogate in this world. Therefore he is not a totally free agent in his social and economic interactions. There is a certain code. The question of interest is one thing, but more important is the total integration of morality in the dealings of any human being in any endeavour he undertakes.

Economics, as we understand it in its classical form, is the satisfaction of the need for goods and services. With Islam, the definition is slightly different. It is the material satisfaction of the need of society according to the role man plays in this world. This entails certain limitations, which make it different from the western concept of total freedom of action.

Trusteeship brings the idea of accountability in this world before humans, and before God in the life hereafter ... We shall have to develop social accounting over against the type of accounting with which we are familiar at the moment... These concepts are not just ethical norms, but have important economic consequences.

In this new approach, we do not claim that we have all the answers or that we have been able to develop all the solutions. We would like to learn from other traditions, and we would like to see others also adopt a more open attitude to the study of the Muslim approach to economics.

Science and Faith : The search for knowledge is a duty in Islam. European scholarship owes a debt to the Muslim world for its earlier leadership in the scientific field. Now, however, "The Muslim World can and should learn from and profit by the West, particularly in the spheres of modern sciences and technology." Muhammad Asad, author of *The Road to Mecca,* is one among many who develop this theme.

Never have the worlds of Islam and the West come so close to one another as today. Cultural imitation, opposed to creativeness, is bound to make a people small... Not that the Muslims could not learn much from the West, especially in the fields of science and technology. But the acquisition of scientific notions and methods is not really "imitation"; and certainly not in the case of a people whose faith commands them to search for knowledge wherever it is to be found. Science is neither Western nor Eastern, for all scientific discoveries are only links in an unending chain of intellectual endeavour which embraces mankind as a whole.

Every scientist builds on the foundations supplied by his predecessors, be they of his own nation or of another; and this process of building, correcting and improving goes on and on, from man to man, from age to age, from civilisation to civilisation, so that the scientific achievements of a particular age or civilisation can never be said to "belong to that age or civilisation." At various times one nation, more vigorous than others, is able to contribute more to the general fund of knowledge; but in the long run the process is shared, and legitimately so, by all. There was a time when the civilisation of the Muslims was more vigorous than the civilisation of Europe.

It transmitted to Europe many technological inventions of a revolutionary nature, and more than that: the very principles of that 'scientific method' on which modern science and civilisation are built. Nevertheless, Jabir ibn Huyyan's fundamental discoveries in chemistry did not make chemistry an "Arabian" science; nor can algebra and trigonometry be described as "Muslim" sciences, although the one was evolved by Al-Khwarizmi and the other by Al-Battani, both of whom were Muslims: just as one cannot speak of an "English" theory of Gravity, although the man who formulated it was an Englishman. All such achievements are the common property of the human race. If, therefore, the Muslims adopt, as adopt they must, modern methods in science and technology they will do no more than follow the evolutionary instinct which causes men to avail themselves of other men's experiences.

Change through Renewal : The Islamic concept of change in society is renewal *(tajdid),* as the key to reform *(islah).*

The Prophet did not start with a system, or with large numbers. He began with change in the hearts of men and women - his wife, his closest friends. The idea of reform is not the modern one, which begins with the outward, trying to reform the world but never man himself.

Africa south of the Sahara has seen a vigorous expansion of Islam during the nineteenth and twentieth centuries. This renewal of Islam in West Africa may be regarded as "a model of *tajdid*", suggests Dr A. R. Doi, Director of the Center for Legal Studies, Ahmadu Bello University, Zaria. The revered Shehu (Sheikh) Uthumanu Dan Fodio (d. 1817), scholar and preacher in what is now Northern Nigeria, was regarded by his thousands of followers as the Renewer *(mujaddid)* of his age. In one of his many books he speaks of the character of such a reformer.

It is related [in a saying of the Prophet] that at the beginning of every century God will send a learned man to the people to renew their faith. The characteristics of this man must be that he commands what is right and forbids what is disapproved of, that he reforms the affairs of the people, and judges between them, and that he assists the truth against vanity and the oppressed against the oppressors, in contrast to the characteristics of the other learned men of his age.

The struggle the Shehu declared against rulers he regarded as corrupt began with preaching (the *jihad* of the word). At the risk of his life he took a stand against an injustice, and, his struggle turned into an open revolt (the *jihad* of the sword). With his brother Abdullah and his son Muhammadu Bello he established a state in the new city of Sokoto. This became the centre of a renaissance of poetry, literature and religious study, as well as of prosperous trade. All three were learned and scholarly men: more than a hundred books by them survive. These were concerned with the application of the precepts of Islam to the practical affairs of home, trade and state, and also with the poems, in Arabic and in the vernacular languages, which helped to make the teachings of Islam live for a population largely illiterate. The memory of Uthumanu Dan Fodio is still a powerful influence among the more than 150 million Muslims in West African countries, and also in the Sudan.

Renewal in this spirit is the aim of the Emir of Kano, HH Al haji Ado Bayero. He sees his responsibilities as extending to the contribution a united Nigeria can make to the world. At the end of Ramadan 1988 he invited chiefs from the south of Nigeria, as well as his northern neighbours, to celebrate the Feast, the Eid-ul-fitr. Together with the Anglican Bishop of Kano, he spoke of uniting peoples of all creeds on the firm ground of moral rectitude, selflessness, and dedication for the betterment of mankind. In a situation tense with recent religious conflict, he and the Bishop gave joint witness to "religion as an agent of unity rather than of division and destruction." Amid the blare of trumpets and the thunder of hooves as thousands of horsemen thronged the ancient city, a note was sounded of quiet faith for the future.

Islam and the West: Over the past hundred years, a renewal of faith and confidence has come to the Muslim world. The forms of this renewal have been manifold: its expressions range from the personal to the running of states, from individual integrity to steps towards a new economic order, from scientific research to art and poetry.

The springs of renewal, or resurgence, in the Muslim world may be discerned in the Quran, in the potency of its teachings and of the basic tenets of Islam. What actually occasioned it, at this time in history, was reaction to the domination of western civilisation, in its political form of imperialism and, more insidiously, in the onslaught of its materialism and secularism.

A reaction had to come. Revulsion against the West was inevitable, and might take controversial forms – not always viewed by Muslims as true to the best in Islam. It was not a reaction against Christianity, but against moral corruption as well as economic and political domination.

In face of the threat of a dominant culture, three possible courses present themselves: rejection, surrender or a selective choice, says Sayyid Abul Hasan Ali Nadwi, Rector of the Nadwat al-*Ulama* Islamic University in Lucknow. One of the most widely read authors of his time, he has written more than 40 books- in Arabic, Urdu and English. His insights into the world situation and the demands it makes on Muslims have done much to challenge the fears and raise the hopes, especially of the younger generation.

In his book, *Western Civilisation - Islam and Muslims,* he analyses the choices that face them.

An unrelenting battle of ideas and ideals is taking place throughout the Muslim world- a clash between the Islamic and the Western concepts of life, values and traditions. The past history of the Islamic countries, the indestructible attachment of the Muslim masses everywhere to Islam, the ideals which inspired them in their struggle for freedom - all these things demand that Islamic values alone should have a claim on their leadership. On the other hand, the intellectual make-up, education and political interests of the ruling classes in Muslim countries require that Western forms of life should be pushed forward.

The attitude of rejection and withdrawal is emphatically futile. It is bound to fail. No nation can aspire to maintain its individuality which lacks faith in itself and is plagued with an inferiority complex. All its efforts to hold its ground against a mighty civilisation, which has also become the dominant trend of the time, must ultimately fail.

In contrast there is the philosophy of defeatism, capitulation, servility. Its advocates are ardent, though immature, disciples of the West. Modernism to them means westernisation.

A man who does not make the West his preceptor and relegate himself to the rank of a pupil, but treats it as an associate, [can] make his own contribution. He ought to know that if he has to learn a great deal from the West, the West too has to learn no less from him. His endeavour should be to bring about a synthesis between the material and spiritual forces of the West and East and then to evolve from it a way of life the West may also be compelled to adopt, and which may serve as an inspiration to the most highly advanced nations of the present day world.

***"Arousing the Conscience of the West"* :** Criticism of western ways does not necessarily regard the fight for values as confined to the Muslim world, nor as irretrievably lost in western society. Dr. Fathi Uthman, former editor of the *Islamic World Review*, in a seminar held at the Oxford Centre for Islamic Studies (February 1987), gave points of common hope and advance, providing grounds for cooperation.

As the shadow of colonialism recedes, he said, new friendships are arising. Business relationships enable economic problems to be tackled together. And above all within the structure of western society there are many positive initiatives, "arousing the conscience of the West and countering the impression of an imminent collapse of standards and values."

Response to such initiatives of change, recognised in the conduct of Christians encountered in the West, was confirmed by a Muslim Brother from the Sudan. "I have moved from condemnation to the realisation that there are people we can and should work with," he said. "Absolute moral standards provide the area of cooperation to achieve the Will of God."

The Unzigzag Way : When you want to understand Islam, where do you go? A learned professor has said that we must go to the dictionary and scholarship, and then to the mosque. Certainly it is necessary to go to these places, but going there alone will be incomplete. Islam is not confined to the mosque- it is a code of conduct and a guidance for everyday life. We have to watch the career of a Muslim who has himself understood the religion of Islam and who practises its principles. Without that watching, the mosque or the textbook will give us only an incomplete understanding.

The Honourable Justice M. M. Ismail, Madras

Islam's conception of life is often put in terms of a road. A road has a beginning and a destination. The individual is somewhere on the road between birth and death. The human race is on the road too -the road from Creation to Judgement.

The millions now turning their faces to Mecca pray many times a day: "Show us the straight way." "Guide us on the straight path." *Al-Fatiha,* the opening chapter *(sura)* of the Quran with its seven verses, is repeated at each of the five times of prayer.

Whole books have been written on these verses. They are the first to be memorised by children, and they are pondered by statesmen. An ex-Prime Minister, asked what was the inspiration behind his success in recent negotiations, went through the Fatiha step by step.

The first volume of one modern "explanatory translation" of the Quran is entirely devoted to this opening chapter. "Let us look at the *Surat Al-Fatiha* as a whole," it says, "and see what type of mind it reflects or tries to build."

"Al-Fatiha": The Opening : In the Name of God, Most Gracious, Most Merciful.

Praise be to God,
The Cherisher and Sustainer of the Worlds;
Most Gracious, Most Merciful; Master of the Day of Judgement.
Thee do we worship, And Thine aid we seek.
Show us the straight way,
The way of those on whom
Thou hast bestowed Thy Grace,
Those whose (portion)
Is not wrath,
And who go not astray.

The Holy Quran, Sura I

Signposts on the Road: The Pillars of Islam : For the traveller who sets out on the road of faith, there are certain signposts or pillars by which to chart his way. The Muslim is taught to mark five such pillars.

The first is his witness to the God he serves: the One God, to whom man must submit or surrender totally. The word *Islam* means such surrender, and *Muslim (Muslima)* is the man or woman who thus submits to God. This "witness" *(shahada)* or creed is:

"There is no god but God (Allah)

And Muhammad is the Prophet of God."

The second of the pillars is prayer.

The third is *Zakat*: the giving of a certain proportion of income for the relief of poverty.

The fourth is the discipline of fasting - from dawn to sunset during the month of Ramadan.

The fifth is the pilgrimage to Mecca - to be performed once in a lifetime by every Muslim able to make the journey.

Of these, the duty which most affects the daily life of the Muslim family is the observance of the five daily times of prayer, starting before sunrise and ending late in the evening. In many of the Muslim homes in which I have stayed, the family are up for the Dawn Prayer that begins the day. It should be performed between dawn and sunrise. My hostess in a Cairo club slipped away to a quiet corner after lunch, so that the midday prayer might not be missed. A cheerful schoolgirl, hurrying in to her home with her books under her arm, went first to pray and then to tea. In the cool of the evening in Bombay's beautiful Hanging Gardens, many of the faithful were praying as the sun set.

The midday prayer on Fridays is the weekly congregational gathering. Shops close, business stops. A sermon precedes the prayers, which are performed together without regard to rank. A gallery or aisle in the Mosque is often set apart for women.

There are many who do not pray, and many for whom it is a mere repetition of a formula. The following quotations come from some of those to whom prayer is a reality - individuals in widely differing circumstances.

Daily Prayers : In his prayers, a Muslim faces the direction of the city of Mecca. When the time comes, in whatever place he happens to be, he turns towards Mecca and says his prayers.

Facing one direction is a symbol of unity of purpose for the millions of Muslims offering their prayers at the same time in the four corners of the earth.

The Muslim says the *Fatiha,* and recites any other portion of the Quran he feels like reciting, because of its particular meaning, or because he happens to remember it. Bowing, and touching the earth with his forehead, he terminates with a formal prayer in which he asks God to bless him and his people "as Thou hast blessed Ibrahim and his people."

The daily prayers are made by practising Muslims individually. A family can join in prayer, or any group which happens to be together. On Fridays, however, the noon prayer should be made collectively.

Voice Within : Prayer reminds man of God and helps him to be receptive to His guidance.

The five daily prayers are the best rest intervals for man in our busy and materialistic world.

The moral foundations of Islam are standards in which human behaviour can be channelled for the good of the individual as well as for the good of the community as a whole. They are not mere preaching stuff which may not keep step with ever-changing conditions. They form together that which we call "conscience" or the good side of us.

The "voice within" reminds us always that God is with us. To believe in God is simply the way to develop this "voice within" by seeking God's remembrance, presence and guidance.

Man Can Choose : The trouble we now see in the world- and in the Muslim world -is the result of listening to self-will when we should listen to God.

If we ask, what does God say in such a crisis as we face today, we can turn to the Holy Quran and find a key in the verse, "God does not change the condition of a people until the people change themselves." Another key is in the *Fatiha,* the prayer we repeat so many times a day. It says, "Guide us in the straight path." This shows us that God wants us to take guidance from Him. If this is so, we have to listen for that guidance. He will not catch us by the ear and drag us along that straight path. We must open our ears to His guidance, which the *Fatiha* makes us ask for.

Man is *ashraf al-makhluqat,* the top of creation, the highest of living beings. We have freedom to think for ourselves, about what is right and what is wrong. If we say everything is under God's control, we imply that He wills evil. You may say a leaf falls to the ground – and God wills it. But with man's actions it is different. He can choose between right and wrong, which lead to heaven and hell. Therefore we need to ask God's guidance along the straight path.

A time of quiet listening and asking for Gods guidance in this way is very important for every Muslim.

Haroun S. Kably,

Plaited Kufic ornamentation

"God gathers mankind for the Day of Judgement"

Advocate, Supreme Court, Delhi, and President, All India Cutchi Memon Community

Thy Lord Hath Not Forsaken Thee : Verses may be chosen from the Quran as optional acts of prayer to suit the circumstances of the believer, his joy and sorrow, gratitude and need.

A television programme in Cairo on the Prophet's Birthday (April 1973) included a talk on courage in adversity by the newly-appointed Sheikh al-Azhar, Dr Abdul Halim Mahmud. The chapter of the Quran named *The Glorious Morning Light* (Sura 93) was read. Afterwards a Palestinian lady, a refugee living in Egypt, said:

As I knit, I pray - just as Gandhi used to say the name of God as he spun. It is the same with the beads you see in my husband's hand. Men say short prayers as they handle them. One of these is, "Your covering and mercy, oh Lord." It means that the inner life is protected. Whatever the circumstances and defeats outside, the life inside our hearts need not be invaded by evil.

One part of the Quran which is often used in our prayers when we are disappointed or disheartened is the sura called *Al-Doha, The Glorious Morning Light.* It is said that these verses were revealed to the Prophet in Mecca, after he had received no revelations for some time and his opponents were mocking him.

By the morning hours

And by the night when it is stillest,

Thy Lord hath not forsaken thee nor doth He hate thee,

And verily the Hereafter will be better for thee than the present,

And verily thy Lord will give unto thee so that thou wilt be content.

Did He not find thee an orphan and protect (thee)?

Did He not find thee wandering and direct (thee)?

Did He not find thee destitute and enrich (thee)?

Therefore the orphan oppress not,

Therefore the beggar drive not away,

Therefore of the bounty of thy Lord be thy discourse.

Mrs Fareeza Taji, Palestine and Cairo

Prayers for Forgiveness and Obedience : The following come from a prayer-book in use in the Sudan.

O God! I ask forgiveness for myself and for my father; for all Muslims, both men and women; for all believers, both men and women; for those of them who are alive and those of them who are dead.

Deal with me and with them, whether soon or late, in the faith, in this world and the next, according to what You deserve. Do not deal with us, O Lord ! according to what we deserve. For You are forgiving, patient, generous, bountiful, tender and merciful.

O God ! in Whose hand are all our affairs, put an end to our neglect of You.

We have turned away from You, and from Your Commands, and from listening to the good things You say.

The crime that has caused this is that we have turned towards people who are no concern of ours. These have drawn us away from the benefit of Your speaking with us, and from our fear of You, in spite of our great need of you.

In this there is nothing but loss.

We pray you to turn our desires towards You. For You alone can rescue us from danger in this world and the next.

From *Al-Ratib*, a book of prayers used by the Imam Muhammad al Mahdi

The Call to Prayer : God is great! God is great!

I testify that there is no god but God!

I testify that Muhammad is God's Prophet!

Come to pray! Come to prosperity!

God is great! There is no god but God!

In the Mosque : Here the believer is a fish in water: the hypocrite is a caged bird.

Inscription on the gate of the Masjid Jami' mosque, Isfahan

The Fast of Ramadan : The Muslim calendar consists of twelve lunar months. Because of this the annual festivals occur at different seasons - thirteen days earlier in each successive year.

The ninth month is the month of fasting, Ramadan. All through it, from the first glimpse of the crescent moon to its reappearance a month later to mark the feast, no food or water may be taken from dawn till sunset.

Before light, the sound of a drum is often heard in the street, with its summons to awake and eat in the twilight, before a white thread can be distinguished from a black, and the day's fast begins. Ramadan is a time of discipline — and also of surprising gaiety, of family visits and neighbourly calls for the *iftar* (break-fast) parties in the evenings when the fast is over.

There are various aspects of Ramadan. One is the recollection of the revelation of the Quran, especially on the "Night of Power" or "Night of Destiny", the 26th-27th of the month. The Prophet's victories - the Battle of Badr and the conquest of Mecca - are celebrated. It is also a time for the healing of quarrels. This is especially associated with the feast at the end of Ramadan. It is customary to greet one's friends by saying, "If I have done you any wrong, please forgive me."

A lady in Djakarta put this into practice. She reached the conclusion that the resentment she held against a friend was in itself wrong — however deeply she felt that she had been injured. She decided to take the opportunity of the feast to set it right on her side.

She went to mutual friends and said, "You know how it is between us. Help me." Together they went to the house, and her companions supported her while she apologised for the ill will she had harboured.

The Turkish editor Ahmet Emin Yalman relates a similar incident.

God forgives, and so must we. That is the purpose of the Bairams (feasts). Their function is to be an occasion of reconciliation. This is effective. For instance, when I was engaged, there was a division in my fiancee's family. I noticed that a certain relative was never seen in their company, though I did not know the cause. When the next feast came, the family went to call on the man, there was a sweet reconciliation and all was well.

"I must clean my heart," is a phrase often heard in connection with this kind of action.

The instruction in the Quran about Ramadan is as follows. It is reproduced from the leaflet sent out for Ramadan 1974 by the Islamic Cultural Centre, London, giving the times of sunrise and sunset in different cities in the United Kingdom, for the benefit of those keeping the Fast.

Ramadan is the (month) in which was sent down the Quran, as a Guide to mankind. Also clear (signs), for guidance and for judgment (between right and wrong). So every one of you who is present (at his home) during mat month should spend it fasting. But if anyone is ill, or on a journey, the prescribed period (should be made up) by days later. God intends every facility for you. He does not want to put you to difficulties. (He wants you) to complete the prescribed period and to glorify Him.

The feast that follows Ramadan lasts three days. It is known as the *'Eid-ul-fitr* (Feast of the Breaking of the Fast).

Payment Due : It is at the end of Ramadan that the yearly payment of alms or poor-tax (*Zakat*) is made. This is defined as "an obligation prescribed by God on those Muslims, men and women, who possess enough means, to distribute a certain percentage of their annual savings or capital in goods or money among the poor and needy."

The basic traditional percentage is 2½ per cent. In recent years *Zakat* has played a large part in plans for an Islamic economic order and a tax system in line with Islamic tradition.

Human Rights and Islam

The fifteenth century of the Islamic era opened on 9 November 1980 AD, (1 Muharram 1401 AH). The year before and the year following this date were a period of intense activity throughout the Muslim world. Behind the turbulent political conflicts of the time Muslim scholars, writers and economists, as well as many of the rank and file of practising Muslims in different walks of life, were seeking to deepen their understanding of their faith.

It was an opportunity, said Dr Inamullah Khan, Secretary General of the World Muslim Congress, "to take stock of the gains and losses of the Muslims in the 1400 years. We should not only talk about our achievements but also our failures and the pitfalls into which we have been falling ... As Islam wants to build an egalitarian and a humanitarian society the two-year Hijra celebration should be for correcting past mistakes in all fields of life, be it educational, cultural, social, not ignoring the very important part that economics play in modern life today."

To bring an eternal message to the attention of mankind involves a continuing battle to clarify its meaning and to purify its expression, in the lives and in the statements of Muslim believers.

Two such statements were issued by the Islamic Council of Europe: the *Universal Islamic Declaration*, April 1980, which stressed that "a universal order can be created only on the basis of a universal faith and not by serving the gods of race, colour, territory or wealth"; followed by the *Universal Islamic Declaration of Human Rights*, September 1981, "based on the Quran and the Sunnah and compiled by eminent Muslim scholars, jurists and representatives of Islamic movements and thought."

The Declaration follows the lines of the Declaration of Human Rights, issued in 1948 by the General Assembly of the United Nations. It has 23 clauses: – the Right to Life, to Freedom, to Equality, to Justice, to Fair Trial etc. There is a basic difference of approach.

The United Nations Declaration starts with "the recognition of the inherent dignity and of the equal and inalienable rights of all members of the human family." The Muslim Declaration looks to "the Divine source and sanction of these rights." "We, as Muslims, believe ... that each one of us is under a bounden duty to spread the teachings of Islam by word and deed, and indeed in all gentle ways, and to make them effective not only in our individual lives but also in the society around us."

The Rights of Minorities are included. "The Quranic principle, 'There is no compulsion in religion', shall govern the religious rights of non-Muslim minorities." The "Right to found a family" (common to both Declarations) is followed by a section on the rights of married women. Explanatory notes point out that throughout the Declaration "person" refers to both the male and female sexes: and also that each of the Rights expressed carries a corresponding duty.

> "This is a declaration for mankind, a guidance and instruction to those who fear God."
> Quran: Sura 3: 138 Al-'Imran

A Note on the Illustrations : The oneness of God and the essential unity of His creation are basic to Islamic art, as they are to all Muslim life and thought. This is reflected in an exactness of mathematical design which gives serenity in architecture and undergirds all the arts.

Light is one: yet when broken by a prism it reveals every shade of colour. The millions of mankind are all equal — all sons of Adam, made of clay - yet in that equality there is scope for the differences of human personality, and never in all history have two individuals been identical. So it is with design: mathematically perfect, yet infinitely varied.

This perfection of pattern is given life in different ways: by the flowing lines of the Arabic script, drawn with the master skill of the calligraphed; by the floral designs that recall the "gardens through which rivers flow" so often described in the Quran; by the reshaping of triangle, square, and circle swept, as it were, by the movement of wind or water.

Bibliography

Adams, C.C. : *Islam and Modernism in Egypt,* Oxford University Press, New York, 1953.

Ahmad, Bherhan : *The Mujaddid's Conception of Tauhid,* Feroz Pub., Lahore, 1940.

Ahmad, Imtiaz : *Divorce and Remarriage among Muslims in India,* Manohar Publishers, New Delhi, 2003.

Ahmad, K. N. : *Muslim Law of Divorce,* Kitab Bhavan, New Delhi, 1988.

Ahmad, Manzuruddin : *Islamic Political System,* Kitab Bhavan, New Delhi, 1991.

Ali, Chiragh : *The Proposed Political Legal and Social Reform under Muslim Rule,* Popular Prakashan, Bombay, 1883.

Badrul, S. : *Muslim Behaviour,* Kitab Bhavan, New Delhi, 1991.

Bahedur, Kalim : *The Jamaat-i-Islami of Pakistan,* Progressive Books, Lahore, 1978.

Baksh, S. K. : *Politics in Islam,* Kitab Bhavan, New Delhi, 2003.

Bawer, Raymond : *The New Man in Soviet Social Psychology,* Oxford, New York, 1990.

Berger, M. : *Islam in Egypt Today : Social and Political Aspects of Popular Religion,* MacMillan, London, 1970.

Bernier, Francois : *Travels in the Mogul Empire*, MacMillan, London, 1916.

Bukhsh, S. K. : *Contribution to the History of Islamic Civilization*, Kitab Bhavan, New Delhi, 2000.

Charles, Howard : *The Constitutionalism*, Great Seal Books, New York, 1947.

Chave, F. : *Islamic Histroriography*, Cambridge University press, New York, 1990.

Davids, Waines : *An Introduction to Islam*, Cambridge University Press, New Delhi, 1995.

Durrani, F.K.K. : *Muhammad (PBUH) the Prophet*, Oxford, New York, 2001.

Enayat, Hamid : *Islam in the Political Process*, Cambridge University Press, Cambridge, 1993.

Engineer, Asghar Ali : *A Rational Approach to Islam*, Gyan Books Pvt. Ltd., New Delhi, 2001.

———: *Islam : Challenge in Twenty-first Century*, Gyan Books Pvt. Ltd., New Delhi, 2004.

Guillaume, A. : *The Traditions of Islam*, Khayats, Beirut, 1966.

Hassan, Ali : *Observations on the Musulmauns of India*, Macmillan & Co., London, 1832.

Helmut, Reifeld : *Islam in South Asia : Adaptation, Accommodation and Conflict*, Social Science Press, New Delhi, 1999.

Houtsma, T. : *Encyclopaedia of Islam*, Macmillan, London, 1934.

Irfan, Habib : *The Agrarian System of Mughal India*, Popular Prakashan, Bombay, 1963.

Jafar, Sharif : *Islam in India*, Oxford, New Delhi, 1972.

James, Burges : *The Muhammadan Architecture of Ahmadabad*, Bernard Quaritch, London,1900.

Jha, V. : *Indian Society: Historical Probings*, Rawat Pub., Delhi, 1974.

Joseph, and Bosworth, C.E. : *The Legacy of Islam,* Oxford University Press, New York, 1979.

Karl, Jaspers : *Man in the Modern Age,* Routledge & Kegan Paul Ltd., London, 1997.

Katharine, Scarfe : *Perception of the Islamic Word,* Cambridge University Press, New Delhi, 1992.

Lewin, Roger : *In the Age of Mankind,* Simithsonian Books, Washington, D.C., 1956.

Lewis, Richards : *Universe,* Harmony Books, New York, 1973.

Martin, Lings : *A Sufi Saint of the Twentieth Century,* Century Pub., London, 1971.

Mirza, Waheed : *The Life and Works of Amir Khusrau,* Kaveri Pub., Calcutta, 1935.

Mortimer, Edward : *Faith and Power, the Politics of Islam,* Oxford, New York, 2002.

Muhammad, Iqbal : *Six Lectures on the Reconstruction of Religious Thought in Islam,* Royal Pub., Lahore, 1930.

Nabith, A. : *The Foundations of the Articles of Faith,* Feroz Pub., Lahore, 1963.

Nasr, Seyyed H. : *An Introduction to Islamic Cosmological Doctrines,* Cambridge, 1964.

Nicholson, R.A. : *Literary History of the Arabs,* Kitab Bhavan, New Delhi, 1994.

Nusservanji, D. : *Zoroastrian Civilization,* Oxford, New York, 1922.

Oage, Charles H. : *The Society,* Macmillan & Co., London, 1959.

Padwick, C.E. : *Muslim Devotions,* MacMillan & Co., London, 1960.

Phillips, O. Hood : *Reform of the Constitution,* MacMillan & Co., London, 1970.

Pierce, R.A.: *Russia in Central Asia, 1867-1917,* University of California, Berkeley, 1960.

Qadir, Abdul, : *Criminal Law of Islam,* Kitab Bhavan, New Delhi, 1999.

Qazi A. Qadir : *The Changing World of Islam,* Royal Pub., Lahore, 1992.

Rizvi, Hasan Askari : *Islami Reassertion : a Socio Poliṭical Study,* Progressive Publishers, Lahore, 1981.

Robert, D. : *Exploring our Living Planet,* National Geographic Society, Washington, 1989.

Saukat, S. : *Human Rights in Islam,* Kitab Bhavan, New Delhi, 2001.

Sharma, Arvind : *Women in World Religion,* New York Press, New York, 1990.

Syed, M. H. : *History of Muslims in India,* Anmol Publications, New Delhi, 2003.

——— : *Islamic Terrorism : Myth or Reality,* Gyan Books, New Delhi, 2002.

Tarn, W. W. : *The Greeks in Bactria and India,* Cambridge, London, 1938.

Thomas, Arnold : *The Legacy of Islam,* Oxford University Press, New York, 2000.

Thompson, H.R. : *Sculptures and Inscriptions of Darius the Great on the Rock of Behistan,* Oxford, London, 1907.

Tritton, A.S. : *The Caliphs and their Non-Muslim Subjects,* Oxford, New York, 1930.

Tutsch, Hans E. : *Facets of Arab Nationalism,* Wayne State University Press, Detroit, 1965.

Underhill, E. : *Mysticism : a Study in the Nature and Development of Man's Spiritual Consciousness,* Oxford, New York, 1956.

Usmani, J.M. : *The Authority of Sunnah,* Kitab Bhavan, New Delhi, 1998.

Von, Edmund : *Modern Islam,* University Press, Los Angeles, 1952.

Von, Grunebaum : *Unity and Variety in Muslim World,* Oxford, New York, 2003.

Waheed, Akhtar : *Sufi Approach to the Problem of Alienation,* Wilson & Co., New Delhi, 1975.

Weiner, Myron : *Sons of the Soil : Migration and Ethnic Conflict in India,* University Press, Prineton, 1978.

Williams, Michael : *Outlines of World Military History,* Oxford, New York, 1996.

Wilson, Lambron : *Traditional Modes of Contemplation and Action,* University Press, Tehran, 1977.

Wolfson, H.A. : *Glimpses of Medieval Indian Culture,* Popular Pub., Bombay, 1959.

Yahanan, Friedmann : *Tolerance and Coercion in Islam : Interfaith Relations in the Muslims Traditions,* Cambridge, New York, 1990.

Yazbeck, Haddad : *Islamic Values in the United States,* Oxford, New York, 1997.

Zaehner, R.C. : *Hindu and Muslim Mysticism,* Oxford, London, 1960.

Zahid, Malik : *Subjects of Quran,* Kitab Bhavan, New Delhi, 1998.

Zahurul, Hasan : *Tarikb-i-Sufiya-i-Gujarat,* Jamil Academy, Ahmadabad, 1981.

Zaki, Azam : *The Ideas of Arab Nationalism,* Cornell University Press, New York,1956.

Index

N

O

P

Q

R

S

T

W

Z

❑❑❑